Perception

A representative theory

Perception

A representative theory

Frank Jackson
La Trobe University, Australia

Cambridge University Press

CAMBRIDGE

LONDON · NEW YORK · MELBOURNE

Published by the Syndics of the Cambridge University Press

The Pitt Building, Trumpington Street, Cambridge CB2 IRP

Bentley House, 200 Euston Road, London NW1 2DB

32 East 57th Street, New York, NY 10022, USA

296 Beaconsfield Parade, Middle Park, Melbourne 3206, Australia

First published 1977

Printed in Great Britain by
Cox & Wyman Ltd
London, Fakenham and Reading

Library of Congress Cataloguing in Publication Data

Jackson, Frank, 1943–

Perception.

Bibliography: p.

Includes index.

1. Perception. I. Title.

BF311.J23   153.7   76–30316

ISBN 0 521 21550 1

To Morag Fraser

Contents

Acknowledgements

I am indebted to many colleagues and friends for many valuable discussions on perception. I would like to mention Alec Hyslop (who converted me to Representationalism), I. T. Oakley, J. J. C. Smart, and D. M. Armstrong. I am particularly indebted to Professor Smart and Professor Armstrong who (despite disagreeing with much of what I say) commented in detail on an earlier version of this book. I am also conscious of a considerable debt to the philosophical example of M. C. Bradley and A. C. Jackson.

In some parts of the book I have drawn to a greater or lesser extent on material I have published elsewhere. The details are given in the bibliography and the relevant places in the text. I am grateful for the kind permission of the editors of *American Philosophical Quarterly*, *Metaphilosophy*, *Mind*, and *Personalist*.

Introduction

0. In this book I argue that the correct philosophical theory of perception is a representative one. By such a theory, I mean one which holds

(i) that the immediate objects of (visual) perception are always mental;

(ii) that there are objects, variously called external, material or physical, which are independent of the existence of sentient creatures;

(iii) that these objects have only the primary qualities;

and

(iv) to (visually) perceive a material object is to be in a certain kind of perceptual state as a causal result of the action of that object.

(The restriction to visual perception – seeing – is to be understood throughout.)

With the exception of clause (ii), these clauses are defended in the chapters that follow. Clause (ii) is, however, an assumption. I assume, that is, that Idealism (Phenomenalism) is false. I take it that we are a very small part of a universe that existed millions of years before we did and will exist millions of years after we have gone. The reason I do not defend the assumption is threefold: first, space; secondly, I have little to add to the criticisms of Idealism by writers like D. M. Armstrong,[1] Don Locke,[2] and J. J. C. Smart;[3] and, thirdly and most importantly, the main reason Idealism has been seriously entertained is the belief that its competitors – Direct Realism and Representationalism – face decisive objections; and I argue that Representationalism does not face decisive objections in chapter six.

Clause (i) is defended at the greatest length – as it ought to be; it is

---

[1] *Perception and the Physical World*, chs. 5 and 6. (Full bibliographical details are given in the bibliography.)

[2] *Perception and Our Knowledge of the External World*, ch. 4.

[3] *Philosophy and Scientific Realism*, ch. 2.

the one which nearly all writers on perception today reject. Its defence requires the conclusions of the first five chapters, the structure of this defence being indicated as we progress through them.

Clause (iii) is defended in chapter five. In this chapter it is argued that scientific investigation of the material world strongly supports the contention that material things have only what I call scientific properties, which turn out to be pretty much Locke's primary qualities.

Clause (iv) is defended and explained in chapter seven. The explanation draws on the sense-datum theory espoused in chapter four.

The role of chapter six is essentially negative: it presents objections to the familiar objections to Representationalism.

1. The philosophical viewpoint from which this work is written is to a considerable extent traditional. In the arguments of the following chapters traditional analytical terms like: 'analysis', '(logical) possibility', 'contingent', 'entailment' and 'necessarily true' play a prominent role.

I cannot defend this viewpoint here, for that would require a book in itself. But I think I should say something about why I adopt it.

One reason is simply that I do not find the criticisms of such concepts by, for instance, Morton White[4] and W. V. Quine[5] convincing. But there is a second reason which should, I feel, carry weight even with those who take Quine's and White's criticisms seriously.

Around the turn of the century, it was known that there was something badly wrong with Newtonian Physics, but it was not known what should be put in its place until Einstein's Theory of Relativity was proposed and became established. However, the physicists of 1900 did not stop work; rather they used the best theory they then had, in the full knowledge that it was inadequate. Likewise, physicists today who believe that certain paradoxes show that there is something fundamental amiss in current quantum theory do not stop using it; rather they use it because it is the best they have to date.

Now it seems to me beyond question that the traditional notions that make up the so-called intensional circle are the best we have to date: there is wide-spread, non-collusive agreement about their application; there are accepted axiom systems embodying the central notion of logical necessity; and we have semantics of a set-theoretic kind for these axiom systems. This is far more than we have for the suggested replacement notions like: paraphrase, degree of revisability, distance

[4] In, e.g., *Towards Reunion in Philosophy*.
[5] In, e.g., 'Two Dogmas of Empiricism'.

from the periphery of experience, and so on. At best, all we have for these notions are preliminary sketches that might serve as bases for fuller explications in the future. Indeed, as has been often noted, the clearest current accounts of these notions appear to presuppose the old notions. For example, the clearest account of the degree of revisability of a statement is in terms of the extent of revisions in a person's beliefs *consequent* upon abandoning that statement. And the relevant notion of consequence appears to be logical consequence, that is, entailment.

In short, it seems to me that someone who refuses to employ the traditional notions at all is like one who says, to borrow a phrase, 'I see it is wrong to build on sand, therefore, I will build on nothing at all.'

In any case, what is quite certain is that, if we are to use the traditional notions, there is no point in using them sloppily just because they face philosophical problems – two approximations take one further from the truth, rather than 'cancelling out'. Or, to borrow a maxim from morals, two wrongs do not make a right. It seems to me quite wrong to put forward analyses to which there are clear counter-examples and then try and excuse this fact by reference to, say, Quine's criticism of synonymy: this is to seek to have one's cake and eat it too. Either one eschews the notions in question altogether or one uses them as precisely as possible.

2. Finally, two matters partly concerning philosophical viewpoint and partly terminology.

Clause (i) of the statement of Representationalism in §o above uses the term 'mental'. The question of how to define the mental is, rightly, highly controversial. All I will attempt here is to describe my usage in as philosophically neutral a way as possible, while going beyond merely giving the usual list: pains, desires, hopes, etc.

I take it that we have a reasonably clear conception of a sentient creature: that of which we (persons) and the higher mammals are prime examples, and rocks are prime non-examples. What I mean by 'mental' is what we *qua* sentient creatures bring to the world; what there could not be if there were no such creatures. Of course there are difficulties here, but we must make a start somewhere; and this account at least enables us to give direction to arguments over whether something is mental: *A*s are mental just if there could be no *A*s if there were no sentient creatures. It is important to notice the generality here: '*A*s', not '*this A*'. My car could not exist without a sentient creature, me – at least in one clear sense, that given by noting that 'My car exists without my existing' is an inconsistent statement. But car*s* could exist without sentient creatures, they could, for example, have been made by automatons or have come into existence spontaneously.

The second matter concerns the usage of 'see'. I will use this in the ordinary sense according to which 'Jones sees the tree', for example, entails that the tree exists; and according to which Macbeth did *not* see a dagger for there was no dagger for him to see, though he may have *thought* he was seeing a dagger and it was, perhaps, *as if* he were.

Of course, from the fact that Macbeth did not see a dagger, it does not follow that he saw nothing. There are two views that can be taken concerning hallucinations.[6] One is that they exist and are seen, but are not, of course, material or physical. On this view, Macbeth saw something, albeit a non-physical something. Alternatively, it can be held that Macbeth saw nothing, and that when under hallucination one sees nothing (relevant) at all, either physical or mental. On this view, one should not really talk about hallucina*tions* at all, for there are none; rather there are cases of hallucina*ting*. (I return to this question at length in chapter three.)

The one thing that I think cannot be said is that 'Macbeth did see something, and that something did not exist',[7] or, concerning hallucinations in general, 'people can and do perceive things which do not exist'.[8] For there are no things – perceived or not – which do not exist. Perhaps when hallucinated one sees nothing – though I will argue against this in chapter three – but one thing is certain: nothing is not a very special, non-existent thing which one sees when hallucinated.

It sometimes seems to be thought that we can side-step the whole issue of whether 'see' has 'success grammar' or 'existential import', by arguing as follows: Let us grant that 'see' as used in current English licences inferring 'D exists' from 'S sees D'. But, for various reasons, this usage is philosophically inconvenient; hence we should conduct our discussion in terms of 'see*', where 'see*' means just what 'see' means, except that 'S sees* D' does not entail 'D exists'.[9]

---

[6] I follow the fairly standard practice of using 'illusion' for cases where something material is seen which looks other than it is, thus the straight stick in water looking bent is an illusion; and of using 'hallucination' for cases where nothing material is seen, thus after-images are hallucinations.

[7] Don Locke, *Perception and Our Knowledge of the External World*, p. 16.

[8] *Ibid.*, p. 17.

[9] I take this to be A. J. Ayer's view in *The Foundations of Empirical Knowledge*, ch. 1.

There is, however, a fundamental problem with such a procedure. Consider someone writing on the secondary qualities who observes that '*X* is red' entails that *X* is coloured, and decides to introduce the term 'red*' to mean precisely what 'red' means except that '*X* is red*' does not entail that *X* is coloured. The question such a procedure obviously raises is whether the deletion of the entailment to '*X* is coloured' leaves anything significant behind. And it is hard to see how to settle this question other than by considering whether 'is *X* red' may be analysed as a conjunction with '*X* is coloured' as one conjunct and some sentence, *P*, not entailing '*X* is coloured' as the other. If it can, '*X* is red*' means *P*; if not, 'red*' has no consistent meaning at all.

Likewise, whether or not there is anything meaningful corresponding to 'see*' depends on whether '*S* sees *D*' can be analysed as a conjunction with one conjunct as '*D* exists', and the other not entailing that *D* exists. Therefore, the question as to whether it is fruitful to introduce 'see*' cannot be raised at the *beginning* of a philosophical discussion of perception, but only after enough has been said to enable an opinion on the possibility of the required kind of conjunctive analyses.

More particularly, the issue turns out to pivot – as we will see in chapters three and four – on whether 'see' is essentially *relational*. '*A* is to the left of *B*' entails that *B* exists, but this is no 'mere verbal convention' or quirk of English usage. For there is no analysing it as '*A* is to the left of* *B* and *B* exists', where '*A* is to the left of* *B*' does not entail that *B* exists – if there were, Logic could dispense with many place relations.

Finally and briefly, I suppose 'see' to be such that '*S* sees *D* and *D*=*D'*' entails that *S* sees *D'*. That is, '*D*' is here subject to substitutivity (of co-referring terms) and so '*S* sees —' is a transparent construction.[10] If I see the friendly-looking dog and the friendly-looking dog is about to attack me, then I see the dog who is about to attack me, whether or not I am fortunate enough to know the fact. This view receives a detailed defence in G. J. Warnock's, 'On What is Seen'.[11]

[10] In the sense defined in W. V. Quine, *Word and Object*, §30.
[11] See also his earlier, 'Seeing', and Fred. I. Dretske, *Seeing and Knowing*, p. 54ff

I

The distinction between mediate and immediate objects of perception

0. Before I can argue that the major claim of the Representative Theory of Perception (RTP) that the immediate objects of perception are always mental, is true, we must see what it means; and, in particular, what 'immediate object of perception' means. This is the concern of this chapter.

1. We talk of seeing things and of seeing *that* . . . : 'I see the tomato', 'I see *that* the tomato is red.' In the first case, 'see' is followed by a singular term putatively naming something; in the second, by a sentence prefixed by 'that'. (We also talk of seeing events, processes, etc.: 'I saw the explosion', 'I saw the steady erosion of the river bank.' But I will concentrate on the first two cases here.)

In starting with the question '*What* are the immediate *objects* of perception', I am opting for the view that seeing things is more basic than seeing-that. The best warrant for such a view would be (i) a successful analysis of seeing-that in terms of seeing things, plus (ii) an argument that showed that the converse – an analysis of seeing things in terms of seeing-that – is impossible. Such a warrant will be offered in chapter 7.

In any case, the distinction between mediate and immediate perception, as conceived here and by traditionally minded writers on perception like G. E. Moore and H. H. Price pertains to perceiving things, not perception-that. For the distinction is introduced as a preamble to discussing *what* we immediately perceive. It is a preliminary to considering the nature of the immediate *objects* of perception. We shall see that some versions of the traditional ways of drawing the mediate–immediate distinction appear to overlook this point.

I believe that the usual formulations of the mediate–immediate distinction fail. I will argue this principally for D. M. Armstrong's formulation in terms of inference and suggestion, for H. H. Price's in terms of doubt, and for G. E. Moore's in terms of the parts not seen. This does not by any means exhaust the many attempts to draw the distinction,[1] but I think it will be sufficiently clear that the kinds of objections that I raise can, if they work at all, be more widely applied.

The general idea behind the distinction is to distinguish seeing houses, cats and mountains, on the one hand, from seeing red triangular shapes and white circular patches, on the other. What is at issue is whether there is an important distinction here, and, if there is, what its importance is. It is not, of course, at issue that statements like 'I see a red, round patch' and 'I see a ship' are both sometimes true.

2. D. M. Armstrong draws the distinction in terms of inference or suggestion, taking as his starting point Berkeley's (in)famous claim in the first dialogue of *Three Dialogues Between Hylas and Philonous* that 'when I hear a coach drive along the streets, immediately I perceive only the sound, but from experience I have had that such a sound is connected with a coach, I am said to hear the coach'.[2]

This is a puzzling claim. Berkeley purports to be talking about hearing the coach, hearing the sound, and about the relation between the two; but what he says is plausible only if construed as being about *believing* (or *knowing*) that one is hearing a sound and hearing a coach. For example, 'the experience I have had that such a sound is connected with a coach' is irrelevant to whether I hear a coach. There is such a thing as hearing a coach for the *first* time, and so, one may hear a coach in the absence of the past experience Berkeley refers to. Past experience is only relevant to the quite separate question of whether I believe or know that the sound is that of a coach, and hence to whether I hear *that* there is a coach outside.

This confusion in Berkeley over whether we are considering the perception of things, or beliefs about perception, or perception-that seems to me to carry over into Armstrong's remarks elucidating Berkeley. For instance, Armstrong argues that

> we can be said to have heard the coach only because we have heard the sound. We may not have paid much attention to the sound, we may have been much more *interested* in the coach than in the sound, but we must have heard the sound in order to hear the coach. But the reverse implication does not hold. Somebody who heard a noise, which was in fact made by a coach, but who was unfamiliar with the

---

[1] E.g., A. White in *G. E. Moore*, ch. 8, distinguishes six methods to be found in Moore's writings alone.

[2] *The Works of George Berkeley*, ed. Luce and Jessop, vol. 2, p. 204.

noise that coaches make, could not say that he heard a coach. Or at any rate he could not say that he knew he was hearing a coach.[3]

But the reverse implication *does* hold. If I hear 'a noise, which was in fact made by a coach', then *ipso facto* I hear the coach – whether or not I am in a position to *say* that I do, or *know* that I do. It seems that both Berkeley and Armstrong are confusing its being true that I hear a coach with my believing or being in a position to say that I hear a coach.

The confusion between perception and belief about perception under-lies the common doctrine that the distinction between mediate and immediate perception is that the latter but not the former involves no inference. Consider, for example, Armstrong's account: 'Immediate perception, then, is perception which involves no element of inference, while mediate perception does involve such an inference';[4] and, later: 'Immediate perception, then, is perception which involves no element of suggestion. We can say if we like that it involves no element of inference, but we must remember the latitudinarian sense of the word 'inference' that is being employed.'[5]

But inference is a notion definable in terms of belief: to infer is at least to believe as a result of . . . (The interesting problems associated with spelling this out are not relevant here.[6]) So to claim that mediate perception, by contradistinction to immediate perception, involves inference is to claim that mediate perception involves certain beliefs that immediate perception does not; and this is false. Hearing the coach does not require any beliefs that hearing the sound does not. There are, so to speak, no additional beliefs which must be 'added on' to hearing the sound to get hearing the coach – if the sound is the sound of a coach, then hearing the sound is hearing the coach regardless of what one believes about whether the sound is that of a coach.

A similar point applies against the formulation in terms of suggestion. Suggestion, in the sense at issue, involves at least putative belief, but one may hear the coach without having any idea that it is a coach that one is hearing; and if one is hearing the sound of a coach, then one is hearing the coach even if the sound in no way suggests a coach to one.

In order to make reasonable sense of the claim that mediate percep-

[3] *Perception and the Physical World*, p. 20.

[4] *Ibid.*, p. 21.

[5] *Ibid.*, p. 21.

[6] But see M. Deutscher, 'A Causal Account of Inferring' in *Contemporary Philosophy in Australia*.

tion involves inference (or suggestion) in a significant way that immediate perception does not, we must modify the claim to something like: *believing* that one is mediately perceiving involves inference while *believing* that one is immediately perceiving does not involve inference; or in terms of the objects of perception rather than the perceiving, X is an immediate object of perception if and only if one may *believe* that one perceives X without carrying out any kind of inference. In terms of this modification, the general idea will be that the sound counts as an immediate object of perception because one does not need to infer in order to believe that one is hearing a sound of a certain kind; while the coach is a mediate object because one does need to infer – from, for example, previously established generalizations about the kind of sound coaches make – in order to believe that one is hearing a coach.

3. There is an enormous amount that could be said here about inference and its connexion with perception but – as these issues do not bear on what follows – I will restrict myself to advancing two objections which can, I believe, be seen to be decisive without our entering into a detailed discussion of inference.

Let us switch from hearing to our primary concern, vision, and put the two objections by reference to a case of seeing a white cat. The idea behind the mediate–immediate distinction is that a certain coloured shape – white, 'cat-shaped', and with fuzzy edges – will be the immediate object of (visual) perception in such a case, and that the cat will be the mediate object of perception.

The first objection (to the account of the distinction given three paragraphs back) arises from the role of the mediate–immediate distinction in arriving at an overall account of perceiving. It is supposed to be a *first* step. Hence, the distinction must be drawn in a way which does not presuppose the answer to later questions. Now consider our white cat seen in pink light. What is the immediate object of perception in this case – a white shape (which looks pink), or a pink shape? The choice between these two answers is notoriously a crucial one, and drawing the distinction in terms of inference pre-empts the choice by forcing the answer most philosophers now reject – namely, a pink shape. For in order to know that one is seeing a white shape which looks pink in the circumstances, one must make reference to facts like (i) that cats are very rarely pink, and (ii) that white objects commonly look pink in this kind of lighting. Hence, precisely the reason – be it good or bad in itself – for saying that believing one is seeing a cat involves inference, namely, the reference to past experience, applies to the belief that one is seeing a white shape; so, *if* the first involves inference, so does the second. Likewise, the familiar point that further investigation might, in a perfectly straight-forward way, force one to abandon one's belief that one is seeing a cat (in favour, for example, of the belief that one is seeing a cleverly-made dummy) applies equally to the belief that one is seeing a white shape which looks pink. We are all familiar with the kind of cases where we would abandon the latter kind of belief in favour, for example, of the belief that what we were seeing really was pink. Sometimes a thing thought to be looking other than it is, is found to be, in fact, looking as it is.

As it happens, I believe that the immediate object of perception in the case of the white cat looking pink is a pink shape. But it is clear that this view must be argued for, as it will be, and not presumed by the very method of drawing the mediate–immediate distinction that is adopted.

The second objection arises from the fact that we are seeking to draw a distinction among objects (things, entities): things like white shapes and sounds being alleged to be in the class of the immediate objects of perception, and things like cats and coaches being alleged to be in the class of the mediate objects of perception. The inference test is disastrously equivocal when applied to objects, as the following argument shows.

Suppose I am looking at the white cat in normal lighting, so that it is not at issue that I am seeing a white shape and that I am seeing a cat; and let us use, following G. E. Moore, 'belongs to' for the relation between the white shape and the cat, whatever that relation turns out to be (perhaps it is identity, or the part-whole relation, or causal – this question can be left to one side here). Now the white shape seen will be *one and the same* as the white shape belonging to the cat. But, on the inference test, the white shape belonging to the cat must be counted as a mediate object of perception if the cat is. *If* inference is involved in believing that one sees a white cat, it must also be involved in believing that one sees a white shape belonging to a white cat; for the latter belief is stronger than the former. Hence, the inference test has the unacceptable consequence that one and the same thing – equally describable as a white shape and as a white shape belonging to a white cat – both is and is not an immediate object of perception.

Clearly, this kind of difficulty will arise for any putative immediate object of perception: the sound is the sound of a coach, and if believing that I hear a coach involves inference, so does believing that I hear the sound of a coach. At best, inference can serve only to distinguish among perceptual statements, descriptions, perception-that, and the like; it cannot serve to distinguish among perceptual *objects*. (In *A Materialist Theory Of The Mind*, Armstrong modifies his view in a way which suggests he would now accept at least part of this conclusion. See page 233.)

It might be thought that a simple modification to the inference test is available to avoid the difficulty just raised. Instead of: *A* is an immediate object of perception for *S* just if '*S* believes that he sees *A*' involves no inference, it might be suggested the inference test be modified to: *A* is an immediate object of perception for *S* just if there is a singular term '*B*', such that $A=B$, and '*S* believes that he sees *B*' involves no inference. But this modification does not really advance matters. Suppose I see a black cat, and this is the only thing I am seeing; then 'the thing I am seeing' designates the cat. And 'I believe that I am seeing the thing I am seeing' does not involve inference. So the modification leads to treating the cat as an immediate object of perception, contrary to intention. A natural reply here is that 'the thing I am seeing' is ambiguous; only if it means 'the thing I am *mediately* seeing' does it designate the cat; if it means 'the thing I am *immediately* seeing', it designates, rather, the black shape. But this reply is, of course, only available to someone who *already* grasps the distinction at issue. It presupposes the distinction, and so cannot be appealed to in elucidating it.

4. In a famous passage in *Perception*, H. H. Price argues as follows:

> When I see a tomato there is much that I can doubt. I can doubt whether it is a tomato that I am seeing, and not a cleverly painted piece of wax. I can doubt whether there is any material thing there at all . . . One thing however I cannot doubt: that there exists a red patch of a round and somewhat bulgy shape.[7]

An immediate problem with this passage is that it appears to beg an important question in the philosophy of perception, namely, whether there is an important distinction between seeing a red patch and there being a red patch which I see, akin to the undeniable distinction between looking for a totally honest man and there being a totally honest man that I am looking for. If there is such a distinction in the perceptual case, Price's central claim becomes very implausible. I may be quite certain that I am looking for the totally honest man, while

[7] *Perception*, p. 3.

entertaining the gravest doubts as to whether *there is* a totally honest man such that I am looking for him. Likewise, *if* the distinction applies in the perceptual case, it might be granted to Price that I cannot doubt that I am seeing a red patch of a round and etc., without it being granted that I cannot doubt that 'there exists a red patch of a round and etc.' which I see.

A consideration of this matter is postponed to chapter 3, for, regardless of how it should be resolved, any attempt to use the (alleged) indubitability of our knowledge that we are seeing red patches as opposed to the obvious fallibility of our knowledge that we are seeing material things like tomatoes, faces the two objections that we raised to the inference test.

(I say 'any attempt' rather than 'Price's attempt' because Price uses the indubitability claim to pick out a relation, that of being directly given, rather than a class of objects. The two approaches converge as the range of this relation is intended to be the class of immediate objects of perception, or, as Price calls them, sense-data.)

Briefly, first, suppose I am looking at a white tomato in red light. Price must hold that I see a red patch, not a white one; for it is obvious that I may doubt that I am seeing a white patch in this situation. Hence, the doubt test begs the same crucial question as the inference test for immediate perception.

Second, the red patch of a round and etc. must be reckoned *one and the same* thing as the red patch of a round etc. belonging to the tomato, and I can, of course, doubt that I am seeing a red patch of a round and etc. belonging to the tomato to at least the extent that I can doubt that I am seeing the tomato. So reference to doubt also fails to pick out anything unequivocally as an immediate object of perception.

As might be expected, similar remarks apply to attempts to draw the mediate–immediate distinction by reference to *going beyond*, as in Don Locke's claim that 'The crucial point about immediate perception is that it does not go beyond what is perceived at the particular moment.'[8] Perhaps we do have here a significant distinction between perceptual *statements*, perhaps there is a sense in which 'I see a red patch', for example, does not go beyond, or, in another favoured phrase, *takes nothing for granted*,[9] while 'I see a tomato' does; but, in any case, we do not have here a way of delimiting the class of immediate objects of perception. For, if the red patch is an immediate object of perception,

8 *Perception and Our Knowledge of the External World*, p. 171.
9 See G. J. Warnock, *Berkeley*, ch. 7.

then – by Leibniz's Law – so is the red patch belonging to, let us say, the prize-winning tomato at this year's Royal Show; and the statement 'I see the (or a) red patch belonging to the prize-winning tomato at this year's Royal Show' is obviously exactly the sort of statement that would be described as going beyond or as taking things for granted. (More precisely, it is, of course, a person asserting the statement who goes beyond or takes for granted.)

5. A quite different way of drawing the mediate–immediate distinction is suggested by the point C. D. Broad, John Wisdom and Moore emphasise in this connexion.[10] Normally, when we see an opaque, material thing, there is a great deal of that thing we do not see (for example, the back and inside). This suggests we define an immediate object of (visual) perception as one we see all of.[11] This suggestion at least has the advantage of avoiding the central problem just raised for accounts in terms of inference and doubt: whether I see all of X or not is independent of how X is described; that is, it is a question about X, not about some description of or statement concerning X.

There is, however, a major drawback to defining immediate objects of perception as those we see all of: it reverses the correct order of argument on perception, it puts the cart before the horse. For how, on this definition, do we settle whether there are any immediate objects of perception? It is non-controversial that there are *mediate* objects of perception, for it is accepted by all parties that we sometimes see things which have parts we do not see (at the time of seeing). But it is highly controversial whether there are things such that we both see them and see all of them, and so, highly controversial as to whether there are any immediate objects of perception according to the suggested definition. Moreover, the answer to this question depends on the nature of what we perceive. If, as in one version of Direct Realism,[12] we always perceive opaque physical objects, then there will be no immediate objects of perception, for it is impossible to see all parts of an opaque physical object. Every such object has a back which one will not be seeing. This is as true of facing surfaces of objects as it is of three-dimensional ones – the fact that a surface is facing one does not remove

---

[10] See, e.g., C. D. Broad, 'Some Elementary Reflections on Sense-Perception', J. Wisdom, *Problems of Mind and Matter*, ch. 9, and G. E. Moore, 'The Nature and Reality of Objects of Perception'.

[11] Cf., D. Locke, *Perception and Our Knowledge of the External World*, p. 175.

[12] That which holds that everything we perceive is physical, as opposed to the version which adds the proviso – except when hallucinated.

its back. On the other hand, *if* after-images are a typical example of what we see, there may, on the definition under consideration, be immediate objects of perception, for it is reasonable to hold that we see all parts of them.

But what we want from the distinction between mediate and immediate objects of perception is a firm base from which to launch an investigation of such questions as whether the immediate objects of perception are always mental, or physical, or whether some are mental and some physical. The definition in question is of no help for this: it makes the answer to whether or not something, X, that I see is an immediate object of perception, depend on first deciding whether X is mental or physical – if mental, there may be no part of X I do not see; if physical (and opaque), there is.

6. In somewhat later writings, Moore introduces the notion of a sense-datum by an essentially ostensive procedure, where, in his usage, 'sense-datum' is a term for the immediate objects of perception, be they mental or physical. For example, in a famous passage he says:

> And in order to point out to the reader what sort of things I mean by sense-data, I need only ask him to look at his own right hand. If he does this, he will be able to pick out something . . . with regard to which he will see that it is, at first sight, a natural view to take that that thing is identical, not, indeed, with his whole right hand, but with that part of its surface which he is actually seeing, but will also (on a little reflection), be able to see that it is doubtful whether it can be identical with the part of the surface of his hand in question. Things of *the sort* (in a certain respect) of which this thing is . . . I mean by sense-data.[13]

I agree with O. K. Bouwsma's criticism,[14] which I take to be essentially the following dilemma. Either we take Moore to be pointing to a part of his hand's surface, or to be pointing to something else. If the first, there is no question of 'a little reflection' (or a lot) leading us to be 'doubtful whether it can be identical with the part of the surface of his hand in question'; for this is a contradiction. If the second, we must *already* understand the notion of a sense-datum and believe it to be distinct from any part of the hand, for there is nothing else relevant (and distinct from the hand) to which Moore might be taken to be pointing.

[13] 'A Defence of Common Sense', p. 54.
[14] 'Moore's Theory of Sense-Data', in *Philosophy of G. E. Moore*.

Moore would probably reply that he was pointing to a certain coloured patch (off white and 'hand-shaped') and leaving it as a matter for further investigation whether this patch is or is not identical with the hand's surface. But how can I be sure that there *is* a relevant, certain coloured patch that I see *unless* we take it to be the physical hand. Presumably, we can be sure that some statement like 'Moore sees a certain coloured patch' is true, but to take it that this entails that *there is* such a coloured patch which he sees is to beg just the kind of question that notion of an immediate object of perception is supposed to be a first step in helping us solve. And, secondly, we are left by this reply quite in the dark as to why this certain, coloured patch should play a basic role in the analysis of perception. Why is seeing a certain, coloured patch more fundamental than seeing part of the surface of a hand? For all Moore says, they are just both things we see, neither being especially prior to the other.

I now turn to the (always more difficult) task of offering a positive account of the distinction.

7. The account I wish to give of the mediate–immediate distinction can be approached by specifying the *in virtue of* relation.

There are many cases where statements to the effect that something is *F*, or something bears *R* to something, may be analysed in terms of some *other* thing being *F* or bearing *R* to something. For instance, to say that a car is red is to say that the body of the car is red: 'This car is red' may be analysed in terms of something distinct from the car, its body, being red. Likewise, anyone who holds that persons are not identical with their bodies is committed to holding that such statements as 'He is tall (heavy, strong)' may be analysed in terms of something distinct from him, his body, being tall (heavy, strong). A relational example is the statement 'The car is touching the kerb': this statement may be analysed in terms of something distinct from the car, namely, some part of the car, touching some part of the kerb.

I will use the expression 'in virtue of' to describe this kind of case. That is, when '*Fa*' may be analysed in terms of *b* being *F*, where $a \neq b$, or '*a* R *b*' in terms of *c* bearing R to *d*, where $a \neq c$ and/or $b \neq d$; I will say that '*Fa*' is true in virtue of *b* being *F*, and '*a* R *b*' is true in virtue of *c* bearing R to *d*. Thus, the car is red in virtue of the body of the car being red; a man is tall in virtue of his body being tall; the car is touching the kerb in virtue of, say, its left front tyre touching the kerb; and so on.

It is important to note that 'in virtue of' is being used to cover cases where a certain kind of systematic analysis is possible; it is not a surrogate for entailment. Saying that 'My car is red' is true in virtue of my car's body being red is not just another way of saying that 'The body of my car is red' entails 'My car is red'; for the converse is also true, 'My car is red' entails 'The body of my car is red', but the car body is not red in virtue of the car being red. The crucial point is that the application of the predicate 'is red' to cars can be analysed in terms of the application of 'is red' to car bodies, but not vice versa. For every red car there must be a red body, but there may be (and are on assembly lines) red car bodies without red cars. Moreover, if my car is my most unreliable possession, then my most unreliable possession is red in virtue of its body being red; but 'My most unreliable possession is red' neither entails, nor is entailed by, 'My most unreliable possession's body is red.'

The 'in virtue of' relation is implicitly involved in many widely entertained philosophical theses. The doctrine that propositions, conceived as abstract entities distinct from sentences, are the fundamental bearers of truth-value, is that a sentence, S, is true *in virtue of* the proposition expressed by that sentence being true, but not vice versa. (And, of course, entailment may run both ways or neither way: 'S is true' entails, and is entailed by, 'The proposition expressed by S is true'; while 'The fourth sentence on the board is true' neither entails, nor is entailed by 'The proposition that snow is white is true' – though, according to the doctrine, if the fourth sentence is 'Snow is white', it is true in virtue of the proposition that snow is white being true.) Likewise, to say that the (singular) causal relation holds between *events* is to say that a statement like 'The stone caused the window to break' is true *in virtue of* some event (involving the stone, presumably) causing the window to break.

There is a use of 'in virtue of' and the like to stand for causal connexions or counterfactual conditions. This is not, of course, our use. No one supposes that the truth of propositions causes the truth of sentences; and nor does the redness of the car body cause the car to be red, the spray painting does that. Likewise, our usage cannot be analysed counterfactually. Suppose my car is touching the kerb in virtue of the front tyre touching the kerb. It may be true that if the front tyre were not touching the kerb, the car would not be; but, equally, it may not be. It may be that if the front tyre were not touching the kerb, then the back tyre would be; and so, the car would still be touching the kerb. The same applies in the proposition case: suppose the fourth sentence is true in virtue of a certain proposition being true. This is consistent with things being such that if this proposition were false, the fourth sentence would still be true; for it may be that the fourth sentence was chosen because it is true, and so, if the proposition were false, the fourth sentence would have been chosen differently.

Thus far, I have given a number of examples of what I mean by 'in virtue of', and a deliberately rather vague definition in terms of *a*'s being *F* being analysable in terms of *b*'s being *F* and *a* and *b* being suitably related. A precise, generally applicable definition is very difficult to achieve. Despite the frequency with which the notion of analysing one thing being so and so in terms of another thing being so and so is appealed to, its explication is highly controversial. In particular, there is an asymmetry in the notion which it is difficult to capture.

Take, for instance, the doctrine that sentences are true in virtue of propositions being true, that is, that the formers' truth is to be analysed in terms of the latters' truth. It is obviously a part of this doctrine that each true sentence bears a relation to some true proposition such that the latter's being true together with the holding of this relation logically entails the former's being true. But there must be more to it than this. For the doctrine is not just that the truth of sentences and propositions is logically interrelated, it is that the truth of sentences derives from, is a matter of, or (as we have put it) the sentence is true in virtue of the proposition being true, and *not* vice versa. In the sentence–proposition case, the explanation for the asymmetry seems to be ontological: for advocates of the doctrine want to say that true propositions could exist without true sentences existing; for instance, if no one had ever written or spoken, there would be no sentences but many truths.

The asymmetry consequent upon this point comes out most clearly (as Melvyn Cann pointed out to me) if one considers the question of order of definition. Given an understanding of '– is true' applied to propositions, one can (according to advocates of the doctrine) obtain a definition of '– is true' applied to sentences thus: a sentence is true just if it expresses a true proposition. The converse, however, is *not* possible. One cannot adequately define '– is true' applied to propositions given its application to sentences. One cannot, for example, say that a proposition is true just if it is expressed by a true sentence, for there are true propositions for which there are no sentences which express them (both in the possible world where there are no sentences, and in the actual world, because there is a non-denumberable infinity of propositions).

Similar remarks apply to our other cases. Given an understanding of '– is red' applied to car bodies, a definition of '– is red' applied to cars can be obtained thus: a car is red just if its body is red. But the converse procedure is not possible because of the possibility (and actuality) of car bodies not attached to cars. Again, '– touches the kerb' applied to cars can be defined in terms of '– touches the kerb' applied to parts of cars, but not conversely. Because no car can touch the kerb without a part of it, the front tyre, say, doing so; but the front tyre can touch the kerb without the car doing so, for it might be detached from the car.

We are now able to spell out *in virtue of* sufficiently for present purposes. An *A* is *F* in virtue of *a B* being *F* if the application of '– is *F*' to an *A* is definable in terms of its application to a *B* and a relation, R, between *A*s and *B*s, but not conversely. This gives us an account for the indefinite case. We obtain an account for the definite case as follows: *This A* is *F* in virtue of *this B* being *F* if (i) an *A* is *F* in virtue of a *B* being *F* (as just defined), (ii) this *A* and this *B* are *F*, and (iii) this *A* and this *B* bear R to each other.

We have noted one way the converse may not be possible: there may be *B*s which lack corresponding *A*s (propositions without sentences, car parts without cars, and so on). There is another. The relation, R, may not be specifiable without circularity. This is the case with our example of the car touching the kerb in virtue of its front tyre doing so; but, for variety, I will illustrate the point with a different example.

I live in Melbourne, a city of Australia; I, therefore, live in Australia. Melbourne and Australia are not identical, nevertheless, I do not live in two different places. Rather, I live in Australia in virtue of living in Melbourne. This example accords with what I have said above. The application of 'I live in –' to countries is clearly definable in terms of its application to parts of countries, but the reverse is not possible because any part of a country might fail to be a part of a country – Melbourne, for instance, is but might not have been a part of Australia.

There is an additional reason why the reverse is not possible in this case. The relevant relation between Melbourne and Australia is that Melbourne is a part of Australia, and the definition of 'I live in —' as applied to a country in terms of its application to a part thereof is achieved by reference to this relation thus: I live in a country just if I live in something which is a part of that country. But a definition of the application of 'I live in —' to some part of a country cannot be achieved by: I live in some particular part of a country just if I live in the country which has that part as a part. For I might live in that country without living in *that* part. It does not follow from my living in Australia and Melbourne being a part of Australia, that I live in Melbourne. Of course, there is a relation between Melbourne and Australia such that it follows from my living in Australia together with Melbourne having this relation to Australia, that I live in Melbourne, namely, *having Melbourne as the part in which I live*. But it would be circular to appeal to this kind of relation in trying to define the application of 'I live in —' to parts of countries in terms of its application to countries.

I hope I have now made what I mean by 'in virtue of' clear enough for what follows. I have laboured the matter to try to allay the suspicions many feel about any attempt to distinguish immediate from mediate perception.

8. We are now in a position to develop a definition of an immediate object of perception (for S at t).

We commonly see things in virtue of seeing *other* things: I see the aircraft flying overhead in virtue of seeing its underside (and the aircraft is not identical with its underside); I see the table I am writing on in virtue of seeing its top; I first see England on the cross-channel ferry in virtue of seeing the white cliffs of Dover; and so on and so forth. Each of these cases fits the account of *in virtue of* given in the preceding section.

Take, for instance, the case of seeing the table in virtue of seeing its top. The top of the table is a reasonably substantial part of the table. And the application of 'I see —' to an opaque, three-dimensional object is definable in terms of its application to a reasonably substantial part, for I am properly said to see an opaque object if I see a reasonably substantial part of it. But the application of 'I see —' to a part of an object cannot be defined in terms of its application to the object to which the part belongs. This is for both of the kinds of reasons noted in the previous section. The particular part might not have been a part of the particular object, and I might have seen the object by seeing some *other* part of it: I might, for instance, have seen the table by seeing the underneath of it.

It follows, therefore, that I see *an* opaque object in virtue of seeing *a* part of it. Moreover, by inspection of the account, it is also true that I see *this* opaque object (the table) in virtue of seeing *this* part (the top). The same line of reasoning obviously applies to the other cases mentioned and, indeed, to a multitude of like ones. That is, we often see things in virtue of seeing other things.

Now for our definition: x is a *mediate object of (visual) perception* (for

S at *t*) iff *S* sees *x* at *t*, and there is a *y* such that ($x \neq y$ and) *S* sees *x* in virtue of seeing *y*. An *immediate object of perception* is one that is not mediate; and we can define the relation of *immediately perceiving* thus: *S* immediately perceives *x* at *t* iff *x* is an immediate object of perception for *S* at *t* (as just defined).

9. It is one thing to provide a definition, quite another to show: (i), that something satisfies it, and, (ii), what kind of thing satisfies it. A full answer to what kinds of things are the immediate objects of perception depends on matters discussed in following chapters, but it is possible to go part of the way at this stage. We have already in effect noted, on the negative side, that reasonably sized, opaque material things are never immediate objects of perception. Any such object will be seen in virtue of seeing some part of that object, for example, the table is seen in virtue of seeing its top.

On the positive side, I will consider three cases in turn. The first is that of seeing a red, round after-image. *If* this is a case of seeing something, as I will argue later (in chapter three), then it quite clearly is a case where there is an immediate object of (visual) perception, namely, the red, round after-image itself; for there is nothing else seen which could plausibly be held to be such that one sees the after-image in virtue of seeing it. Perhaps one sees the wall behind, the side of one's nose, and the like, but obviously the after-image is not seen in virtue of seeing any of them. Therefore, provided after-images are seen, we have shown that something satisfies our definition; and, clearly, for hallucinations in general, *if* they are part of what is seen, then they are immediate objects of perception.

The second case I consider is that of veridical perception. Suppose I I stand in front of a white wall; then if I look at it in reasonably normal circumstances, I will see a largish, white expanse. That is, one true answer to the question What do I see? will be – a white expanse. There will, of course, be other true answers – like, a wall, and the painted surface of a wall; but I do not think it can seriously be denied that a white expanse is one true answer, and so, that there is at least one white expanse which is seen. I say 'at least one', because on some theories there will be more than one; but, on all sane theories, there is at least one white expanse seen.

Moreover, I do not think it can be seriously denied that at least one of the white expanses seen is an immediate object of perception as defined here; because it follows regardless of the theory of perception assumed. If Direct Realism is true, then what is seen is a white expanse identical with the facing surface of the wall, the wall, and nothing else relevant. Clearly, the wall is seen in virtue of seeing the facing surface, and hence is not an immediate object of perception; but the facing surface is not seen in virtue of seeing the wall (for the same kinds of reasons that applied to the table case earlier). And, as far as Direct Realism is concerned, there will be nothing else seen which could at all plausibly be that which the facing surface is seen in virtue of seeing. Hence, the Direct Realist must acknowledge that the facing surface is an immediate object of perception. But the facing surface is, according to him, one and the same as the white expanse, so he must acknowledge the white expanse ('the', as there is only one according to him) as the immediate object of perception.

If Representationalism is true, then, depending on the version, there may be two white expanses which are seen – one mental, the other facing surface of the wall causally responsible for the mental one (or, better, responsible for *having* the mental one) – or, on representative theories which deny that colour properly speaking qualifies physical things, just one. In either case, the mental one will have to be regarded by the representationalist as an immediate object of perception as we have defined it; for the mental entity, if seen as postulated on the theory, is evidently not seen in virtue of seeing something else. It is not, for instance, seen in virtue of seeing the object which, according to the theory, causes one to experience the white expanse. On the other hand, the wall is seen in virtue of seeing the white expanse; for seeing material objects can, according to him, be analysed in terms of seeing mental entities belonging to them. That is, he holds that the application of '*S* sees —' to something material can be defined in terms of its application to something mental, but not conversely – because, for instance, the mental thing might exist and be seen without the material one existing or being seen.

Both the Representationalist and the Direct Realist, therefore, must acknowledge that in the case of veridical perception there is an immediate object of perception and that it is a coloured expanse – while, of course, disagreeing profoundly about the ontological status of this coloured expanse. Similar remarks apply to Idealism.

The final case I consider is that of illusion. Suppose the white wall of the previous case is being illuminated by a red light and consequently looks pink. Again, it is quite certain that there is a coloured expanse which is being seen and is an immediate object of perception. What *is* controversial is whether two coloured expanses, one white and one pink, are seen or only one, white expanse is seen. If there is only one expanse, this will be the immediate object of perception, for we cannot be seeing it in virtue of seeing the pink one, there being no pink expanse. On the other hand, if there are two, the immediate object of perception will obviously (from the considerations above) be the mental, pink one. In either case, therefore, there is an immediate object of perception, and it is a coloured expanse.

The upshot, therefore, is that in every case where something is seen – hallucination (if that is a case), illusion and the veridical case – there is a coloured expanse which is seen and not in virtue of seeing anything else; that is, whenever something is seen, there is an immediate object of perception and it is always a coloured shape or expanse.

10. It will make the significance of this conclusion clearer, and, possibly, forestall some objections if I draw attention to certain things I am *not* saying when I say that whenever a person sees something, there is a coloured expanse which he sees and which is an immediate object of perception for him.

First, in saying that the immediate objects of perception are always coloured expanses, I am not saying that they are *merely* coloured expanses, that they have *only* the properties of shape, extension, and colour. I am not, for example, expressing any view one way or the other on whether R. Firth is right to claim 'that such qualities as simplicity, regularity, harmoniousness, clumsiness, gracefulness . . . can also have the same phenomenological status as colour and shape'.[15] What I am claiming, and all I need for the argument of the following chapters, is that the immediate objects of perception have *at least* colour, shape, and extension.

Second, though I do hold that it is certain that opaque, three-dimensional physical objects like tomatoes are not immediate objects of perception, I do not hold, and need not, that perceiving a physical object, say the tomato, is a two-fold process starting with the perception of a red shape and finishing with the tomato. If I see a red shape which belongs to the tomato, then I see the tomato, regardless of whether I believe that I am, or am conscious of seeing a tomato, or see the shape *as* belonging to a tomato, and so on. There is – as we, in effect, noted in §2 – nothing that needs to be added to seeing the patch to get seeing the tomato.

There is, of course, a manifest difference between seeing the red patch (and so, the tomato), and such things as: taking it that one is see-

[15] R. Firth, 'Sense-Data and the Percept Theory', p. 221.

ing the tomato, being conscious of seeing the tomato, seeing the patch *as* related to a tomato, and so on. But these latter, though important, are not important for the theses I wish to defend here; and, hence, will not be discussed in any detail.

There has, I think, been a tendency to confuse what it is to perceive a material object with: what it is to take it that one is seeing a material object, seeing something as being a certain kind of material object, being conscious that one is seeing a material object of a particular type, and so on. To give a recent example, T. L. S. Sprigge, in advancing what he describes as the traditional empiricist stance, holds that

> it is proper to distinguish *two factors* in each case of perception, first, the sensing of a certain sense-datum, second, the putting of some interpretation upon this sense-datum of a kind such that, if it is correct, or at least correct enough, the two factors together will constitute perception of some material thing.[16]

I think Sprigge is right to distinguish the two factors (and our arguments later will support his description of one of them in terms of sense-data); but, surely, he is wrong to say that two factors together 'constitute perception of some material thing'. For what constitutes perception of some material thing can occur without any appropriate interpretation occurring.

I can see the headmaster without knowing that I am; I can see him even without realising that I am seeing a person – I may mistake him for a realistic dummy planted in a student rag. Again, I may see a red patch on the wall but take it that I am seeing a red after-image – even as radical a mistake in interpretation as this does not rule out my in fact seeing the red patch.

Third, I am not denying the familiar and important point that, in many circumstances, we find it much easier to specify the physical objects we see than the coloured shapes we see; nor that sometimes we remember seeing some physical thing without being able to remember what corresponding coloured shape we saw. My definition of *immediate object of perception* does not entail that immediate objects of perception are easier to specify or remember than mediate objects; and, hence, though I say that every physical object is seen in virtue of seeing some coloured expanse, this does not commit me to saying that the coloured shape in question is easier to specify or remember than the physical object (and in many cases it certainly is not).

[16] *Facts, Words, and Beliefs*, p. 3, my italics.

Consider a parallel: suppose Jones lives in Detroit, and so, in America. In the terminology used in this chapter, he lives in America in virtue of living in Detroit, just as we saw that I live in Australia in virtue of living in Melbourne. But this in no way entails that it is easier for me to specify or remember the city Jones lives in than the country he lives in. And, of course, we are commonly more certain of the country someone lives in than the part thereof.

Fourthly and similarly, I am not committed to denying the occurrence of what is sometimes called unconscious perception. Armstrong describes a case thus,

> I am driving along an unfamiliar street, and I pass a hoarding. When I reach the end of the street I am asked what it was that the hoarding was advertising. *To my surprise* I am able to answer; to my surprise, because I was not conscious of seeing what was on the hoarding when I passed it, I did not notice it at the time. Should we say, nevertheless, that I *did* see it ?[17]

Armstrong answers, yes, to his final question, and this seems at least as reasonable as any other answer. 'But how can you contemplate this answer, given that he remembers only what was advertised and nothing of the colour or shape of the advertisement; for you are committed to saying that if he sees the hoarding, then he sees a coloured expanse.' But it is evidently absurd to hold that he saw the hoarding without seeing the front face of the hoarding (that is where the advertisement was) and *that* is a coloured expanse. So *if* the case is to be described as seeing the hoarding, it must be allowed that a coloured expanse was seen without in any way registering.

'But how can something register, without what it is true in virtue of registering ?' Well, suppose our subject had also been asked if there was a black cross painted somewhere on the face of the hoarding. It seems quite possible that he should be able to answer, Yes, without being able to say *where* on the hoarding the cross was painted. But the cross *must* have been somewhere on the hoarding, thus it seems we can (visually) register that something is the case without registering what it is the case in virtue of.

Fifthly, as will be obvious from the tenor of the preceding, the notion of an immediate object of perception I am concerned with is quite distinct from the notion of what is *directly given* or of what one is

---

[17] *Perception and the Physical World*, p. 123.

directly aware, at least on the usual understanding of these expressions. For I do not maintain any of the following:

(i) that my belief that I am seeing the tomato must derive from believing that I am seeing the red shape which is the immediate object of perception.

(ii) that my belief that I am seeing the tomato *must* be less certain than my belief that I am seeing the red shape.

(iii) that a necessary condition of seeing the tomato is being *aware* of the red shape.

Not only am I not maintaining any of (i)–(iii), I in fact take them to be false. My reasons for this are the usual ones so will just be summarised. Take (i): First, I may, of course, see the tomato without believing I see it – perhaps I think it is a wax dummy, or perhaps I see it without in any way noticing it. Second, suppose I both see the tomato and believe that I see it, must my belief that I see the tomato derive from believing that I see the red shape? Well, of course, it may; but there seem clear cases to show that it need not so derive. Suppose I glance briefly into the kitchen and see a bowl of fruit and vegetables containing a tomato. And suppose I am then asked whether I saw a tomato and whether it was red or green (that is, was ripe or unripe). It seems clear that I might be able to answer the first query without being able to answer the second; that is, it is possible that I noticed seeing the tomato without noticing in any way the colour (which I must, of course, have seen). Hence, it is possible that I believe that I see the tomato without believing that I see a red shape (though I *am* seeing a red shape). The case just described may seem contrived, but I think similar cases arise fairly often. Suppose I am walking along a country lane at the beginning of autumn deep in thought. Then there will normally be *very* many things – hundreds of leaves, for example – that I see without noticing them at all, and so, without believing that I am seeing them; but there will also be many things – more leaves, for example – which I see and notice sufficiently to believe, perhaps very briefly, that I am seeing them, but not sufficiently to have any opinion on their colour: I see many of the leaves and am aware that I am seeing them, without being aware of whether they have 'turned' yet, that is, without being aware of whether they are green, yellow or red.

These kinds of case – of briefly glancing at an object (in our case, a leaf or a tomato) and noticing its identity more than its colour – show also that (ii) and (iii) are false: I may, obviously, be more sure that I am seeing a tomato or a leaf than a red shape and be unaware (in any natural meaning of that term) of the red shape in such a case.

I am not, though, denying that if *at the time of knowingly seeing* an object I am asked to specify the relevant coloured shape or apparent coloured shape, I will, except in bizarre circumstances,[18] be able to give a clear answer. There is a capacity of human beings, which we might call 'directing one's attention to one's perceptual experience' or 'putting oneself in the phenomenological frame of mind', the exercise of which enables us to pick out a coloured shape corresponding to any physical object we are seeing.

Nor am I denying the familiar point that one cannot see something without its looking some way (in particular, some colour or shape) to one. Likewise, I am not denying that seeing presupposes seeing as. Every leaf seen on my walk must look some colour and shape to me and must be seen as having some colour and shape by me at the time of seeing. But, just as I may see something without noticing it, without believing that I see it, so something may look some way to me (or be seen as . . .) without my noticing this in any way. As I drove quickly through the village, perhaps I saw the third house on the left without noticing or believing that I did. If so, the house must have looked some way to me, but I may not have noticed what way that was.

11. My insistence above that the notion of an immediate object of perception as defined here is not intended to play anything like its usual *epistemological* role, might give rise to the objection that if I refuse to give the immediate objects of perception their usual epistemological role, then I am simply side-stepping the major issue and, perhaps, leaving the immediate objects without any significant role at all to play in the philosophy of perception.

The first part of my answer to this charge is simply that we cannot do everything at once. The questions that arise in *analysing* statements of visual perception will keep us busy enough. The second part, and the main part, of my answer is that – important and interesting though epistemological questions are – they are secondary to analysis in an important respect. By this I do not mean that we cannot know a statement to be true without first knowing its analysis. That is an absurd position. Whether or not we know the analysis of statements about the minds of other persons, such statements as 'Jones is in pain' are sometimes known to be true. What I mean is that in order to have a *general*

[18] Like that of seeing a just perceptible star, where concentrating on seeing the star makes it 'disappear' from the night sky.

theory of *how* we know, we must have at least the beginnings of an analysis. I may know that Jones is in pain, but I cannot even start on an explanation of *how* I know this, without taking a position on the analysis or meaning of such statements. For example, if I explain our knowledge on analogical grounds, I am assuming the analytical thesis that psychological predicates mean the same when applied to myself and to others. If I explain our knowledge by reference to the fact that Jones is behaving in the kind of manner that is used to teach the meaning of 'is in pain' to children, then I am assuming some analytical connexion between meaning and manner of teaching; and so on.

Therefore, though questions as to the epistemic relations between statements like 'I see a red patch' and 'I see a tomato' are extremely important, it seems a reasonable procedure to first tackle the question of the analysis of 'I see a tomato.' And the role I see for the immediate objects of perception is that of providing a starting point from which to answer this latter question. It is for similar reasons that I eschew such questions as: What is it not just to see a tomato, but to be *conscious of* seeing one, or, What is it to *interpret* one's perceptual experience as being of a tomato – questions like those I argued above tended to be confused with the question of what it is to see a tomato. These questions are obviously important (and relate to psychology as well as to philosophy), but are surely questions that presuppose what it is to see a tomato (being conscious of seeing a tomato involves seeing a tomato, for instance), and so, may reasonably be postponed.

12. It is common to introduce the term 'sense-datum' (or 'sense-impression', 'sensum', etc.) at this point as a convenient term for the immediate objects of perception. There are two reasons why I do not follow this practice. Visual sense-data – as traditionally conceived, and as conceived later in this work – are both what is seen whenever seeing occurs, and the bearers of the *apparent* properties (if the white wall looks blue, the corresponding sense-datum *is* blue). Regarding the first point, I have argued that whenever there is something which is seen, there is an immediate object of perception which is seen; but this is silent on whether there are cases of seeing which are not cases where something is seen. Regarding the second point, I have argued that the immediate objects of perception are coloured expanses, that is, that every immediate object of visual perception has some colour and some shape; but the issue of *what* colour and *what* shape has been left open.

13. A final comment. The view being advanced here is an *analytical*

expansion view, not a *two meanings* one. I have argued that though we see opaque, material things of reasonable volume, they are never the immediate objects of perception for a person at a time. But this is *not* to say that we see material objects in a different sense from that in which we see the immediate objects; it is, rather, to advance as an analytical thesis that to see a reasonable-sized, opaque material object *is* to see something distinct from that object, the relevant immediate object of perception (whatever the ontological status of the latter may turn out to be).

In 'Sense-Data', Benson Mates argues that we must concede that 'see' has two senses (at least), as follows:

> Suppose that Smith and Jones are looking at the Campanile from different points of view; the light is good and neither of them has any difficulty seeing it. We consider the assertion:
> (1) Smith and Jones see the same thing.
> Is it true or false? Well, on the one hand, *of course* it is true, for *ex hypothesi* Smith and Jones both see the Campanile. On the other hand, since what anyone sees in a given situation depends upon his perspective, the lighting, and the whole structure and state of his nervous system, it is equally obvious that what Smith sees under these circumstances is not even 'congruent' let alone literally identical, with what is seen by Jones. Now no sentence can be both true and false when taken in the same sense; consequently we are led to the conclusion that sentence (1) has more than one sense. And it is natural to single out the verb 'see' as the culprit, to say that there are two (or, at least two) senses of 'see'.[19]

But the fact that there is both a case for saying (1) is true, and a case for saying it is false, does not show that there is a hidden ambiguity (located by Mates in 'see'); rather, it shows the need for analytical expansion. Jones and Smith see the same thing, the Campanile, in virtue of seeing different things, different aspects or whatever. Suppose Jones lives in Los Angeles and Smith in New York, do they live in the same place? In order to answer this question, we do not need to postulate two meanings for 'live in'. All we need to say is that they live in the same place, USA, in virtue of living in different places, Los Angeles and New York. In other words, they live in the *same country*, but different cities; and, likewise, they see the same *extended object*, but

[19] 'Sense-Data', p. 230. In my discussion of this passage, I am indebted to Alec Hyslop.

different *aspects*: there is no need to postulate ambiguity, only a need to spell things out.

Perhaps it is worth putting the matter in semi-formal terms. Mates is suggesting that we have both

$(\exists x)$ [Jones and Smith see x],

$\sim (\exists x)$ [Jones and Smith see x],

as true sentences; and, hence, that 'see' in each must carry a different meaning.

But what in fact we have as true together in the situation he describes are

$(\exists x)$ [x is a material thing of reasonable volume & Jones and Smith see x]

and $\sim (\exists x)$ [x is an aspect of a material thing & Jones and Smith see x] and the overall situation is best described by

$(\exists x)\,(\exists y)\,(\exists z)$ [$x \neq y$ & x and y are aspects of z & Jones sees x & Smith sees y & (hence) Jones and Smith see z].

There is no putative contradiction here that calls for resolution by identifying an equivocation.

14. To conclude, we now have an account of what an immediate object of (visual) perception is. It is something seen, but not in virtue of seeing anything else. It is always a coloured shape, though the arguments of later chapters are needed before we can say in every case what colour and what shape it has. The account is doubly 'topic-neutral' in that it leaves as matters for further investigation, (i), whether the immediate object is mental or physical, and, (ii), the precise relation – causal, part–whole, or whatever – that holds between the immediate object of perception and a material object which is seen in virtue of seeing it. I now turn to the required further investigation.

2

Three uses of 'looks'

0. We now know some things about the immediate objects of visual perception, but, as noted in chapter 1, §12, we cannot yet say that they are sense-data. Before we can say this we need both an account of hallucinations and an analysis of a class of 'looks' statements. The first arises out of the discussion of the next chapter on the existence of mental objects, the second out of chapter 4 on the case for sense-data; but before the second is possible, we need to identify precisely the relevant class of 'looks' statements and to establish certain theses about the statements in this class. Accordingly, it is the principal task of this chapter to characterize the sense of 'look' (and 'appear') for which we argue in chapter four that the sense-datum theory is true; the sense of 'look', that is, on which '*S* looks *F* to *X*' entails that *X* is immediately seeing something *F*.

1. Leaving aside obviously non-visual uses of 'look' as in 'It looks as if the government will be re-elected', it is plausible to distinguish three uses of 'look' (and 'appear') which I will call *epistemic, comparative*, and *phenomenal*.[1]

The epistemic use is propositional in that statements containing 'looks' so used are in (or can naturally be cast into) the form 'It looks as if *p*', where '*p*' is a sentence expressing a proposition: examples are 'It looks as if the sun is sinking into the sea', 'It looks as if these tomatoes are ripe', and 'It looks as if it is about to rain.'

Suppose I say, in front of a house whose bell has not been answered and whose curtains are drawn 'They appear to be away' or, in our standard form, 'It looks as if they are away'; then I am expressing the fact that a certain body of *visually* acquired evidence – in this case, drawn curtains and unanswered bell – supports the proposition that they are away. Again, suppose I say, looking at the approaching thunder clouds, 'It looks as if it will rain soon'; then I am saying that what I can see supports the proposition that it will soon rain. It is this usage which naturally shades in to the non-perceptual usage exempli-

[1] Cf., R. Chisholm, *Perceiving*, ch. 4.

fied by 'It looks as if the government will be re-elected.' This non-perceptual usage is just the epistemic 'looks' with the provision that the supporting evidence be visual deleted.

It seems to me a mistake to analyse the epistemic use in terms of tentative, guarded, etc. assent to '*p*'. A. M. Quinton says of the case where I say that they appear to be away that 'I am simply asserting in a guarded, tentative, qualified way that they are away.'[2] But if this were the case, it would be *inconsistent* to say 'They appear to be away, but I happen to know that they are hiding in the attic.' We often say that it looks as if *p* when we know for certain that not-*p*. Our account handles such cases by describing them as cases where we take it that though a certain body of visual evidence supports that *p*, other (non-visual) evidence makes it certain that not-*p*.

Moreover, our account explains the conditions under which we with-draw 'It looks as if . . .' claims. Suppose that, in the case where I say that it looks as if it will rain soon, it is pointed out to me that thunder clouds in this part of the world never produce rain – the rain always falls on the other side of the mountain. Then I will withdraw my claim, that is, I will take it that my statement *was* false; but I will not, of course, take it that it was false that I tentatively assented to its being about to rain.

This is not to deny the obvious fact that sometimes what we are *doing* when we say 'It looks as if *p*' is indicating tentative assent to '*p*'. This is entirely consistent with our analysis. Saying that some proposition is supported is one common way of indicating tentative assent. Likewise, sometimes what we are *doing* when we say '*p*' by itself is indicating belief that *p*, but this does not imply the absurd view that '*p*' and 'I believe that *p*' mean the same.

2. In addition to the use of 'looks' which naturally takes a sentence expressing a proposition, there is the use that is followed by 'like' and an indefinite singular term: 'It looks like a cow', 'It looks like a tomato', 'It looks like a red thing does at dusk', and so on. This is the comparative use, so-called because 'It looks like an *F*' seems just to mean that it looks the way *F*s normally do; that is, 'looks like an *F*' expands to 'looks like an *F* (normally) does'.

Now the way an *F* normally looks is a *relative* notion, relative to cir-cumstances: the way an *F* looks in one set of circumstances may be very different from the way an *F* looks in another set of circumstances.

[2] A. Quinton, *The Nature of Things*, p. 180. This doctrine receives its best known expression in Quinton's earlier 'The Problem of Perception'.

Hence, whenever someone utters a sentence of the form 'X looks like an F', he must be understood as having some set of circumstances in mind – usually either 'normal' circumstances or the circumstances obtaining at the time of utterance. Thus I may say of a man one thousand yards away that his head looks like a dot. This does not mean his head looks the way a dot does at one thousand yards, but the way a dot does in normal circumstances for viewing a dot, that is, close up. But if I say a man's head at a thousand yards looks like a woman's, I do not mean that a man's head at a thousand yards looks like a woman's head does in normal circumstances; I mean it looks like a woman's at a thousand yards. Thus, to avoid possible ambiguities, we will include reference to the circumstances when these are not entirely clear.

There is a further respect in which the way an F normally looks is relative, namely, to persons: the way an F normally looks in a given set of circumstances to one person may be very different to the way it looks to another person in the same circumstances. So that when someone utters a sentence of the form 'X looks like an F does in C', he must have in mind some person – usually either the 'normal' person or himself. For example, when I say that Irish tweed looks like Harris tweed, I mean to normal persons; and when an expert on tweeds says they look quite different, he means to a tweed expert. Again, a red–green colour-blind person may say that a red stop light looks like a green one (to him), or, when telling a normally sighted person about the Highway Code, that they look different (to normal persons). Therefore, to be fully explicit, the comparative use needs to be specified in terms of the schema: 'X looks like an F normally does in C to S', where X is the thing in question, F is a kind of thing (cow, dog, red thing), C is the circumstances (bright daylight, dusk), and S is a person.

One standard way that one's eyes provide evidence for there being an F before one, is for it to look the way it normally does when there is an F. Thus, in many cases, we are equally happy to say either 'It looks as if there is a cow before me' (epistemic) or 'It looks like a cow before me' (comparative). But the two are obviously not equivalent. Suppose I am confronted by a papier-mâché cow which looks just like a cow – the right shape, colour, etc., but which is obviously made of papier-mâché (like Madame Tussaud's wax-works, which are life-like but obviously wax); then the model will look like a cow but it will not look as if there is a cow before me.

Also we frequently use expressions which are ambiguous between the comparative and epistemic uses. 'The dog looks dangerous' may mean 'It looks as if the dog is dangerous' (epistemic) or 'The dog looks like a dangerous dog' (comparative), depending on the context, tone of voice, emphasis and so on.

3. The final use of 'looks' I distinguish is the *phenomenological* or, for brevity, the *phenomenal*. It is sometimes doubted whether there is any such use, but, in the sense I will give the term, what is open to doubt is not the existence of the phenomenological use but, rather, whether it is analysable in terms of concepts pertaining to the epistemic or comparative uses.

The phenomenal use is characterized by being explicitly tied to terms for colour, shape, and/or distance: 'It looks *blue* to me', 'It looks *triangular*', 'The tree looks closer *than* the house', 'The top line looks *longer than* the bottom line', 'There looks to be a *red square* in the middle of the white wall', and so on. That is, instead of terms like 'cow', 'house', 'happy', we have, in the phenomenal use, terms like 'red', 'square', and 'longer than'.

We shall be principally concerned with the phenomenal use of 'looks' in what follows. It is the analysis of this use which leads to sense-data. It has been widely supposed of late that we can, strictly speaking, do without this use in that it can be analysed in other and more basic notions which relate to the first two uses. Two general ideas are abroad: that 'looks red' or 'looks square' can be analysed in comparative style in terms of looking the way red or square things normally look, and that 'looks red' or 'looks square' can be analysed in epistemic style in terms of belief. The remainder of this chapter will be devoted to arguing that both ideas are mistaken.

4. There is a more radical and a less radical approach to a comparative style of analysis of looking red.

In *Locke, Berkeley, Hume*, Jonathan Bennett holds that 'He has a red sense-datum' means 'It is with him, as though he were seeing something red', where 'It is with him as though he were seeing something . . .' is to be understood as like 'He is sensorily affected in the way he usually is when he perceives a . . .'[3] Translated to the analysis of looking, this suggests we might understand '*X* looks *F* to *S*' as '*X* produces in *S* the kind of sensory state he is usually in when he

---

[3] J. Bennett, *Locke, Berkeley, Hume*, p. 33. Similar suggestions are common in defences of the Mind–Brain Identity Theory, see, e.g., J. J. C. Smart, *Philosophy and Scientific Realism*, p. 94.

perceives an *F*.' I call this a more radical approach because the word 'look' does not appear in the analysis. If Bennett had suggested that '*X* looks *F* to *S*' means '*X looks* the way *F*s usually do to *S*', or something like this, this would be an example of the less radical approach in which reference to looks is retained in the analysis.

The more reductive character of the radical approach is obviously philosophically attractive, but, at the same time, it leaves the door open to what appear to be decisive counter-examples. Suppose I am totally red colour-blind; red things look grey to me, or, perhaps, they do not look any way at all to me. And suppose I take a job where it is very important for me to be able to pick out red things successfully. Then the following is not just imaginable, it might be concretely realised. Utilising the fact that light reflected from red objects has a special wave-length distribution, a scientist designs a 'black box' which produces a distinctive sound in the presence of red objects. I wear this box strapped to my head and pick out red objects by means of the sound. When I hear the sound, I will be in the kind of sensory state I usually am in when I see a red thing (though red things do not look red to me, I can, of course, still see them), but, quite obviously, nothing will be looking red to me.

In the rest of this section, I will be concerned solely with the less radical approach which retains reference to looking in the analysis. Clearly, if, as I will argue, the less radical approach fails, so must the more radical.

We noted in §2 that comparative looks-statements need to be understood in terms of the schema '*X* looks like an *F* normally does in *C* to *S*.' How might such a schema be deployed to give an account of

(1) *X* looks red to me.

Does (1) perhaps mean something like

(2) *X* looks the way red things normally look to me in normal circumstances.

Before we discuss whether (1) and (2) are equivalent, two points should be noted. First, if (2) is to be worth our consideration, an at least moderately objectivist stance must be taken about colour. If 'red thing' means nothing more than 'thing which looks red in . . .' the replacement of (1) by something like (2) would achieve nothing to the philosophical point. For the purposes of discussion, I will take such a stance in this chapter. (And, of course, we could have focussed on shape instead of colour.) Second, the reference to red things in (2) cannot be eliminated by reference to a list of paradigmatically red things like geranium petals, ripe tomatoes, and blood. For it is entirely contingent what things are red. The world might have been such that everything which is green were red, and conversely; and, moreover, there might, of course, have been no red things at all. In either case, the truth values of (2) with 'red things' replaced by a list of things which are red would differ from that of (1). Hence, (2) with 'red things' so replaced cannot constitute an analysis of (1).

I will now argue that (1) and (2) are not equivalent on the ground that (1) may be true when (2) is false, and on the ground that (2) may be true when (1) is false. I start by looking at cases which suggest that (1) may be true when (2) is false.

Hume pointed out that there might be a disparity between the colours we can conceive of and those that are in fact represented in the world.[4] Likewise, there might be a disparity between the colours objects have and those they look to have. For example, there might be a shade of red which objects look to have at sunset but which no object actually has. Indeed, for all I know, there is. It could even be the case that there were no red objects at all, although objects looked red on occasion. This case shows that (1) may be true when (2) is false, for it shows that X may look red to me even though nothing is red; but then X cannot be looking the way red things normally do to me, or, indeed, the way red things normally do to anyone.

It may be suggested that this kind of case can be handled counter-factually. *If* there were any red things, they *would* look the way X looks to me when X looks red to me. There are two difficulties with this suggestion. First, to say that X looks red to me is to say something about how things *actually are*, it is not to say anything about how things *would be* if the world were different. Consider a world created by a Cartesian evil demon who hates red things but tolerates non-red things looking red on odd occasions. Perhaps he has resolved to destroy the world if any red things come into existence. In this world, things look red on odd occasions, but nothing looks the way red things would if there were any; for if there were any, nothing would look any way to anyone. Second, I may have eyes which are very sensitive to red, so that if there were any red things, they would completely dazzle me. But certain things look red to me in special circumstances – say, white walls at sunset. That is, my eyes cannot tolerate red

---

[4] Hume observed that a particular shade of blue might not be represented in the world, but could be conceived of by extrapolation from those shades represented.

things (or could not, if there were any), in the way that an albino's eyes cannot tolerate bright light; but things sometimes look red to me. In this case, certain things look red to me but these things do not look the way red things would look to me.

The case for saying that (2) may be true when (1) is false is that someone might, like the totally colour-blind, see the world in shades of grey, but, unlike the totally colour-blind, have extremely good 'grey vision'; in particular, he might be able to make among the greys the same number of discriminations normal people make in the whole colour spectrum. (I am here indebted to Michael Bradley.) Such a person might well see red objects as a unique shade of grey, and for such a person it might well be true that X looks the way red things normally look to him in normal circumstances, namely, that special shade of grey, without it being true that X looks red to him.

Apart from these difficulties, there is the notorious problem of explicating *normal circumstances* in (2). In everyday chat about colour, we take reasonably bright daylight as normal circumstances, but this quite obviously will not do in (2). (1) does not mean anything like

(3) X looks the way red things normally look to me in daylight.

I might (some people do) have very sensitive eyes which are completely dazzled by daylight, so that the way red things look to me in daylight is not red at all, rather looking red is the way red things look to me under low intensity illumination.

There is only one specification of normal circumstances which avoids this kind of problem, that which identifies normal circumstances as those in which red things look red to me. But inserting this specification in (2), makes (2) hopelessly circular as an account of (1).

It has been suggested to me that 'normal circumstances for a person' might be defined as those in which that person can make the most colour discriminations. Thus daylight counts as normal circumstances for most people, but, for our person with very sensitive eyes, low-intensity illumination counts as normal circumstances. But this account of normal circumstances gives manifestly wrong answers when inserted in (2). The circumstances under which a maximum number of colour discriminations are possible are those which *exaggerate* colour differences, that is, are those circumstances in which things look more different in colour than they really are; and so are circumstances in which objects do *not* look the colour they are. For example, examining objects under a very powerful optical-microscope enables many more colour discriminations than examining them in daylight, but under such circumstances objects do not look the colour they are.[5]

Sometimes comparative analyses of (1) make reference to other people. Thus (1) might be analysed along the lines of

(4) *X* looks to me the way red things look to most people in normal circumstances.

(This suggestion was put to me by Michael Tye, see his 'The Adverbial Theory'.) It is, in fact, possible to extend our objections to (2) and (3) as analyses of (1) so that they apply also to (4), but it is unnecessary to do so. Nothing like (4) can be right. The number of persons that do, did, and will exist is *logically independent* of the colour things look to have. In particular, *X* might look red to me even though no one else did, does, or will exist; and so, the analysis of (1) must not make reference to others. Of course, the correct analysis of something like

(5) 'Red' is the correct word in English to describe how *X* looks to me.

may well involve reference to others, for it may well be a necessary truth that English is a public language. But (5) is very different from our concern, (1): (5) is about a language and would not be true if the English language had never developed; while statements like (1) are not about the English language, were true before anyone had a language at all, and would be true even if English had never developed.

5. Can the phenomenal use of 'looks' be analysed in epistemic terms, in particular, in terms of belief?

Prima facie, '*X* looks *F* to *S*' cannot be analysed in terms of *S*'s beliefs. Something can equally look red (square) to me when I am convinced that it is red (square), that it is not red (square), or when I have no idea whether or not it is red (square). However, it has been argued with considerable ingenuity that this appearance is misleading, and that a belief analysis, albeit a fairly complex one, is possible.

The most recent and detailed view of this kind is due to George Pitcher,[6] and I will concentrate on his account. My criticisms will, however, be concerned with the general thrust of the account rather than with the fine detail, and so, if successful against his account, are equally

---

[5] As Berkeley observed in the *First Dialogue*, see D. M. Armstrong, 'Colour-Realism and the Argument from Microscopes', in *Contemporary Philosophy in Australia*.

[6] See his *A Theory of Perception*, part II.

applicable to the similar accounts offered by D. M. Armstrong and J. W. Roxbee-Cox.[7]

A preliminary point: supporters of the belief analysis of looking and/or seeing differ over whether it is believing, acquiring belief or causally-receiving belief that is crucial. Our criticisms will, however, be independent of this difference and I will, consequently, suppress it in what follows.

Evidently, an advocate of a belief analysis of 'looks *F*' must claim, first, that whenever a 'looks'-statement is true, an appropriate belief-statement is true; and, secondly and conversely, that whenever that belief-statement is true, the 'looks'-statement is true. It is, however, very easy to describe cases which appear to refute both of these claims. I will start by considering apparent counter-examples to the first claim.

6. Consider the Muller–Lyer figure below.

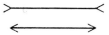

The two lines are the same length, but the top line looks longer than the bottom line. Moreover, I know with complete certainty that the lines are the same length. (I am familiar with this kind of illusion and have just measured the lines.) Therefore, I neither believe nor am inclined to believe that the top line is longer than the bottom line. A similar case is where I am looking at a wall I know to be white with blue-tinted glasses on. The wall looks blue, but I neither believe nor am inclined to believe that the wall is blue.

Pitcher attempts to handle the problem posed by these cases by suggesting that there is a *suppressed inclination to believe* in such cases. Pitcher divides his analysis of looking in terms of believing into three cases: First Cases, where when it looks so-and-so to *S*, *S* believes that it is so-and-so; Middle Cases, where when it looks so-and-so to *S*, *S* is inclined to believe that it is so-and-so; and Last Cases, where *S* merely has a suppressed inclination to believe. Clearly, the two cases we have just described count as Last Cases on Pitcher's classification.

Is it true that there is a suppressed inclination to believe in our two cases? To decide this question, we must decide what Pitcher means by a suppressed inclination to believe. I think that Pitcher's account of the matter contains a serious obscurity.

[7] D. M. Armstrong, *Perception and the Physical World*, and *A Materialist Theory of the Mind*; J. W. Roxbee-Cox, 'An Analysis of Perceiving in Terms of the Causation of Beliefs I'.

In normal English usage, a suppressed so-and-so is a sometime so-and-so. A suppressed newspaper was once a non-suppressed newspaper. But in our two cases there may never have been a belief or inclination to believe: for example, it was not that I was inclined to believe the wall blue when I first put on the glasses and then suppressed the inclination, rather I never had the inclination at all. So that Pitcher cannot be taken to be giving the usual meaning to the words in question. But this makes it hard to see what he can mean by a suppressed inclination to believe. A totally destroyed house is not a house which was once a normal house and is now a special sort of house, a totally destroyed one. It is essential to our understanding of talk 'about' destroyed houses that it be understood as talk about non-destroyed houses which no longer exist. The same appears to be true of suppressed inclinations to believe: talk of them is essentially talk of sometime inclinations, inclinations that once were but are no longer.

Pitcher attempts to illustrate what he means by citing the following

> Suppose, for example, that an appealing child accused of a misdeed tells you that he didn't do it, but that you have overwhelmingly good evidence that he did. It may well be that you *want* to believe the child, but can't. If so, your attitude towards what he says is weaker, even, than being inclined to believe it. You do have an immediate impulse to believe it, but you (reluctantly) suppress it: we may say that you have a suppressed inclination to believe what the child says, although in fact you believe the opposite.[8]

I cannot see that this case helps in any way. The correct thing to say about it is that you *want*, or would *like*, to believe the child. Now, of course, wants and desires are closely tied to inclinations on one meaning of 'inclination', but not on the meaning that is relevant here. When the wall looks blue, I do not *want* or *desire* it to be blue. The sense of 'inclination' relevant here is that tied to tendency and likelihood, where to say, for example, 'I am inclined to believe him' means that I tend to believe him or think it likely that he is telling the truth, rather than that I want to believe him.

A further difficulty in the way of construing what Pitcher means by a suppressed inclination is his elucidatory footnote: 'I do not mean, of course, that the inclination is *totally* suppressed, i.e., that it is suppressed, so to speak, out of consciousness altogether. I mean only that

[8] *A Theory of Perception*, p. 93.

it is partially, and perhaps even mostly, suppressed.'[9] But Pitcher cannot afford to insist that the inclination is not 'totally suppressed'. In our two cases, I have no inclination whatever to believe that the top line is longer, or that the wall is blue: I am as certain as I am of anything that neither is the case.

In discussing cases similar to our two, Armstrong talks *counter-factually*. He says, for example, that

> In such cases of perception without belief and even without inclination to believe, it is possible to formulate a true counter-factual statement of the form 'But for the fact that the perceiver had other, independent, beliefs about the world, he would have acquired certain beliefs – the beliefs corresponding to the content of his perception.[10]

I think this is the only way to make good sense of talk of suppressed inclinations to believe. That is, what must be claimed by Pitcher is what is in fact claimed by Armstrong: although I have no inclination to believe that the wall is blue, I would believe it blue if I did not already know . . . ; and though I have no inclination to believe the top line is longer, I would believe it to be longer if I did not already know . . .

This suggestion looks promising in rough outline, but there are enormous difficulties in the way of filling in the details. And it is essential to fill in the details. For there will, of course, be sentences 'p', 'q', such that, in the case of the wall, 'If p, then I would believe that the wall were blue' and 'If q, then I would believe that the wall were white'; and the wall does not (and cannot) look both blue and white.

Consider the Muller–Lyer case. What counterfactual can plausibly be invoked to handle this case? G. N. A. Vesey suggests that 'if I hadn't good reason . . . to believe them [the two lines] to be equal, I would, on looking at them, believe them to be unequal';[11] where the kind of good reason Vesey has in mind is measuring the lines and finding them to be equal. The problem here is that what Vesey claims seems to be false. Even if I had not measured the lines, or otherwise determined that the lines were equal, I would not have believed that the top line was longer than the bottom; I would, rather, have reserved judgement. This is not because I am familiar with the Muller–Lyer illusion, but is a result of the fact that it is obvious that the 'wings' at

---

[9] *Ibid.*, p. 93.
[10] *A Materialist Theory of the Mind*, p. 222.
[11] G. N. A. Vesey, 'Analysing Seeing (II)', p. 134.

the end of the lines are going to have a distorting effect. The *first* time I was presented with the illusion, and before I had measured the lines, I noted that the top line looked longer, but did not thereby believe that it was longer. And this is almost universally the case. Every student presented with the Muller–Lyer figure for the first time realises that, though the top line looks longer, it would be foolhardy to suppose that it was in fact longer.

A similar point holds in the case of the white wall looking blue through blue glasses. It looks blue, but I know it is white. Would I believe that the wall was blue if I did not happen to know it was white? Of course not, I know I am wearing blue glasses, and so, I know that the wall's looking blue shows nothing about its real colour. But suppose I had not known that I was wearing blue glasses, what would I have believed then if I had not known the wall was white. Must it in this case be true that I would have believed that the wall was blue? There is no *must* about it. I might have noticed that my hand looked blue and so have suspected that the circumstances were such as to make non-blue things look blue (without knowing that my glasses were the cause); I might have believed that the wall was being illuminated by a blue lamp; or there might have been something about a friend's smile that alerted me to the possibility that there was something strange about the circumstances; and so on and so forth.

I think the most that can confidently be claimed in the way of relevant counterfactuals in the case where the wall looks blue, is something like: if I had not known or been fairly certain that the wall was white and if I had believed that the circumstances were such that objects look the colour they are, then I would have believed that the wall was blue. But such a counterfactual achieves nothing in the way of a belief analysis of 'looks', for it itself contains 'looks', the very term whose analysis is being sought. Moreover, the following counterfactual is equally true: if I had not known or been fairly certain that the wall was white and if I had believed the circumstances were such that objects do *not* look the colour they are, then I would *not* have believed that the wall was blue (or white, either).

What about the case where I have no belief one way or the other about whether the circumstances are such that objects look the colour they are? The only way to answer this question is to consider a case. Suppose that, as part of a psychology experiment, I am blindfolded and led into a room which I know is such that either the lighting is normal or the lighting is such as to radically alter the colour things look to have, and suppose that when the blindfold is removed I am unable to determine which of these two possibilities obtains. Then I will be in, precisely, the situation where I have no belief one way or the other about whether the circumstances are such that objects look the colour they are. Now suppose that a certain wall looks blue, what will I believe about the colour it is – obviously, absolutely nothing!

It might be objected that because it is a necessary truth of some kind that things normally look as they are, I must take it, in the case just described, that if the wall looks blue, then it is blue: because I have no particular evidence for or against things being as they look in this case, I must accept the general presumption in favour of things being as they appear. However, in a later chapter (chapter 5) I argue that the scientific picture of the material world as made up of widely-separated, colourless particles ought to be accepted. If this is right, then it is not even a *truth*, let alone a necessary truth, that things normally look as they are. Moreover, even if it is a necessary truth that things normally look as they are, it quite certainly is not a necessary truth that anyone *believes* that it is a necessary truth; therefore, in the kind of case just described, I may well note that the wall looks blue while refraining from believing, or being disposed to believe, that it is blue, because I do not believe that it is any kind of necessary truth that things usually look as they are.

7. We have been considering whether looking entails believing, I now turn to the question of whether believing entails looking. To make the discussion as simple as possible, I will restrict it to Pitcher's first cases, cases where the subject actually believes. Thus, we will be considering whether we can state conditions on a person's beliefs, rather than on his inclinations (suppressed or otherwise) to believe, which entail that something looks some way to him.

It is, to start with, quite obvious that I can believe (or retain the belief, or acquire the belief, or causally-receive the belief) that there is, say, something red in front of me without anything looking red to me or its looking to me that there is something red before me. Perhaps my eyes are shut, but I have been told there is something red before me by someone I trust; or perhaps I remember it; or perhaps I am short-sighted and cannot see the object, but can read a note much nearer to me telling me about the object; or perhaps I can see the object and it looks black, but I know that in the circumstances red things look black, and so I believe that there is something red in front of me; and so on and so forth.

Belief theorists have attempted to handle this difficulty in three ways: (i) by reference to the range of acquired beliefs, (ii) by appeal to the role of the sense-organs, (iii) by reference to the ground of the relevant beliefs – or by some combination of these ways. I will examine each in turn.[12]

(i) When something looks F to me, it does not just look F; it also looks G and H and . . . For example, a tomato on the mantelpiece which looks red to me will also look to have a certain shape, to be a certain distance away, to be so far from the edge of the mantelpiece, to be well or badly lit, and so on and so forth. Hence, a belief theorist should give an account of looking F, not in terms of a belief, but in terms of a whole range of acquired beliefs which includes the belief that something is F as one belief among many. On the other hand, when I am told or read from a note that there is something red in front of me, I will only acquire the one belief, not the whole range required for there to be something looking red to me.

There are, however, a number of difficulties for this attempt to handle the case of believing so-and-so without looking so-and-so. First, the note might have been much longer. It might have contained sufficient additional information to generate in the reader the whole range of beliefs corresponding to something looking red. Likewise, the person telling me that there is something red in front of me might also have told me about the shape, position relative to the mantelpiece, distance from me etc., of the thing in question. Secondly, this attempt goes no way towards handling the case where I believe the object is red because it looks black and I know that red things look black in the circumstances. For, in such a case, I will normally acquire the whole range of beliefs. Thirdly, there are cases where something looks red without there being a spread of beliefs. Perhaps I glance very briefly at the object and only notice the apparent colour and virtually nothing else. Perhaps the room is almost dark and all I can see is an indistinct red glow at an indeterminate distance from me. Or perhaps I am looking down a long, dark tunnel and can see only an indistinct red shape at the end. In all these cases, there will not be the wide range of beliefs allegedly always corresponding to something looking some way, and, in particular, the range might well be smaller than that provided by the note or by being told of the red looking object.

[12] Armstrong emphasises (ii) in *Perception and the Physical World*, though the emphasis is all but eliminated in *A Materialist Theory of the Mind*. Pitcher emphasises (i) and (ii). Roxbee-Cox emphasises (iii) and (ii).

(ii) The commonest way of trying to meet the difficulty about belief without looking is to invoke the fact that, when I believe that something is F because it looks F to me, my belief is caused by the operation of an object *on my eyes*.[13] Thus, according to this suggestion, the cases of being told and of remembering that there is something red in front of me do not count as cases of something looking red to me because my belief is not acquired by using my eyes. But the suggestion, at least as it stands, fails entirely to meet the case of believing that there is something red in front of me as a result of reading the note or as a result of its looking black in circumstances known to be such that red things look black: both of these are cases of beliefs acquired by using one's eyes.

In response to this kind of difficulty, Pitcher makes what seems to me to be a desperation move. He suggests that the beliefs acquired be *perceptual beliefs*, which he defines thus: 'by a perceptual belief that there is an x at u I mean one that a person has when, in First Cases, it looks (in the phenomenal sense) to him as though there is an x at u'.[14]

Our discussion has been in terms of the 'looks' F construction. If we translate Pitcher's account of a perceptual belief into the construction we have been concerned with, we obtain something like: a perceptual belief that something is F is one that a person has when, in First Cases, something looks F to him.

The objection to be made here is obvious. The proffered account of a perceptual belief is manifestly circular. It is in terms of the very notion whose elucidation is being sought, that of something looking F.

From the remarks on the page following the above quotation, I am certain that Pitcher would reply to this circularity charge along the following lines: 'The circularity in my account doesn't matter because the main rival to my account, the Sense-datum theory, is equally circular. On the Sense-datum theory, looking square (red) is analysed in

---

[13] Sometimes the suggestion seems to be that, in addition to the belief being caused via the eyes, the belief be that it itself is caused via the eyes. What is required is both that one believe as a result of the operation of the eyes, and that one believe that one believes as a result of the operation of the eyes. This additional requirement seems too strong: surely young children and animals have things look various ways to them without having any 'meta-beliefs' about the causation of the resulting beliefs. In any case, the objections that follow, with obvious amendments, could be applied to the stronger version.

[14] *A Theory of Perception*, p. 90.

terms of immediately perceiving a square (red) sense-datum. But what is a square (red) sense-datum? Surely, all the theorist can say is that it is the kind of sense-datum one has when something looks square (red).'

But this is like arguing that defining 'bachelor' as 'unmarried man' is circular because 'unmarried man' means 'bachelor'. Of course it does; that is why the definition is correct. What is at issue when we consider the question of circularity is whether the individual (semantically significant) *parts* of the proffered analysis are both distinct from and more basic than what is being analysed. In the case of the definition of 'bachelor', this clearly obtains. The relevant parts are 'un-', 'married', and 'man', and they are each distinct in meaning from, and more basic than, 'bachelor'.

Likewise, the sense-datum theorist can happily admit that 'square (red) sense-datum' means something like 'sense-datum one has when something looks square (red)', while, at the same time, avoiding the charge of circularity by insisting that both 'square' ('red') and 'sense-datum' are meaningful parts of 'square (red) sense-datum', neither of which has a meaning that can only be explained in terms of that of 'looks square (red)'. There would be nothing wrong (as far as circularity goes) with Pitcher's account of a perceptual belief if it contained *ingredients* which *together* constituted looking *F*; the trouble is that looking *F is* one of the ingredients.

Moreover, Pitcher's account of perceptual belief undermines the ontological significance of his belief analysis of looking. One of the main aims of any belief analysis of perception is to avoid the Sense-datum theory's commitment to the existence of something *F* when something looks *F* to someone. The belief analysis achieves this because, despite the considerable controversy over the semantic structure of belief statements, we know enough about them to know that a statement like 'I believe (am inclined to believe) that there is something *F* in front of me' can be true without there being anything *F* in front of me. However, if the belief in question is not merely a common or garden one, but, rather, a special kind – a perceptual belief, where a perceptual belief is defined in terms of looking *F* – then the whole question of ontological commitment to there being an *F* is thrown back into the melting-pot.

A further problem for the analysis of looking in terms of beliefs acquired by using one's eyes is how to define the eyes. If the eyes are specified in physiological terms, as a certain physiological structure described in medical text books which is typically stimulated by light, absurd results follow. Take, for example, people blind from birth. It is obviously possible that medical scientists of the future develop a portable piece of 'hardware', carried in the hand and wired appropriately to the brain, which enables such persons to see and make it possible for things to look various ways to them. It would be absurd for philosophers to tell medical scientists that this is impossible. Furthermore, visual experiences can (and do) occur without the use of the eyes. Small electric currents applied directly to the right parts of the brain cause a variety of visual experiences.

A more promising definition of the eyes in this context is as that which typically gives rise to beliefs about *both* colour *and* shape.[15] What, on this approach, makes my belief that there is something red in front of me constitute something looking red is its being caused by the action of something which typically gives rise to beliefs about both colour and shape. Thus the belief I acquire as a result of feeling something concerning its shape does not constitute a case of looking because feeling typically gives rise to beliefs about shape, texture, and temperature, but not about colour. Likewise, the note's informing me that there is something red in front of me does not constitute something looking red because the note is (or may be) silent on the matter of shape.

Clearly there is something right here. Vision does typically put colour and shape together – a fact, incidentally, reflected in the Sense-datum theory defended in chapter 4 by defining visual sense-data as those having both shape and colour. Nevertheless, there is no real help for the belief analysis in this point. Suppose I acquire information about the world around me from computer print-outs, where the computer has been specially constructed so as to always give information about colour and shape together. And suppose the computer prints out that there is something red and round in front of me, and I so believe. This belief is acquired by a means typically giving rise to beliefs concerning both colour and shape, but, nevertheless, does not constitute something looking red (or square) to me. Moreover, this latest suggestion evidently goes no way towards meeting the case where I believe that there is something red in front of me because it looks black to me and I know that in these circumstances red things look black. Here my belief is acquired by a means typically giving rise

---

[15] I take the idea from discussion of related issues in J. W. Roxbee-Cox, 'Distinguishing the Senses'; see also H. P. Grice, 'Some Remarks on the Senses'.

to beliefs concerning both shape and colour, namely, via the eyes, but nothing looks red to me.

(iii) The final way I will consider of trying to meet the 'belief without looking' case turns on the nature of the *ground* of the belief. When I believe that there is something red in front of me because I read this on a note, there is, in an obvious sense, a ground for this belief of mine; that is, there is a set of beliefs – such as that there is a note on which a certain sentence is written and that the sentence was written by someone reliable – on which my belief that there is something red in front of me rests. The suggestion we are now considering is that what marks off those beliefs which constitute looking so-and-so is that they are not grounded: when I believe that there is something red in front of me because it looks red, my belief is not grounded on any other belief of mine.

This final suggestion seems to me to fare no better than the others. First, it fails to cover the memory case. Believing something because you remember it is a classic example of an ungrounded belief. When you remember that $2 + 2 = 4$, there is no other belief of yours on which your belief that $2 + 2 = 4$ rests – though there may, of course, be other beliefs of yours concerning the reliability of your memory on which your (meta-)belief that your belief that $2 + 2 = 4$ is reliable rests. Hence, when I believe that there is something red in front of me because I remember that there is, my belief is ungrounded; however, nothing need look red to me.

Secondly, contra the suggestion, when I believe that something red is in front of me because something looks red, there does seem to be a ground, namely, my belief that something looks red and that things look as they are in the circumstances that obtain. This is a belief of mine and grounds my belief that there is something red in front of me – it answers the question '*Why* do you believe that there is something red in front of you?' (Of course, my belief that something is *looking* red to me is not grounded.) The only reason one could have for denying this would have to lie in the doctrine that looking so-and-so never constitutes a ground. But an advocate of the suggestion under consideration cannot afford to hold this (implausible) doctrine. Because he would then have to count the case where something looks black to me and I believe that there is something red in front of me because I know the circumstances are such that red things look black, as a case of ungrounded belief; for my belief is based on something looking so and-so. And he cannot afford to do this, because nothing looks red to me in this case.

I think we must conclude from all this that the phenomenal use of 'looks' is strongly distinct from the epistemic and comparative uses. From now on when I use 'looks' (or 'appears') in the absence of explicit contrary indication, it will be in the phenomenal sense, the sense relevant to the defence of the Sense-datum theory in chapter 4.

8. There is one final matter that should be mentioned. I have characterized the phenomenal use of 'looks' as that explicitly tied to terms for colour, shape, and/or distance. It has, however, sometimes been suggested that the case of shape is rather special and, in particular, that some occurrences of 'looks F', where 'F' is a term for shape, can be analysed in a special way not applicable to the other cases. For example, Vesey suggests that the sense in which round plates look oval when viewed at an angle is given thus: 'if one put a transparent screen at right angles to one's line of vision, between oneself and the plate, and drew on it the outline of the plate seen through the screen, the shape drawn would be oval'.[16]

In similar vein, he adds later on the same page: 'A straight staff, half immersed at an angle in water, looks, from many points of view as if it were bent or broken at the water level. If one drew the outline of the staff on a transparent screen one would draw a bent or broken line.'[17]

The same general idea is sometimes put in terms of cameras. 'If one photographed the plate (stick), the print would contain an oval (bent) shape.' But it cannot possibly be maintained that the sense in which the plate looks oval or the stick bent is given by reference to corresponding shapes on photographs. The shape obtained on a photographic print is a function of the complex internal construction of the camera; the meaning of statements concerning the shape things look to have is not. For instance, a change in the internal construction of cameras would lead to a change in the shapes on photographic prints, but not thereby to a change in how things look.

Likewise, it seems to me that the facts about transparent screens and the related facts of perspective drawing and projective geometry do not in any way constitute an account of the *meaning* of the 'looks'-statements in question. Consider the plate held at an angle: the shape

[16] G. N. A. Vesey, *Perception*, p. 11.
[17] A similar suggestion is to be found in Armstrong, *Perception and the Physical World*, p. 12, see also the references footnoted there.

drawn on the transparent screen is an appropriate oval *only if* the screen is held at *right angles* to one's line of vision. If the screen is held at some other angle, the shape drawn will be too oval or too round; indeed, if the screen is held parallel to the plate, the shape drawn will be the same as that of the plate, namely, round.

That is to say, '*S* looks oval to me' cannot possibly be analysed as '*S* marks out an oval shape on a transparent screen', it must be analysed as '*S* marks out an oval shape on a transparent screen held at right angles to the line of vision.' But why choose to hold the screen at right angles to the line of vision, why this particular alignment? (And, if the account is being expressed in projective terms, why choose the shape projected on a plane perpendicular to the line of vision?) Only two answers seem possible. One is because that alignment gives the right answer, which makes it clear that to offer the above analysis is to put the cart before the horse; the other is because light travels in straight lines, and so, along the line of vision. But this is evidently an empirical fact about light, not part of the meaning of certain 'looks'-statements: scientists discovered it by taking careful measurements, rather than by discussing among themselves the meaning of '*S* looks oval to me.'

Moreover, if I put on distorting glasses, or if the reflected light is bent in some manner, the shape the plate looks to have will in general alter; but the shape marked out on the transparent screen or projected on the perpendicular plane will remain unaltered. Similar difficulties apply in the case of the straight stick looking bent. If the transparent sheet is in the water as well as the stick and appropriately positioned, the line marked out on it will be straight, not bent; and if I put on distorting glasses, the line marked out on the transparent sheet will be unaltered, while the shape the stick looks to have will change.

9. To conclude, we now have one preliminary to our case for sense-data in chapter four out of the way. We have an account of the relevant sense of 'looks', that according to which I will argue that when something looks *F*, a sense-datum is *F*; and also arguments – which we will need to refer back to later – against comparative and epistemic analyses of this sense of 'looks'. The remaining preliminary is the business of the next chapter.

3

The existence of mental objects*

o. It is now time to give the account of visual hallucinations adverted to in chapter 2, §o. In chapter 1, my comments on hallucinations were characteristically conditional. I distinguished the non-controversial claim that statements like 'I see a red after-image', 'Drunkards see pink, rat-like shapes', and 'The travellers saw a mirage' are, on occasion, true, from the highly controversial claim that when such statements are true, *there are* red after-images, pink shapes, mirages, and so on which are seen. And I avoided the controversy by talking conditionally, by restricting myself to saying that *if* the visual hallucinations are part of what there is, then they are examples of immediate objects of (visual) perception. I can avoid the controversy no longer: it is time to argue that hallucinations are part of what there is, that 'a red after-image', 'a mirage', 'a rainbow' are not merely nominal substantives, but actually name things, and, in particular, name a special sub-set of the immediate objects of perception.

The issues that arise when discussing the existence of hallucinations parallel those that arise when discussing the existence of the bodily sensations, a matter of interest in itself; hence, I have discussed the two questions together in this chapter. It might, however, be urged that there is a simple and decisive consideration which shows that hallucinations do not exist which does not apply to the bodily sensations. It is sometimes urged that it is part of the meaning of the word 'hallucination' that when someone is under an hallucination he is not seeing anything at all, and so that it is simply a matter of definition that visual hallucinations, in the sense of what is seen when hallucinated, do not exist.[1] But, of course, what is true by definition is that nothing *physical* or *material* is seen when hallucinating, and so, that visual hallucinations are not physical things. Therefore, it is simply a matter of definition that if the drunkard who seems to be seeing pink rats is hallucinating,

---

* The first half of this chapter derives from my 'On The Adverbial Analysis of Visual Experience' and from 'The Existence of Mental Objects'.
[1] See, e.g., N. Brown, 'Sense Data and Physical Objects', p. 182.

there are no pink *rats* which he is seeing; and, likewise, Macbeth was not seeing a *dagger*. But the definition of an hallucination leaves open the possibility that something non-physical, that is, mental, is seen when hallucination occurs. As far as the definition is concerned, there may be pink rat-like (mental) shapes which are seen by drunkards, and there may have been a mental image seen by Macbeth which he mistakenly took to be a dagger.

1. We will, then, be concerned in this chapter with two kinds of mental objects: the bodily sensations – such things as pains, itches, and throbs; and the visual hallucinations – such things as after-images and mirages. There is a very widespread view that, while there are things like the *having* of bodily sensations and the *experiencing* of after-images, there are, strictly speaking, no such things as bodily sensations and after-images. What exists includes the experiencing of pains and after-images, but not the pains and after-images themselves.

This denial of mental objects is particularly associated with contemporary versions of Materialism wherein it is the having of a pain and the experiencing of an after-image which are identified with a process in the brain – it being considered unnecessary to say what kind of thing the pain and the image are, on the ground that they are no kind of thing at all.[2] But the denial is appealing for Dualists too, and, as Keith Campbell observes, 'the program to eliminate mental objects is almost common ground in the philosophy of mind'.[3] Despite this near unanimity, I believe that there are substantial considerations favouring the existence of mental objects and the associated act–object account of having sensations and visual hallucinations (the account of which distinguishes the having from what is had and allows both as existing); indeed, I believe that the arguments that follow force us to acknowledge that mental objects exist.

A word of clarification: when I say that sensations and images exist, I mean just that. I do not mean that they exist independently of persons (or sentient creatures in general). It is reasonable to hold that sensations and after-images cannot exist unowned, that for every such there is necessarily a person who has it; but this does not in itself show that sensations and after-images are not examples of existent mental objects. It is an open philosophical question whether 'What exists?' and 'What

[2] See, e.g., J. J. C. Smart, *Philosophy and Scientific Realism*, p. 97; and D. M. Armstrong, *A Materialist Theory of the Mind*, p. 117. The point is particularly emphasised by Jaegwon Kim, 'Properties, Laws, and the Identity Theory'.

[3] *Body and Mind*, p. 62.

exists independently?' are really the same questions. It is one to be settled by looking at the individual cases and, in particular, the case of sensations and after-images – as we will be doing in this chapter. 'Everything is a substance (in the Aristotelean sense)' is a substantial philosophical claim, not a tautology.

2. We certainly talk and write as if there were mental objects: '*There is* a pain in my foot', '*This* after-image is brighter than *that* one', '*The itch* gets worse when I eat tomatoes', and so on.

This settles nothing as it stands. We once talked as if there were demons, and we now often talk about the average family or the next waltz; and yet there are no demons, average families or waltzes. These three examples illustrate three ways to show that there are no things of a certain kind. We were wrong about demons, because many statements we took to be true turned out false: epilepsy is *not* caused by demons, for example. There is no average family because statements that appear to be about this family can be given a reductive style of analysis in terms of the many non-average families that there are. The case with waltzes is slightly different. Presumably, 'The waltz is about to start' can be given a reductive analysis in terms of certain people being about to move in certain distinctive ways; but to show that there are no waltzes we do not need to go as far as this. It is sufficient to observe that 'The waltz is about to start' can be construed as 'People are about to start waltzing', 'The waltz is romantic' as 'People get romantic when they waltz', and so on. We do not need to give a full-scale analysis of statements about waltzing, we only need to know enough about the meaning of 'waltz' to know that statements apparently about waltzes can be, and are best, re-cast as being about people waltzing. The same is, in fact, true of the average family. We can show that 'The average family owns 0·9 pets' does not commit us to there being a family with a most peculiar pet, by pointing out that the statement may be analysed as 'The number of pets divided by the number of families equals 0·9'; but we can achieve the same goal without a full-scale analysis, by pointing out that the statement may be written as 'The average number of pets in a family is 0·9.' Here the crucial term 'average' reappears and so the analysis is only partial, but enough has been done to make it clear that there need be no family with 0·9 pets.

3. In similar vein, there are three ways we might seek to show that there are no mental objects: by showing that all statements of the form, '*S* has a pain (itch, after-image, etc.) of kind *F*' are false; by producing a

reductive analysis of such statements, for example, of a behaviourist or topic-neutral kind, which eliminates the relevant psychological terms; or, finally, by offering a partial analysis (a recasting which better displays logical form or semantic structure) of these psychological statements, and which, while not eliminating all mentalist vocabulary, shows that these statements are not really about mental objects.

Of the first strategy, I will just say that I am sure it is mistaken, but I do not know how to prove that it is. For I do not know of any premises which are more obvious than that it is sometimes true that we are in pain, having a red after-image, and so on, from which a proof might be constructed.

The second strategy has been much discussed in connexion with the translation versions of Materialism advanced by J. J. C. Smart and D. M. Armstrong. I am afraid that Behaviourist analyses and the topic-neutral development of them by Smart and Armstrong in terms of typical causes of behaviour and typical effects of stimuli, strike me as very implausible. I agree with Alvin Plantinga's comment that 'no one has produced even one example of a mental-state-ascribing proposition that is equivalent to some behaviour-cum-circumstances proposition; nor has anyone suggested even the ghost of a reason for supposing that there are such examples',[4] a comment which also seems to me to apply to the topic-neutral descendants of Behaviourism (though, let me add, they are certainly preferable to their ancestor). Moreover, my reasons for finding them implausible are familiar;[5] hence, I will simply take it as read that the second strategy fails.

I will, therefore, concentrate on the third strategy in this chapter. I am sure the popularity of the denial of mental objects is due to the belief that it can be sustained by a relatively simple re-casting of sensation statements without recourse to anything as implausible as a wholesale rejection of the truth of such statements, and without recourse to anything as difficult as a full-scale behaviourist or topic-neutral analysis of psychological statements.

With one exception, our discussion of the third strategy applies equally to statements about bodily sensations and statements about visual images. The exception is Bruce Aune's attempt to re-cast

---

[4] Plantinga, *God and Other Minds*, p. 191. For a similar view see D. Davidson, 'Mental Events'.

[5] From, e.g., Campbell, *op. cit.*, ch. 5; Jerome Shaffer, *Philosophy of Mind*, ch. 2; M. C. Bradley, 'Sensations, Brain-Processes, and Colours'; and S. J. Noren, 'Smart's Materialism: The Identity Theory and Translation'.

statements putatively about bodily sensations as statements about parts of the body.

4. Aune urges that sensations can be regarded as properties of, or relations with, the body thus:

> I have a pain *in my arm*, asserts no more than, and may be rephrased as, 'My arm pains me' or 'My arm hurts'. And these latter locutions, far from suggesting that pain is a peculiar object that may be here or there, imply that it is rather a feature, in some sense, of a part of one's body.[6]

If one favours 'My arm hurts' as the reconstrual of 'I have a pain in my arm', one is treating sensations as properties or qualities of parts of the body; if one favours 'My arm pains me', one is treating sensations as relations between persons and parts of their bodies.

A common objection to both views has been that sensations are private while properties and relations are public. But, first, it is not entirely clear that sensations are private; and, secondly, it is very far from clear that it is essential to either the notion of a property or of a relation that it be public. It is, however, quite clear that it is essential to the notion of a property that it cannot be instantiated in the absence of a bearer, and essential to the notion of a relation that it cannot obtain in the absence of relata. And this will be sufficient to show that the two views are untenable. The argument will be developed for the relation view alone, as it applies *mutatis mutandis* to the property view.

The phantom limb phenomenon shows that it is possible to have bodily sensations outside of one's body. But if bodily sensations are to be understood in terms of relations between persons and parts of the body, this is impossible; as it is impossible for a relation to hold in the absence of its relata. It is impossible for me to be standing next to the Taj Mahal in the absence of the Taj Mahal. Likewise, if sensation statements essentially related persons to parts of their bodies, they could not be true in the absence of appropriate parts of the body.

It might be objected that pains in phantom limbs are not located outside the body. But if pains in phantom limbs are not where they feel to be, that is, where a limb used to be, then they are, presumably, either nowhere, or in the stump, and it cannot be maintained that having a pain in one's phantom limb is having either nowhere or one's stump

---

[6] B. Aune, *Knowledge, Mind, and Nature*, p. 130.

hurting one. The first because it is nonsense, and the second because it is the translation of a quite different statement according to the view in question, namely, of 'I have a pain in my stump.' Perhaps, as a matter of fact, pains said to be in phantom limbs are really in stumps, but the point remains that Aune's theory does not enable us to translate statements about pains in phantom limbs into relational statements relating persons to parts of the body, because 'I have a pain in my stump' is evidently not equivalent to 'I have a pain in my phantom limb.' (Of course, if one took the view, as I do, that disembodied existence is logically possible, Aune's view could be immediately dismissed. 'I have a pain' cannot be translated as '$(\exists x)$ [x is a part of my body & x hurts me]', for the latter but not the former, entails that I have a body.)

One might try to save Aune's kind of theory by invoking the psychologists' notion of a body-image, and say that to have a pain in some place is to have the body-image at that place hurting one. This avoids the phantom limb objection because in such cases the body image extends beyond the body. It, nevertheless, leads nowhere. Apart from the suspicion of circularity – what is the body-image apart from the total locus of the bodily sensations – the body-image is not a physical body (if it were, invoking it would be useless as a reply to the phantom limb objection), and to reify it is to commit oneself to mental objects as much as reifying the sensations themselves.

There is a further problem for Aune's account arising from the occasional disparity between the location of a pain and the location of its cause. Appropriate stimulation of appropriate brain regions gives rise to pains in various parts of the body; and, as a matter of common experience, disturbances in the mouth can cause pains in the ears. These pains which are remote from their causes are commonly called referred pains. They are uncommon but not rare; and, of course, they might be common. If they were common, pains would not play as useful a role in signalling bodily damage as they now do; but it cannot possibly be maintained that it is logically necessary that pains are useful. Their usefulness is a consequence of Evolution not of Logic.

According to Aune, to have a pain in one's foot at t is to bear the paining relation to one's foot at t. Now Aune must hold that this relation is *internal* in the same way as, for example, 'is redder than'. If X is redder than Y at t_1, but not at t_2, then either or both X and Y must have changed between t_1 and t_2 – in particular, one or both must have changed colour. It is not possible that X and Y each be the same colour at t_2 as they were at t_1, yet their colour relationship be different at the two times. Likewise, it seems clear that if my foot pains me now, then either I or my foot must have changed between an earlier time when my foot was not paining me and now.

The problem this presents Aune is that the pain in question may be a referred one, so that the cause is not in the foot; and if the cause is remote from the foot, clearly the foot may be totally unchanged as far as physical features go. This means that either I myself, the person, changes, or that the foot changes with respect to some non-physical, that is, mental, feature. But the latter entails that something in the foot has mental features, and something with mental features is a mental object. And mental objects are just what Aune is seeking to avoid. It is, therefore, clear that Aune must adopt the former view that I, the person, changes. Now for a person to change is for a person to go from one *state* to another *state*. So that if Aune takes the view that the person changes he is, in effect, seeking to avoid mental objects by taking the view that having a pain is not a matter of being related to a pain, but of being in a certain mental state; that is, he is offering an account of sensations as states of persons.[7] I argue against such a state theory in §7, 8, 9 below.

5. I now turn to examples of strategy three which are equally applicable to sensations and hallucinations. I will start by talking in terms of the former and switch later, for variety, to the latter.

The following passage from Thomas Nagel's paper, 'Physicalism', makes a convenient starting point:

> although it is undeniable that pains exist and people have them, it is also clear that this describes a condition of one entity, the person, rather than a relation between two entities, a person and a pain. For pains to exist *is* for people to have them.
>
> . . . we may regard the ascription of properties to a sensation simply as part of the specification of a psychological state's being ascribed to the person. When we assert that a person has a sensation of a certain description B, this is not to be taken as asserting that there exist an x and a y such that x is a person and y is a sensation and $B(y)$ and x has y. Rather we are to take it as asserting the existence of only one thing, x, such that x is a person, and moreover $C(x)$, where C is the attribute 'has a sensation of description B' . . . Any ascription of properties to them [sensations] is to be taken simply as part of the

---

[7] Which he, in fact, does, *ibid.*, p. 132.

ascription of other attributes to the person who has them – as *specifying* those attributes.[8]

Nagel's general idea here is clear enough. It is to switch from predicates on or descriptions of sensations, to predicates on or descriptions of persons: strictly, nothing is painful, but many things are persons with painful sensations. What is not so clear is just how Nagel supposes the switch he recommends serves to dispose of sensations.

Consider, for example, my brother. Every description of my brother can be transposed to a description of me without meaning loss: 'My brother is tall', for instance, goes to 'I have a tall brother.'[9] But the possibility of switching from 'is tall' as a predicate on my brother to 'has a tall brother' as a predicate on me is clearly irrelevant to the question of my brother's existence. What matters is the way we ought to understand the predicate 'has a tall brother'; the answer in this case being that it is to be understood as formed from a relation by filling an argument place with a singular term. Likewise, what is crucial for whether sensations exist is not just that a statement like 'My pain is severe' can be rendered as 'I have a severe pain', but whether or not it can be so rendered with the predicate 'has a severe pain' understood other than as containing 'a pain' functioning as a singular term filling an argument place in the relation 'x has y'.

The general position here is like that concerning whether there are literally objects of belief – entities such that to believe is to be appropriately related to these entities. We can always switch from predicates on beliefs to predicates on persons, as in the switch from 'His belief is unusual' to 'He has an unusual belief', but this possibility is, in itself, compatible with the relational view of belief.

6. Can we, then, view the semantic structure of 'has a painful sensation' and the like so as not to commit ourselves to there being painful sensations; in particular, so that 'a sensation' is not, strictly speaking, a singular term?

The simplest such view would be the view which sees nothing; the

[8] 'Physicalism', p. 342. I have no doubt that Nagel would argue in precisely the same way for hallucinations.

[9] It may be objected that this only holds if I refer to my brother as my brother. Suppose my brother is the life of the party. 'The life of the party is tall' cannot be translated into a statement about me. But the same applies to sensations. There are ways of referring to sensations other than as sensations; for example, as that which is the subject of this chapter, or by giving them proper names – or at least there are if there are sensations, and to suppose otherwise would beg the question at issue.

view, that is, that sensation predicates on persons have no semantic structure at all; a view we might express by writing 'has-a-painful-sensation' or 'hasapainfulsensation'. On a view of this kind, we can only talk of the meaning of sensation predicates as a whole, for the meanings of the parts of such predicates do not in any way contribute to the meaning of the whole.

This is holism gone mad. Consider the two predicates 'has a burning pain' and 'has a burning itch'. It is perfectly obvious that the meanings of these two predicates are related, and that this relation is a function of the common term 'burning': if they did not have this term in common, the relation would not be the same. But to concede that the appearance of 'burning' in *both* is semantically significant is to concede that its appearance in *either* is, which is to concede that the predicates are semantically structured. Likewise, the occurrence of 'leg' in both of 'has a tingle in his leg' and 'has an ache in his leg' obviously contributes to the meaning relation between the predicates and *a fortitori* to the meaning of each of the predicates. (There is also the question raised by Donald Davidson – for example, in 'Theories of Meaning and Learnable Languages' – of whether languages with indefinitely many primitive predicates of this kind could be learnt.)

Given that a no-structure theory of sensation predicates would be a pyrrhic victory for the theorist who wishes to deny that there are mental objects, what theories remain open to him? Just two seem to have either currency or plausibility: the first I will call the state theory, the second the adverbial theory.

7. Those who deny that there are mental objects commonly make considerable use of terms like 'state', 'condition' and 'process'. For instance, Nagel urges that to say that a person has a pain 'describes a *condition* of one entity, the person', and again 'we may regard the ascription of properties to a sensation simply as part of the specification of a psychological *state*'s being ascribed to the person'.[10] And Campbell claims that 'Descriptions of men mentioning pains, after-images, or pangs of remorse are not relational descriptions connecting men with pains, etc., but complex descriptions of the men's *condition*, mentioning *events* or *processes* but not relating one object to another.'[11]

This suggests a state theory of sensation statements of the following kind. 'I have a throbbing, painful sensation in my knee' does not relate me to my sensation, saying of it that it is throbbing, painful and in my

[10] From earlier quote, my emphasis.
[11] *Op. cit.*, p. 62.

knee; rather it is about me and a state of mine (or condition or process or event etc. essentially involving me – the differences between all these are not important here): it says that I am in a throbbing, painful, in my knee sensation-state; it is, if you like, the sensing, not the sensation which has the properties. A possible parallel is, 'The walk tired me'; presumably, it is the walking rather than the walk which does the tiring, and the statement is thus really about my walking, not my walk.

The obvious question to ask at this point is whether the state theory really achieves anything, for a person and a state of the person are distinct things (a person may be in many different states at the one time, for instance). There does not, therefore, appear to be any significant ontological reduction being effected. On the act–object theory which countenances mental objects by construing sensation statements as relational, 'I have a painful sensation' is explicated as '$(\exists x)$ [I have x & x is painful & x is a sensation]'; while on the state theory we get something like '$(\exists x)$ [I am in x & x is a sensation-state & x is painful]'; and so, the gain appears to be verbal rather than ontological.

I think the state theorist has some sort of reply if he distinguishes *unitary* states from *relational* states. A unitary state of a person is a state of that person not essentially involving anything over and above that person. My being happy, to take a psychological example, and my being warm, to take a physical example, are both unitary states of mine. There is a natural, if philosophically difficult, sense in which my being happy or being warm at some time are not things over and above and distinct from me at that time. This is essentially linked to the connexion between the counting principles for persons and their unitary states – for a given person at a time, there cannot be more than one unitary state of a given kind. For instance, there cannot be more cases of persons being warm (happy) in a room than there are persons. If this were not so, if there might be two unitary states of a given kind for one person at one time, there would be no sense to the claim that such states were, in some substantial sense, nothing over and above the one subject in these states.

Therefore, if the state theorist insists that the sensation states – the sensings – are unitary, rather than relational states like being happy *at* . . . or being warmer *than* . . , it appears he has a theory significantly distinct from the act–object theory.

He also has a theory exposed to two serious objections. I will call the first, the many-property objection, and the second, the complement objection.

8. The many-property objection arises from the fact that we ascribe many things to our sensations: a sensation may be painful *and* burning *and* in the foot. How can a state theorist handle this?

The state theorist recasts 'I have an F sensation' as 'I am in an F sensation-state.' Hence, the obvious account for him to give of 'I have a sensation which is F and G' is 'I am in a sensation-state which is F and G.'

But this conjunctive style of account faces a decisive difficulty. Suppose I have a sensation which is F and a sensation which is G, then, on the state theory, I am in a sensation-state which is F and in one which is G. But there may at a given time be only one such unitary state for a given person; therefore, I am in a sensation state which is F and G. But the latter is the state theorist's account of 'I have a sensation which is F and G.' Hence, the conjunctive style of account has as a consequence that 'I have a sensation which is F and a sensation which is G' entails 'I have a sensation which is F and G', which is quite wrong. The latter entails the former, but not conversely; for I may have one sensation which is F and, at the same time, another which is G. That is, having, for example, a burning, painful sensation in the foot is being conflated with having a burning sensation and painful sensation and a sensation in the foot.

It is important to appreciate that it serves no purpose for the state theorist to try to avoid this consequence by renouncing the commitment to there being at most one sensing or sensation-state for a given person at a given time. If we may have many sensings for one person at a time, sensings must clearly be strongly distinct from persons and to have a sensation will be, as on the act–object theory, to be related to something other than oneself. The theory will be nothing more than the verbal recommendation to use the word 'state' rather than the word 'object'.

What the state theorist must do is give a different account from the conjunctive one of how his theory handles statements that a particular sensation is F and G and . . . A number of different answers are possible, but it turns out that the various possibilities are essentially the same as those that arise in the discussion of the corresponding objection to the adverbial theory and so I will postpone the matter until then.

9. The complement objection to the state theory is a special case of a general way of showing that some term does not qualify a given thing. We show that if the term did, so might its complement.

For example, the view that truth is a property of sentence *types* may be refuted by noting that 'is true' and its complement 'is not true' may apply to one and the same sentence type depending on the meanings given to the constituent terms of that type. Thus, 'He is a bachelor' may be true if by 'bachelor' is meant bachelor of arts but false otherwise (and, likewise, true or false depending on who is meant by 'He'). And there are, of course, two characteristic responses to this kind of observation: to look for a new entity to be the bearer of truth-value, like eternal sentences or propositions; or to argue that we are dealing with a relational predicate – like 'is true in L' or 'is true said by S at t' – rather than a one-place predicate. A second example, more mundane but closer to current concerns, is the view that 'school-age' in 'I have a school-age child' qualifies having a child rather than the child; that is, that being of school-age is, strictly, a property of having children rather than of children. One way of showing that this view is false is to observe that 'I have a school-age child' and 'I have a non-school-age child' are both true. But nothing, including the having of children, can be both F and non-F, hence it is a child, not the having of it, which is or is not of school-age (and there must be at least two children).

In parallel with the child case, it may be the case that 'I have a painful sensation' and 'I have a non-painful sensation' are both true at the one time, hence we cannot construe being painful or not as a characteristic of the having of the pain rather than the pain. For if we did, we would have a state – in this case, a sensing – being both F and non-F.

As with the first objection, there are a number of replies that might be made on behalf of the state theory which are essentially the same as the replies to the corresponding objection to the adverbial theory, and will thus be discussed then.

10. Two digressions. First, the possibility of having different kinds of sensations at the one time also seems to me to undermine the analogy commonly drawn between sensations, colours, and wax impressions by those who wish to deny that there are mental objects.

On the way to his adverbial theory to be discussed below, C. J. Ducasse suggests colour predicates as a model for sensation predicates: the relation between 'has a severe pain in his foot' and 'has a sensation' is like that between 'is bright red' and 'is coloured'.[12]

In what I take to be similar vein, Descartes suggests that we view sensations on the model of impressions in wax: 'I allow only so much difference between the soul and its ideas as there is between a

[12] *Nature, Matter and Minds*, see ch. 13.

piece of wax and the various shapes it can assume.'[13] Presumably the notion here is that, as far as ontology goes, for a person to have a particular kind of sensation is like a piece of wax assuming a particular shape.

But it is impossible for one object to be two different colours or shapes at once. Though we may say that an apple is both red and green, by this we mean that one part is red and a *different* part is green; likewise, a statue may be different shapes at a time only in the sense that different parts are different shapes. The analogies, therefore, fail at a crucial point.

It might be objected that, though the analogies fail, they do not do so at a crucial point. However, I think it can be shown that the disanalogy pointed to is crucial. The point of suggesting an analogy between, say, 'X is bright red' and 'X has a severe pain' is to suggest that we view the semantic role of 'severe' as paralleling that of 'bright'. 'Bright' does not stand for a feature of what 'red' denotes; instead it serves to describe X more precisely, to identify more closely or delimit the class to which X belongs: X belongs not just to the class of red things, but to a proper sub-class of that class – the class of bright red things as opposed to, say, the class of dark red things. This is why X cannot be both bright red and dark red at the same time: 'bright' and 'dark' serve to say different, incompatible things *about X*. Likewise, if 'severe' served, by analogy with 'bright', to say something about X rather than about a pain in 'X has a severe pain', X could not have both a severe and a mild pain at the same time, for this would involve *one* thing, X, having incompatible characteristics. By way of contrast, the act–object theory has no trouble here. 'Severe' in 'X has a severe pain' serves to say something about a pain on this theory, and all that needs to be said of the case where X has a severe pain and a mild pain is that there must be *two* pains, one mild, one severe – which is precisely what theorists who deny that there are mental objects cannot say, for they cannot say that there are any pains at all.

The second digression concerns a point drawn to my attention by Keith Campbell. In my discussion of the state theory, I have assumed that persons *qua* persons really exist, for I have treated the theory as analysing mental objects away in favour of states of *persons*. And if one adopted a Humean-style bundle theory of the person according to which persons are 'convenient fictions' and statements putatively about them are analysable in terms of sets of individual mental experiences

[13] *Descartes: Philosophical Writings*, p. 288.

bearing some common relation to each other, then my case against the state theory would be undermined. My reply to this objection is that a bundle theory of the person is only as good as its account of the relation between the individual experiences in virtue of which they constitute a person. And, to date, no remotely plausible account of this relation has been offerred. (See Armstrong, *A Materialist Theory of the Mind*, p. 55 ff.)

11. I now come to the most widely canvassed theory of those which deny that there are mental objects, the so-called adverbial theory held by, for example, Ducasse, R. M. Chisholm, and Aune.[14] Our discussion will be couched principally in terms of our main concern, visual images, in particular, for concreteness, after-images, as a change from bodily sensations.

The basic idea behind the theory is to utilise the fact that, on standard views, after-images, sensations, and the like, cannot exist when not sensed by some person (sentient creature), in order to reconstrue statements which purport to be about sensations, after-images and so on, as being about the way or mode in which some person is sensing. Thus, 'I have a red after-image' becomes 'I sense red-ly', and 'I have a pain' becomes 'I sense painfully', and so on.

A parallel often appealed to in presentations of the adverbial analysis is the elimination of talk putatively about smiles in favour of talk about the manner of smiling; as in the recasting of 'Mary wore a seductive smile' as 'Mary smiled seductively.' Similarly, it is pointed out that one way of showing that we need not acknowledge the existence of limps or dances is to note that 'He has an unusual limp' and 'Patrick dances a magnificent waltz' may be transcribed to 'He limps unusually' and 'Patrick waltzes magnificently', respectively.

The two objections I will be raising against the adverbial theory parallel the two raised against the state theory. This will surprise no one who accepts Donald Davidson's general approach to adverbs,[15] for on this approach there will be no significant difference between the state and the adverbial theories – except, perhaps, that the adverbial theory will have events in place of states, a difference which is not important in this context. I want, however, to keep my objections as independent as possible of the controversial issues surrounding the whole question of the semantics for adverbial modification.

[14] Ducasse, *Nature, Matter and Minds*, R. M. Chisholm, *Perceiving*, B. Aune, *op. cit.*

[15] See 'The Logical Form of Action Sentences'.

12. Our statements about after-images are not just to the effect that an image is red, or square, or whatever; they are also to the effect that an image is red *and* square *and* . . . The first objection I will be raising for the adverbial theory turns on this point that an after-image has many properties, and will be referred to as the many-property problem.

It seems to me that adverbial theorists have been rather reticent about how they handle this problem. It is clear enough that their view is that to have an after-image which is *F*, is to sense *F*-ly – the attribute, *F*, goes to the mode or manner, *F*-ly. But it is not clear just what account would be offered of having an after-image which is *F* and *G*. Do both of the (in their view, apparent) attributes go to separate modes, so that to have an after-image which is *F* and *G* is analysed as sensing *F*-ly and *G*-ly; or do we have a new compound mode, *F-G*-ly? It seems to me that both these answers, and the variants on them, face substantial difficulties.

Suppose having an *F*, *G* after-image is analysed as sensing *F*-ly and *G*-ly.[16] This conjunctive style of answer has the advantage of explaining the entailment from 'I have a red, square after-image' to 'I have a red after-image'; for it will correspond to the entailment from 'I sense red-ly and square-ly' to 'I sense red-ly.'

But if this answer is adopted, it will be impossible for the adverbial theorist to distinguish the two very different states of affairs of having a red, square after-image at the same time as having a green, round one, from that of having a green, square after-image at the same time as having a red, round one; because both will have to be accounted the same, namely, as sensing red-ly and round-ly and square-ly and green-ly. In essence, the point is that we must be able to distinguish the statements: 'I have an *F* and a *G* after-image', and 'I have a *F*, *G* after-image', and the conjunctive answer does not appear to be able to do this.

In discussion of this objection, it has been suggested to me (by Edward Madden) that the adverbial theorist might have recourse to the point that when I have a red, square after-image at the same time as a green, round one, they must (as we say) be in different places in my visual field: the red one will be, for instance, to the left of the green one. But how can this help the adverbial theorist? For 'I have a red after-image to the left of a green one' raises the same problem; namely, that it

[16] This is the obvious interpretation of Ducasse, *Nature, Mind, and Death*, ch. 13, §22.

cannot be analysed conjunctively as 'I sense red-ly and to-the-left-ly and green-ly'; for that is equivalent to 'I sense green-ly and to-the-left-ly and red-ly', which would be the analysis of 'I have a green after-image to the left of a red one.' (And, likewise, for 'there-ly' and 'here-ly' in place of 'to-the-left-ly'.)

Perhaps the thought is that when applied to after-images terms like 'red' and 'square' are *incomplete*, they demand supplication with a term indicating location in a visual field. But this cannot be right. I can know perfectly well what saying someone has a red or a square after-image means without having any idea at all of the location of the after-image. Moreover, it is evidently not possible to give an exhaustive list, p_1, $\dots, p_n$, of all the parts of a person's visual field that might be occupied by one of his after-images. So that 'I have a red after-image' cannot be analysed as 'I sense red-p_1-ly or $\dots$ or red-p_n-ly.' The best that can be done is '$(\exists x)$ [x is a part of my visual field and I sense red-x-ly]', which – leaving aside the question of interpreting quantification into adverbial modification – commits the adverbial theorist to the existence of a species of mental object, namely, parts of visual fields, and so undermines the whole rationale behind his theory.

13. What other answers might the adverbial theorist give to the many-property problem? One answer might take its starting point from the ambiguity of a statement like 'He spoke impressively quickly.' Here 'impressively' can be taken as modifying 'spoke', in which case we are regarding the statement conjunctively – as equivalent to 'He spoke impressively and quickly.' Alternatively and more naturally, 'impressively' can be read as modifying 'quickly' – just as 'very' modifies 'quickly' not 'spoke' in 'He spoke very quickly.' Likewise, the adverbial theorist might argue, we should translate 'I have an F, G after-image' as 'I sense F-ly G-ly', where the latter is not to be read conjunctively with 'F-ly' and 'G-ly' both modifying 'sense', but with just one adverb, say 'G-ly', modifying 'sense' and the other, 'F-ly', modifying 'G-ly'.

There seem to me to be two objections which, taken together, are decisive against this answer to the many-property problem. First, if we consider an actual example, for instance, the analysis of 'I have a red, square after-image' as 'I sense red-ly square-ly', it is hard to see how one could in a non-arbitrary manner decide which adverb modified which. Does 'red-ly' modify 'square-ly', or vice versa? I cannot see any way of settling such a question rationally: it is, for example, equally impossible to have a colourless, shaped after-image as it is to have a shapeless, coloured after-image; and, further, it seems to make no difference which order one reads the adverbs in.

Secondly, suppose the adverbial theorist finds a suitable ground for settling the question as to which adverb modifies which, and suppose it is 'red-ly' which modifies 'square-ly'; then he is faced with the absurd consequence that 'red' takes a different meaning in 'I have a red after-image' to that it takes in 'I have a red, square after-image'. For in the former, on the adverbial theory itself, 'red' indicates a mode of sensing, the former statement translating to 'I sense red-ly'; while in the latter statement 'red' does not stand for a mode of sensing at all, because the latter statement, on the theory, translates to 'I sense red-ly square-ly', with the 'red-ly' understood as modifying 'square-ly' and *not* 'sensing'. There are, of course, cases where the one adverb some-times modifies a verb and sometimes another adverb: witness our earlier example, 'impressively' – in 'He spoke impressively' it modifies 'spoke', and in 'He spoke impressively quickly' it modifies 'quickly' (on the most natural reading). But this is of no assistance to the adver-bial theorist. It is clear that 'impressively' plays a different, though related role in the two statements – this is why 'He spoke impres-sively quickly' does not entail 'He spoke impressively' – while, on the contrary, it is clear that 'red' plays the same role in 'I have a red after-image' and 'I have a red, square after-image.' This is why the latter does entail the former, and why having a red, square after-image is properly described as a special case of having a red after-image.

14. Although W. Sellars does not address himself directly to the many-properties question, he does use a suggestive notation in this connexion.[17] When talking of having a red, triangular sense-impres-sion, he talks of sensing red-triangular-ly. The precise significance of the hyphenation is not made explicit, but an obvious interpretation of it is as indicating that red-triangular-ly is not a mode of sensing having red-ly as a component; it is, rather, a quite new mode of sensing; and so the meaning of 'red-triangular-ly' is not to be viewed as being built out of independently semantically significant components like 'red' and 'triangular'; and likewise for 'green-square-ly', etc.[18]

[17] In, e.g., 'Reply to Aune', in *Intentionality, Minds and Perception*; and *Science and Metaphysics*. In 'The Adverbial Theory of the Objects of Sensation', Sellars argues that what follows is *not* his view. But it is, in any case, worth con-sideration. In the latter paper, Sellars emphasises the role of comparative analy-ses in his adverbial theory. These are criticised in §19, below.

[18] A view of this kind is explicitly advanced by G. Pitcher in 'Minds and Ideas in Berkeley'.

Put thus baldly, this view obviously faces in more acute form the difficulty just considered. Having a red, triangular after-image is a special case of having a red after-image, hence any adverbial theorist must treat sensing red-triangular-ly as a special case of sensing red-ly. But on this view in question, sensing red-triangular-ly fails to have sensing red-ly as even a component.

The view might, however, be refined. In discussions of the step from 'This is a horse's head' to 'This is a head', it is sometimes suggested that the latter should be read as 'This is a head of something', so that the step can be viewed as Existential Generalization. In similar vein, it might be suggested that 'I have a red after-image' should be expanded to 'I have a red after-image of some shape', and consequently its adverbial translation should be expanded to 'I sense red-some-shape-ly.' On this view, red-ly is not a mode of sensing at all. The modes of sensing are red-triangular-ly, red-square-ly, green-round-ly, and so on, and sensing red-ly is to be understood as sensing red-square-ly or red-round-ly or red- . . .-ly.

There seem to be two serious difficulties facing this suggestion (apart from the difficulty of giving a precise construal of the dots). The first is that the modification appears to undermine the adverbial theorist's claim to be offering a philosophically perspicuous account of after-images. When I have a red, square after-image, the redness and the squareness appear as discriminable elements in my experience; and hence elements that it is desirable to have reflected in distinct elements of any offered analysis. The act–object analysis of having an after-image clearly meets this desideratum: to have a red, square after-image is to be in a certain relation to a mental object which has as distinct properties redness and squareness. The adverbial theory, on the modification in question, does not; for having a red, square after-image is accounted as sensing red-square-ly, where the hyphenation indicates that this mode of sensing is not to be further broken up into distinct elements. Indeed, on this view, someone who remarks on the common feature in having a red, square after-image and having a red, round after-image is making a plain mistake – the first is sensing red-square-ly, the second sensing red-round-ly, which are different, and that is that. But, far from being a plain mistake, the remark looks like an evident truth.

The second objection[19] derives from the point that there are indefinitely many things that may be said about one's after-images. An

[19] This objection can also be applied to the suggestion discussed in §13.

after-image may be red, red and square, red and square and fuzzy at the edges, red and square and fuzzy at the edges and to the left of a blue after-image, and so on.

Now consider how the adverbial theory should handle 'I have a red, square, fuzzy after-image.' It cannot analyse this as 'I sense red-square-ly and fuzzy-ly', for essentially the same reasons as the conjunctive account had to be rejected. In brief, such a treatment would conflate 'I have a red, square, fuzzy after-image' with 'I have a red, square after-image and a fuzzy after-image.' Should the theory then abandon the view that red-square-ly is a fundamental mode of sensing, and adopt the view that red-square-fuzzy-ly is a fundamental mode of sensing? On this further modification, 'I have a red, square fuzzy after-image' would go to 'I sense red-square-fuzzy-ly'; and 'I have a red, square after-image' would be analysed as, roughly, 'I sense red-square-fuzzy-ly or I sense red-square-sharp-ly.' Thus, on this further modification, red-square-ly, green-round-ly, and so on, are no longer modes of sensing; rather red-square-fuzzy-ly, green-round-sharp-ly, and so on, will be the various ways of sensing.

However, in view of the point this objection started with, this process of modification will continue without end. For any n that the adverbial theorist offers an analysis of 'I have an $F_1, \ldots, F_n$ after-image' as I sense F_1- ... -F_n-ly', he can be challenged for his analysis of 'I have an $F_1, \ldots, F_{n+1}$ after-image'; and so, for the reasons above, be forced to abandon F_1- ... -F_n-ly in favour of F_1- ... -F_n-F_{n+1}-ly as a basic mode of sensing. This means that the adverbial theorist cannot ever give even a single example of a basic mode of sensing, and thus cannot ever complete even one of his adverbial analyses; and even if he could, would, moreover, end up with a theory no better than the no-structure one rejected earlier.

15. I suspect that some adverbial theorists who have written down expressions like 'red-square-fuzzy-ly', have meant by the hyphenation no more than that mode of sensing associated with what we normally, and in their view misleadingly, call having a red, square, fuzzy after-image. But this is not to give us a theory we can oppose to the act–object theory; it is merely to express the hope that such a theory may be forthcoming. It is not to argue or show that we can do without mental objects; it is just to say that we can, for the central question of how to interpret the hyphenation is left unanswered except for a reference to the very theory being denied.

16. My second objection to the adverbial theory is, in essence, the

complement objection transferred from the state theory to the adverbial. Just as it is not possible for something to be *F* and non-*F* at the same time, it is not possible for a person at a given time to *V* both *F*-ly and non-*F*-ly. I can sing badly easily enough, but I cannot sing both well and badly at the same time; I can run quickly, but not both quickly and slowly; and I can inspect carefully, but not both carefully and carelessly; and so on and so forth.

Therefore, to have an after-image which is *F* cannot be to sense *F*-ly; for it is manifestly possible to have an after-image which is *F* at the same time as one which is non-*F*: I may have a red and a green after-image at the same time, or a square and a round one at the same time; while it is not possible to sense *F*-ly and non-*F*-ly at the same time. (And likewise for the bodily sensations.)

The only reply which appears to have any real plausibility here is to urge that, though one cannot *V* both *F*-ly and non-*F*-ly at a given time, one can *V* *F*-ly with respect to *A* and *V* non-*F*-ly with respect to *B*. For instance, I can, during a concerto, listen happily to the strings and unhappily to the piano. And that when I have a red and a non-red after-image together, I am sensing red-ly with respect to one thing and non-red-ly with respect to another. But what are these things with respect to which I am sensing, for there need, of course, be no appropriate physical things in the offing? It is hard to see what they could be other than the mental objects of the act–object theory.

17. Two lines of objection to the arguments just given might be thought to arise from Terence Parsons' 'Some Problems Concerning the Logic of Grammatical Modifiers'.[20]

(i) Parsons claims that:

(1) John wrote painstakingly and illegibly.

and

(2) John wrote painstakingly and John wrote illegibly.

are not equivalent because – though (1) entails (2) – (2) does not entail (1). He gives two cases which he claims show (2) may be true when (1) is false:

> if there were two separate past occasions on which John wrote, on one of which he wrote painstakingly, and on the other of which he wrote illegibly, but no past occasion on which he did both at once . . . Also if on one and the same occasion he wrote painstakingly with one hand and illegibly with the other. [p. 331]

[20] I am indebted to Barry Taylor for drawing my attention to the relevance of this paper.

This might appear to threaten my arguments in two ways. First, in my discussion of the conjunctive reply to the many property problem, I was clearly working under the general assumption that there is no significant distinction between a statement like (1) and the corresponding statement like (2). Second, Parsons' second case where (2) may be true while (1) is false, could easily be modified to threaten the principle that one cannot V F-ly and non-F-ly at the same time, and so my discussion of complementation *vis-à-vis* the adverbial theory. The modification would be to consider a case where John wrote illegibly with his left hand while writing legibly with his right; would he then be writing legibly and illegibly at the same time?

The threat, however, is more apparent than real. This is obvious in the first case Parsons gives, because it involves considering *different* times of writing; and our discussion of the conjunctive reply involved just *one* time – we noted the possibility of having different visual images at the *same* time. In short, it is sufficient for us if 'John *is writing* painstakingly and illegibly' is equivalent to 'John *is writing* painstakingly and John is writing illegibly', and the first case does not threaten this equivalence.

With the second case we must remember that we are dealing with something that can be judged both overall and in a particular aspect. Normally, when we say that Jones wrote illegibly, we mean that overall the writing was illegible, not that every word was illegible (likewise, a speech may be impressive without every part of it being impressive). In this sense, 'Jones wrote illegibly with one hand (his left, say)', does not entail that Jones wrote illegibly, for most of the writing may have been with his right hand in elegant copperplate; and similarly for 'painstakingly'. And in this sense Parsons will be right that it is possible that Jones wrote painstakingly with one hand and illegibly with the other without (1) being true, but equally this is possible without (2) being true, so the case fails to establish that (2) may be true without (1) being true.

On the other hand, if we take 'Jones wrote illegibly' to count as true if any part or aspect of Jones' writing was illegible, and likewise for 'painstakingly'; then if Jones wrote painstakingly with one hand and illegibly with the other, (2) must be true, but so will (1); and so there is still no case for denying that (2) entails (1).

Parallel remarks apply to the possibility of writing illegibly and legibly. It is not, in the overall sense, possible to write, on a given occasion, both legibly and illegibly (though it is possible to write in a manner which deserves neither epithet). It *is* possible that *one* aspect of one's writing be legible and *another* be illegible. But we noted in §16 that the possibility of V-ing F-ly with respect to A while V-ing non-F-ly with respect to B is of no use to the adverbial theory, for the only plausible candidates for A and B in the sensing case are mental objects.

In general, whether or not one agrees with my discussion of (1) and (2), there is little comfort for the adverbial theorist in Parsons' remarks. The case for distinguishing (1) and (2) rests heavily on there being something *more* involved than just the person (John's hand as well as John); and the adverbial theorist's aim is to effect an ontic reduction to the person alone in his account of sensing.

(ii) The second line of objection concerns the 'predicate-modifier' formal semantics for adverbs given by Parsons. By contrast with Davidson's event-predicate treatment,[21] these semantics view adverbs as functions on predicates; and it might be thought that they could be appealed to by the adverbial theorist to elucidate 'green-triangular-ly' and so on in a way which acknowledged structure without facing the problems of the conjunctive treatment.

The 'predicate-modifier' theorist must, however, see a certain *intensionality* in *all* adverbs. 'x senses' and 'x breathes' are (we may suppose) co-extensional. But John does not breathe slowly if and only if he senses slowly, and the adverbial theorist will not allow that he breathes red-ly if he senses red-ly. Without going into the details,[22] this means that possible worlds (and beings) other than the actual must be invoked in predicate-modifier semantics. Hence, they achieve nothing for the adverbial theory. Perhaps (perhaps) we need possibilia for the elucidation of modal statements, but 'I have a pain' and 'I have a red image' are statements about the actual world, if any are. Moreover, appeal to possibilia would make a mockery of any claim of the adverbial theory to greater ontological economy than the act–object.

It may be objected to this last argument that because extension (in the actual world) is notoriously insufficient to determine intension, any adequate semantic theory – even for non-modal statements – requires acknowledging possible worlds and beings other than the actual.

In order to meet this objection it is necessary to sketch (very briefly) a possible-world semantics. 'A is red' is true if and only if A belongs to the class of red things. But this class does not determine the intension of

---

[21] In the paper cited in footnote 15.
[22] But see David Lewis, 'General Semantics', especially p. 28.

'red'. The latter is determined (more nearly, anyway) by the class of possible red things, which we can view as the union of the classes of red things in each possible world. Hence, the intension of 'red' may be viewed as a function with the set of possible worlds as its domain and the set of red things in all possible worlds as its range, which goes from each possible world to the set of red things in that possible world: that is, the value of [red] at w is the set of red things in w (where [...] is the intension of ...).

We can now say that 'A is red' is true in w if and only if A belongs to the value of [red] at w. The important point to notice here is that the evidently non-modal nature of 'A is red' is reflected in the fact that the value of [red] at w has as its members only the red things *in w*, and the value of [red] at *other* worlds is *irrelevant*. By contrast, 'A is necessarily red' is true in w if and only if A belongs to the value of [red] in all worlds (or all worlds accessible to w, or something along these lines) and these truth-conditions do involve red things outside w.

In similar vein, the truth-conditions for 'Jones walks' will be along the lines of: 'Jones walks' is true in w if and only if Jones belongs to the value of [walks] at w, where [walks] is a function from each possible world to the set of walkers in that world. What about 'Jones walks slowly'? According to the predicate-modifier approach, [slowly] is a function from one intension to another, that is, on the possible-world conception, a function from one function to another function. But the intensional aspect noted earlier means that it cannot be said that 'Jones walks slowly' is true in w if and only if Jones belongs to the value of [slowly] at the value of [walks] at w. Because, for any w in which every walker is a thinker and *vice versa*, the value of [walks] at w will be identical with the value of [thinks] at w; and so, for every such w, we will have every slow walker a slow thinker, and *vice versa*. This unacceptable consequence can only be avoided by taking the value of [walks] at worlds *other than w* into account in giving the truth-conditions in w for 'Jones walks slowly.' And this is wrong. Even if one grants the possible worlds of the semantics just sketched, 'Jones walks slowly' ought – like 'A is red' and unlike modal statements – to be given truth-conditions in a possible-world w involving only how things are in *that* world.

18. To this stage, we have been concentrating on short-comings in alternatives to the act–object theory. I want now to mention and develop a positive advantage of the theory.

Many of the terms that we use to describe material things may also be used to describe visual hallucinations: both may be said to be red, triangular, moving, and so on. This is not true to the same extent in the case of bodily sensations: pains and itches are not triangular or red, and chairs and tables are not severe or intense. However, certain spatial locutions apply equally to both: both an ache and a bone may be said to be in the foot or in the hand.

How is this striking fact to be explained? Obviously, it is not a linguistic accident, a fantastic fluke in the development of English (and, of course, a similar situation exists in French, German, Russian, etc.) that 'triangular', for example, may apply equally to an after-image and a figure in chalk on the black-board, or that 'in my foot' may apply equally to a pain and a blood vessel.

The simplest explanation, and, thus, in the absence of strong contrary indications, the best, is that both after-images and chalk figures may have the same property, that of being triangular, and, hence, may warrant the same linguistic description; and, likewise, both pains and blood vessels may have the same property, that of being located in the foot, and, hence, may warrant the same linguistic description. But this explanation is only available to one who acknowledges the existence of after-images and pains. For if they do not exist, they cannot have any properties at all, and, *a fortiori*, cannot have the same property as a chalk figure or a blood vessel.

Essentially the same point can be put in terms of meanings (and so in a manner more neutral concerning realism about properties). The simplest theory is that 'triangular' and 'in the foot', for example, mean the same when applied to mental objects and material objects. What I am saying about the chalk figure when I say it is triangular is the same as what I am saying about the after-image when I say that it is triangular. Likewise, when I say that my pain is in my foot I am making the same claim about my pain as I make about a blood vessel when I say that it is in my foot. And this theory is available only to one who acknowledges that *there is* an after-image and that *there is* a pain. For if after-images and pains do not exist, they cannot possibly be said to be triangular or in the foot in the sense that chalk figures and blood vessels may be.

This question of the properties that mental objects have (to put the matter in its realist guise), as well as bearing on the existence of such objects, also bears of course on their nature. There is little philosophical bite to the bald assertion that there are mental objects, that in itself is just an affirmation of pluralism about the mind. The bite comes with our claim that these mental objects really are red, triangular, in the foot, or whatever.

This argument for mental objects will provoke two related lines of reply. First, that there are good reasons, independent of whether pains and after-images exist, for denying the univocality thesis just sketched, for denying, that is, that 'red', 'square', 'five inches across', and the like mean the same when applied to visual hallucinations as they do when applied to physical objects; and for denying that 'in my foot', 'in my stomach', and the like mean the same when applied to bodily sensations as they do when applied to physical objects. Secondly, that, in support of the denial of univocality, it is possible to give intuitively plausible *special* analyses of the meanings of the terms in question when applied to visual hallucinations and bodily sensations. For instance, it might be suggested that the meaning of 'in my foot' in 'I have a pain in my foot' is captured by analysing the latter as 'I have a pain of the kind typically caused by a disturbance in my foot'; and that the meaning of 'red' ('square') in 'I have a red (square) visual image' is captured by analysing the latter as 'Something is going on in me like what goes on in me when I see something red (square).'

19. Both lines of reply seem to me to be particularly weak in the visual hallucination case.

(i) Though it is commonly asserted that univocality fails for hallucinations, it is hard to find any real arguments for the claim – other than arguments against the existence of hallucinations as mental objects, either based on adverbial or state theories of the kind we have already rejected or on behaviouristic analyses that we have agreed to have been shown mistaken elsewhere.

It has, of course, been widely maintained that the application of terms like 'red' and 'square' to visual hallucinations is *logically secondary* to their application to physical things. But this is a separate question to the univocality one. What is meant by saying that the application of, say, 'square' to visual hallucinations is logically secondary is something like (the matter is not always entirely clear) one or more of: 'square' could not apply to hallucinations unless it also applied to physical objects; one could not learn 'square' as applied to hallucinations prior to learning its application to physical objects; there could not be a language containing 'square' which applied to hallucinations but not physical objects. Now, whether or not such claims are correct (and I find them less plausible than many do), they relate to the conditions of *application* of terms to hallucinations, not to the nature (that is, meaning) of *what* is applied. Hence, they are separate from the issue of univocality. That is, the fact (if it is a fact) that the application of a term to *A*s is logically secondary to its application to *B*s does not entail that the meaning of the term is different when applied to *A*s.

It is, I think, a confusion of the issues of univocality and logical secondariness which leads P. T. Geach in *Mental Acts* to the surely absurdly extreme position that temporal predicates like 'before', 'now', 'lasts for five minutes' are equivocal in their application to mental and physical things: 'though time-determinations . . . can really be ascribed to sensations . . . nevertheless we are not saying the same thing when ascribing them to sensation as when we apply them in the physical world' (p. 128). Although this claim that, for instance, 'preceded' in 'The red after-image preceded the green one' means something different from what it means in 'The explosion preceded the flash' is extremely implausible; a claim like that our use of 'preceded' in the first statement is logically secondary to its use in the second is not. I suspect that Geach has slid from the latter to the former.

There is, moreover, good reason for accepting univocality in the case of visual hallucinations. As J. L. Austin emphasises in *Sense and Sensibilia*, we are only rarely deceived by our visual hallucinations. Nevertheless, we are sometimes deceived, and, more commonly, are sometimes undecided. I may take a mirage for a real oasis, or I may simply not know whether I am seeing a mirage or an oasis; I may take a red after-image to be a faded red blob of paint on the wall, or I may simply not know whether what I am seeing is an after-image or a paint blob; or I may take a phosphene (what happens when a certain part of the brain has a very small electric current passed through it) to be a real flash of light, or I may simply not know whether it is a phosphene or a flash of light.

The cases where I am undecided seem to me to provide substantial support for univocality. Suppose I just cannot tell whether the bright yellow flash is a phosphene or a flash of light. Then I will not know whether to describe my experience as seeing a yellow flash of light or as having an hallucination of one; but I will know that 'bright yellow' is the term to use to describe my experience *whether or not* it is a phosphene or a flash of light. But to deny univocality is to adopt a *two* meanings doctrine: 'bright yellow' takes two meanings, one when applied to physical things like light flashes, another when applied to hallucinations like phosphenes; accordingly, one cannot know the meaning of 'bright yellow' unless one knows whether it is being applied to something physical or to a visual hallucination. And, hence, it is a consequence of denying univocality that, in the case we have described, I do not know what 'bright yellow' means; because I do not know whether or not I am hallucinating. This is absurd. Clearly, I know precisely what I mean by saying that I am seeing a bright yellow flash, even though I do not know whether the flash is a light flash or a hallucination, and I do not need to find out whether it is or is not a phosphene in order to find out what I meant.

By way of contrast, with a word like 'burning' which does take one meaning applied to a bodily sensation, say, an itch, and another (related) meaning when applied to a physical thing, say, a fire, one does not know what is meant if someone says that something is burning unless one knows whether the something is mental or physical. It might be suggested that I do know the meaning of 'burning' even if I do not know to what it is being applied; for I know that either it means what it does when applied to something mental, or what it does when applied to something physical. But this is to concede that I do not know the meaning of 'burning' at all in such a case. I know what the two possibilities are, but not which one obtains – knowing the two possibilities for the next Prime Minister is *not* knowing who the next Prime Minister will be. Likewise, the denier of univocality cannot hold that I know the meaning of 'bright yellow' in the case of the previous paragraph on the ground that I know that 'bright yellow' either means what it does when applied to light flashes or what it means when applied to phosphenes. This is not knowing what 'bright yellow' means, it is merely knowing what it *might* mean.

(ii) The difficulties for analysing 'I have a red (square) visual image' along the lines of 'Something is going on in me like what goes on in me when I see something red (square)' parallel those raised for comparative analyses of the phenomenal use of 'looks' in chapter 2, §4. I will, therefore, just summarise them.

Not only is it possible, but people actually have visual images whose colours are distinct from those of any physical objects they have ever seen, and likewise for shapes; they have, therefore, images which are *F* without being in a state of the kind normally brought about in them by seeing things which are *F* (and without having something going on in them like what etc., and so on for the various formulations). Moreover, it is clear that not only might the colour or shape of a person's image differ from that of any physical object he has seen, it might differ from that of any object there is. Therefore, it does not help to point out that the state will at least be of the kind normally brought about in people in general by seeing things which are *F* (and, further, there might not be any other people).

Moreover, it does not help this style of analysis to point out that the state will be of the kind that *would* be brought about *if* one were to see an *F*. There is nothing contradictory about a totally colour-blind person having coloured images. Indeed, some psychologists believe that there are such people, that is, that there are people who are all the time in the kind of situation all of us are in at dusk – able to have coloured images, but with everything physical looking grey. Such a person will have an image which is, say, red, while being in a state which, because of his colour-blindness, is unlike the state he is in when (or would be in if he was) seeing something red.

Contrariwise, a person may be in a state of the kind normally caused in him by seeing an *F*, without having an image which is *F*. This follows immediately from the case described in chapter 2, §4.

20. The two lines of reply of §18 have more bite in the case of bodily sensations. A number of initially attractive arguments have been offered for denying the univocality of location idioms as applied to physical things and bodily sensations. And this denial of univocality has been supported by not implausible analyses of the location element in statements concerning bodily sensations. Nevertheless, I think that on inspection the initial attractiveness of the arguments for denying univocality disappears and that serious problems emerge for the proferred analyses of the location element, so that both lines of reply fail even in the bodily sensation case. I will start by considering the arguments for denying univocality of location, for holding, that is, that sensations are not literally located in the way that physical things are.

(i) It is often supposed that the well-known phantom limb phenomena which we were concerned with in §4 show that bodily sensations are not located in the literal sense. J. J. C. Smart, for instance, argues as follows.

> we can characterise a pain, for example, as 'in my right thumb' or 'under my breast bone'. What is meant by this? It is quite clearly not that my pain is in my thumb or under my breast bone in the literal sense . . . This is obvious when we consider that I might have a pain 'in my thumb' even though my thumb had been amputated.[23]

[23] *Philosophy and Scientific Realism*, p. 103. In my discussion of this and the following objections, I am much indebted to M. C. Bradley, 'Two Arguments Against the Identity Thesis', part II.

This certainly shows that not all sensations are located in parts of the body. But it is hard to see the bearing of this on the question of whether sensations are located *simpliciter*. Why not take the phantom limb phenomenon as showing that, though most sensations are located in parts of the body, not all are; some are located in regions near, but outside, the body? Alternatively, (though, in my view, implausibly) the phantom limb phenomenon could be taken as a case of radical mis-location: the pain is taken to be outside the body, but is really in the body, say, in the stump. In either case, the phantom limb phenomenon does not show that sensations are not literally located.

(ii) In chapter xx of *Principles of Psychology*, William James con-cedes the plausibility of the view being defended here. Concerning the differences between qualitatively identical sensations differently located, he observes that 'The most natural and immediate answer to make is that they [the differences] are unlikenesses of *place* pure and simple.' (§ 'The Meaning of Localization')

He then, however, argues that this answer faces 'an insuperable logical difficulty':

> No single *quale* of sensation can, by itself, amount to a consciousness of *position*. Suppose no feeling but that of a single point ever to be awakened. Could that possibly be the feeling of any special *whereness* or *thereness*? Certainly not. *Only when a second point is felt to arise can the first one acquire a determination of up, down, right or left, and these determinations are all relative to that second point.* Each point, so far as it is *placed, is* then only by virtue of what it *is not*, namely, by virtue of another point. This is as much as to say that position has nothing *intrinsic* about it . . . *a feeling of place cannot possibly form an immanent element in any single isolated sensation.* [Later in same section, author's emphasis.]

I think there is a crucial ambiguity in this passage as to whether James is taking a relational stance about position in general, or just about the position of sensations. For example, when he says that 'position has nothing intrinsic about it', is he talking about position in general or about the position of sensations in particular? If he is talking about position in general, then his warrant for saying that no quale or immanent element of a sensation can constitute its location, will be clear enough. If position in general is relational, then no thing, be it mental or physical, a pain or a chair, can have the position it does in virtue of an intrinsic property. But it is hard to see how this constitutes a difficulty for one who holds that sensations are literally located. Of course, if one took the view that sensations have only intrinsic qualities, or that only the intrinsic qualities or quale of sensations can be known, it would follow either that they are not located or that their location cannot be known. But there is no indication that James takes this view, which is, anyhow, absurd.

On the other hand, it may be that in this passage James is advancing a particular relational thesis intended to apply just to sensations. For example, the claim that 'each point' is placed only by virtue of its relation to 'another point', appears to be about sensation points or points of feeling to the effect that sensations are located only by reference to other sensations. On this view, the location of a sensation would be a matter of its bearing certain relations to other sensations; and if it were adopted, the doctrine that sensations are literally located in parts of the body would have to be abandoned. For on this latter doctrine, a pain in my foot is so located because of its relation to my foot, not because of its relation to other sensations.

James seems, however, to provide no reason to adopt the view that sensations are located solely in virtue of their relations to other sensations. For instance, the point that no single quale of sensation can constitute a consciousness of position does not provide a reason; for it bears only on whether location for sensations is relational, not on the relata of that relation.

Likewise, James' very plausible claim (in the second and third sentences of the quotation) that if one had only ever been aware of one point, that awareness could not have contained an awareness of position, does not provide a reason. For it applies equally to material things. If I had only ever been aware of one material thing, say a chair, I could not have been aware of that thing as having some location. Awareness of position involves, it is plausible to say, awareness of more than one thing, and, hence, awareness of the location of a bodily sensation involves awareness of something other than that sensation; but it does not follow that that other thing must itself be a sensation. And not only does this not follow, it is in itself implausible. I am now aware of an ache in my left knee, but I have no other bodily sensation, and so am not aware of its location in relation to any other current sensation. Perhaps it will be urged that my awareness of the location of my ache – though not dependent on my awareness of some other current sensation – is dependent on my awareness of the location of past, remembered sensations. But this claim is very implausible.

Amnesiacs, for example, do not have trouble locating their first few sensations after awakening, though they may not remember the location of any past sensations.

(iii) It is sometimes urged that bodily sensations are only 'intensionally' located, because they are where they *feel* to be. A pain in the leg is a pain which feels to be in the leg. Now the phantom limb phenomenon shows that this cannot be quite right, for it shows that some pains which feel to be in a leg are not. But, in any case, it is hard to see how the point counts against the literal location of bodily sensations. Many material objects are located where they appear to be, and are, none the less, literally located there.

Perhaps the point the advocates of this argument have in mind is the (alleged) impossibility of being mistaken about where a sensation feels to be, and so, about where a sensation is, by contrast with the manifest possibility of mistake about the location of material things. But even if we grant the alleged point of difference, why must we construe this as a difference in the sense in which sensations and material things are located? Why not construe it as simply a difference between material things and sensations?

Moreover, there is good reason for denying that our knowledge of the location of our sensations is incorrigible. In §21, cases are described which show conclusively that we can be mistaken about where our own sensations are located.

(iv) Finally, some arguments that can be discussed more briefly. Sometimes it is emphasised that doctors do not detect pains and itches in parts of the body. But, of course, they do – by feeling them in their own case, and by being told about them in their patients'. What doctors do not do is come across sensations during surgery in the way they come across blood vessels, nerves, and so forth. But why accept the principle that everything located in the body can be discovered by surgical procedure? Surely, unless one is to beg the whole question at issue, sensations are a *prima facie* counter-example to this principle.

It also seems to me to be mistaken to argue that bodily sensations cannot be in parts of the body because they are in the mind.[24] The sense in which sensations are in the mind is that they cannot exist without the mind (or person) existing – they are incapable of independent existence. Hence, saying that a sensation is in the mind is not assigning it a location incompatible with its being in a part of the body. Nor is there a difficulty here over logical connexions between distinct

[24] See, e.g., D. M. Armstrong, *A Materialist Theory of the Mind*, p. 316.

existences.[25] True, if my pain is a located item and if it is dependent on my mind, distinct things are logically connected – which violates one empiricist dogma. But it is equally true that if my pain is *not* located, distinct things are logically connected; for, on any sane view, the mind is not identical with any particular sensation, whether or not sensations are located.

Likewise, it seems to me that there is little force in the consideration that absolutely precise locations cannot be given to one's bodily sensa · tions. The same holds true for clouds and cities. Moreover, on the most widely held interpretation of Quantum Mechanics, the fundamental particles lack an absolutely precise location in the normal sense, and yet they are certainly located. (These particles also provide an example of located items not detected during surgery.)

Finally, there seems to me to be little force in the argument that pains cannot be located in the same sense as physiological occurrences on the ground that we determine the location of the former quite differently from the way we determine the location of the latter.[26] I determine the location of things I see quite differently from how I determine the location of things only you see: I look in the first case, I ask you in the second. Visible things have their location determined quite differently from invisible, tangible things; and electrons have their location determined quite differently from mountains. But in none of these cases do we regard the location idiom as equivocal. The differences are to be explained by the differences in the nature of the things located, not by differences in the sense in which they are located.

21. We now come to the question of whether the location element in sensation statements is susceptible to special analysis: analysis which removes the appearance that sensations are items literally located in parts of the body.

(i) In *Intention*, G. E. M. Anscombe says: 'it [is] difficult to guess what you mean . . . if you say that your foot, not your hand, is very sore, but it is your hand you nurse, and you have no fear of or objection to an inconsiderate handling of your foot, and yet you point to your foot as the sore part: and so on' (p. 14).

We agreed in §3 to take it for granted that no full-scale behaviourist account of psychological statements is possible. But this is consistent with the possibility of a behaviourist style of analysis of a particular part of certain psychological statements. For instance, 'He is in

---

[25] The aspect of the matter Armstrong emphasises in *Bodily Sensations*, see p. 78.
[26] I take this argument fom Jenny Teichman, *The Mind and the Soul*, p. 75.

uncontrollable pain' cannot be fully analysed behaviourally, but evidently the meaning of 'uncontrollable' can be handled in behavioural terms. Likewise, this passage from Anscombe might be used as the basis for suggesting that the location part of sensation statements can be translated behaviourally, that 'I have a pain in my foot', for example, is equivalent to something like 'I have a pain which disposes me to nurse my foot, direct attention to my foot . . .' I will advance two objections to this analysis (apart from the obvious one that it is hard to see how to extend the analysis so as to cover bodily sensations which are mildly pleasurable).

First, though it is true that usually when one has a pain in a part of one's body, one is disposed to nurse that part and otherwise behave in a manner that might reasonably be described as directed towards that part, this appears to be a consequence of something purely contingent – namely, that nursing the relevant part normally relieves the pain, and, generally, that to relieve the pain it is necessary to direct one's attention to where the pain is. But this is not, of course, universally the case. The way to relieve those ear pains caused by disturbances in the mouth is to direct attention to the mouth rather than the ear; and the way to relieve the pains in the arm caused by disturbances in the heart is to direct attention to the heart; and, in general, the way to relieve referred pains is to concentrate on the place of the cause rather than on the place of the pain. Moreover, with the development of analgesics, it is becoming more and more common to direct attention, in effect, to the brain rather than to where the pain or the cause is. It appears, therefore, that though appropriately directed behaviour is correlated with pain location, it is not in any way constitutive of such location: the correlation is far from universal and might not obtain at all.

The second objection derives from a point made by K. Baier. He argues that we can mis-locate our pains, as follows:

> Under certain conditions of observation, as when he is not allowed to see the relevant parts of his body, a person may make claims about where on his body he was pricked and where he felt the pain, claims concerning which he later accepts corrections. When told by the experimenter or when allowed to explore the area with his own finger or to watch as he is being pricked again in the same place, he admits that the pains (and the pricks) were not in the place where he first said they were.[27]

[27] 'The Place of a Pain', pp. 142–3.

Another, more mundane case leading to the same conclusion is where you bend down to scratch an itch or rub an ache on the shin and find that it was not quite where you started scratching or rubbing. Moreover, it is possible to become confused in certain extreme situations about which leg is one's left and which one's right, and so, to have a pain in the right leg while thinking it is in the left leg.

As Baier points out, this possibility of error provides a particularly clear difficulty for behaviourist analyses of location. When we have the location of a pain wrong, our behaviour will normally be directed to the wrong place. The possibility of error also rules out suggestions like: the place of a pain is where I would point to if asked.[28] If asked, I may point to the wrong place. (Additionally and obviously, I may also point to the wrong place because I wish to mislead, am embarrassed, or whatever.)

(ii) The other obvious way of attempting to find an analysis of pain location is to start from the fact that pains are commonly where their causes are. But referred pains, to which we have already alluded, are clear counter-examples to analysing 'I have a pain in my foot' as 'I have a pain whose cause is in my foot.' Moreover, though 'Every pain has a cause' is true, there is nothing contradictory about uncaused pains, and, in particular, about an uncaused pain in the foot; that is, it is not a necessary truth that a pain in my foot has a cause.

It might be suggested that instead of saying that a pain in the foot is a pain whose cause is in the foot, we say that a pain in the foot is a pain of *the kind typically* caused by a disturbance in the foot (and, we might add, of the kind typically relieved by massaging the foot).[29] But, first, pains in the foot do not seem to have any particular phenomenal quality which makes them form a kind (as critics of R. H. Lotze's Local Sign theory[30] have emphasised). And, second, sufferers from pains in phantom limbs not uncommonly suffer severe pains 'therein' for many years. These pains are caused by disturbances in the stump, and are, thus, clearly of the kind typically caused by a disturbance in the stump, yet they do not have the pain in the stump. In similar vein, we can imagine a 'brave new world' in which pleasurable sensations are typically caused by direct stimulation of the brain while remaining distributed about the body.

---

[28] This is one possible interpretation of L. Wittgenstein's remarks in *Blue and Brown Books*, p. 50.

[29] See, e.g., G. Ryle, *The Concept of Mind*, p. 105.

[30] Presented in his *Outlines of Psychology*, part I, ch. 4.

The obvious tactic at this point is to switch from the place of the cause to the *believed* place of the cause. Now we sometimes know that a pain is a referred one, so that 'I have a pain in my foot' is not equivalent to 'I have a pain whose cause I believe to be in my foot' – I may know that the cause is not in my foot; and I may know this for certain, so that there is no inclination on my part to believe that the cause is in my foot. But, it might be urged, the analysis should be put counterfactually: if I had not known the cause was elsewhere, I would have believed the cause was in my foot. I think it is clear enough that this suggestion faces the same general problem that the counterfactual rendition of the notion of a suppressed inclination to believe faced in chapter 2, §6.

Perhaps 'I had a pain in my foot' entails that if I had not known that the cause of my pain was not in my foot and if I had believed that the cause of a pain and the place of a pain were generally the same in these sorts of circumstances, then I would have believed that the cause of my pain was in my foot. But this is worthless as an analysis for it refers to the very notion, *the place of a pain*, for which an analysis is being sought. And it is certainly not the case that 'I had a pain in my foot' entails that if I had not known that the cause of my pain was not in my foot, then I would have believed that the cause was in my foot; for one way of not knowing that the cause is not in my foot is having no opinion on whether the cause is or is not in my foot, so it might well have been the case that if I had not known the cause was not in my foot, I would neither have believed that it was or that it was not in my foot. In addition, we have the usual problem with counterfactual analyses of the categorical. Surely to say that I have a pain in my foot is to say how things are, not how things would be if things were different.

Baier's point about the possibility of error concerning the place of a pain also constitutes a serious problem for the analysis in question. Believing, as I do, that the cause of a pain is usually where the pain is, when I am in error about the place of a pain I will mis-locate the cause. I will believe it is where I *wrongly* think the pain is.

Baier, naturally, is cognizant of this difficulty, and in his own analysis of pain-location in terms of the believed place of cause he adds a special *unless* clause to give the following:

'The place of someone's pain' means 'The place where, going by the feeling of pain alone, the sufferer would be inclined to say *the cause* of his pain seemed to him to be unless, in the light of further experience by sight and touch, he would be inclined to say it really was in some other place.' [*op. cit.*, p. 149]

But what does 'going by the feeling of pain alone' amount to? Disturbances in the heart give rise to characteristic pains in the arms and in parts of the chest remote from the heart (often the parts of the chest are where the sufferer mistakenly thinks his heart is). *Going by the feeling alone*, those who experience these pains are inclined to say that the cause is in their heart – which is where their pains are not. I suspect that Baier really means by 'going by the feeling alone', going by *where* the pain feels to be – the aspect of the pain we are supposed to attend to when we go by feeling alone is not its severity, or its burning quality, not the kind of pain it is, but rather its location or its felt location. But this is to put the cart before the horse. We are seeking an understanding of what it means to say that a pain has a certain location, and we are not going to achieve this by presupposing a grasp of what it means to say that a pain has a certain felt location; for in order to understand 'feels to be in my foot' we need an understanding of 'feels . . .' *and* 'in my foot' as applied to sensations.

Moreover, despite the 'unless' clause, Baier's analysis is also exposed to the objection deriving from his own point about the possibility of mis-location. If we can be wrong about the location of a pain going on feeling alone – the point on which we and Baier are agreed – then we can surely also be wrong after subsequent investigation by sight and touch. It is generally agreed that the everpresent logical possibility of perceptual illusion makes the deliverances of sight and touch fallible. Consequently, once the possibility of mistake about pain location is granted, how could subsequent perceptual investigation possibly yield *logically* indubitable knowledge of location? Therefore, despite the 'unless' clause, Baier has left open the possibility of mistaken belief about the place of a pain, and so, the possibility that a subject has a pain in one place, but, despite subsequent investigation by sight and touch, has a mistaken belief about its location and is inclined, consequently, to locate the cause of the pain at a place remote from where the pain really is.

At this point, a radical reply might be suggested. Instead of seeking ever more complex accounts of pain-location in terms of cause, belief, and/or behaviour, it might be suggested that we return to the simple view that 'I have a pain in my foot' means 'I have a pain whose cause is in my foot', and describe cases of referred pain as cases of radical mis-location. When, as we say, I have a pain in my ear caused by a disturbance in my mouth, I really have a pain in my mouth which I mistakenly think is in my ear.[31]

This cannot be right. I may (indeed, I normally do) know that the cause is in my mouth. But 'The cause is in my mouth' is the proferred analysis of 'The pain is in my mouth'. Hence, an advocate of this radical reply cannot say that mis-location has occurred. I have the place of the cause right, and that, on his view, is having the place of the pain right. Further, one thing that is beyond contest is that the pain feels to be in the ear; the cause, however, may not. I may feel the gum disturbance which causes the pain; that is, the cause of the pain may be felt in the gum, and so, in the mouth. But, then, how can the advocate of the view under discussion explain how the pain fails to be felt in the mouth? For on his view there is nothing more to a pain being in the mouth than its cause being in the mouth, and I feel the cause there.

22. This is all I want to say for now in defence of the existence of mental objects. Certain difficulties that have been raised for allowing them as part of what there is parallel those raised against sense-data, and will be considered in the latter context (in chapter 4, §12ff.).

Once mental objects are admitted, the account to be offered of visual hallucinations is obvious. First, we noted in chapter 1, §8 that if visual hallucinations exist, they are immediate objects of perception. They do exist, hence they are immediately perceived. Second, when under hallucination, one is not thereby seeing any physical object, by definition. Therefore, to be under hallucination is to immediately see a mental object which is coloured and shaped and which does not correspond to any physical thing. For instance, seeing an after-image is a hallucination because the coloured, shaped image that is seen does not correspond to any physical reality. (The precise significance of 'does not correspond to any physical reality' is discussed in chapter 7, §10ff.)

23. I want to finish this chapter by considering and rejecting a very general kind of objection to the way the question of the existence of mental objects has been discussed. The objection might be summed up in the slogan: Paraphrase cannot create or destroy entities. The sense of the objection is that whether mental objects exist is a question about the *world*, not a question about language or statements; yet throughout the chapter I talk of whether certain parts of certain statements can be analysed this way or that way, of whether this word or phrase is like an adverb, of whether that word is a name and so on. I talk, that is, about

---

[31] Keith Campbell suggested an approach of this kind to pains in phantom limbs to me, but I do not think he would accept this wider application.

language, about the possibility of analyses and paraphrases and re-castings of logical form, rather than the things themselves.

I think two things need to be emphasised in reply to this. First, of course paraphrase cannot create or destroy mental objects. Pains exist or do not exist regardless of whether anyone has ever carried out a certain paraphrase; and they would exist or not whether or not we had developed a language with statements to be the subject of philosophical analysis. What paraphrase can create or destroy is the *case for or against* believing in certain entities. A parallel is a comprehensive wave theory of light: if such could be made out, it would destroy the case for believing in the corpuscles of the corpuscular theory, but not the corpuscles themselves. The latter either exist or not independent of our theories – it is the reasonableness of believing that they exist that depends on our theories. Likewise, our discussion of language was a discussion of the reasonableness of *accepting* that there are mental objects; and if our discussion was successful, it did not make any mental objects; what it made was a case for believing that there are mental objects.

Secondly, our concern was not with any old statements. It was with *true* statements, statements that tell us how it is; and our concern was with just what they do tell us. If 'I have a red after-image' is true, what it tells us is that I have a red after-image, and what this in turn amounts to depends on what reading should be given to the statement. If, as we argued, it is to be understood on the act–object model, it tells us that there is something red which I have. But if the adverbial theory is right, it tells us how I am sensing and does not require for its truth that there be an object being sensed. This does not mean that empirical matters are irrelevant to the existence of after-images. It is an empirical fact that 'I have a red after-image' and the like are true on occasion; and if they were never true, there would not be any after-images or pains regardless of our earlier arguments. The analysis of statements enters the picture only when we have accepted the truths and are concerned with their implications for what there is.

4

The case for sense-data

o. Following chapter 1, §12, to accept (visual) sense-data is to accept that (i) whenever seeing occurs, there is a coloured patch which is the immediate object of perception, and (ii) that this coloured patch bears the apparent properties. Claim (i) has already been established. In chapter 1, we argued that the immediate objects of (visual) perception are coloured patches, and we observed that there is always an immediate object in cases of veridical and illusory perception. And in chapter 3, we concluded that there is also an immediate object in the case of hallucination. There is, thus, when seeing occurs, always an immediate object of perception which is a coloured patch.

The task of this chapter is, then, to establish claim (ii). This claim is obviously correct in cases of veridical perception, for in these cases the apparent properties coincide with the real ones. If I am looking at a white, square object that looks white and square, no-one will quarrel with the claim that the immediate object of perception is white and square (unless they reject the whole mediate–immediate distinction). Likewise, the real and apparent properties coincide in the hallucination case. An after-image which looks red and square is red and square. (In saying this, I am not asserting that our knowledge of after-images is incorrigible: being wrong about an after-image's colour, if this is possible, is a matter of being wrong about the colour it looks to have.) The controversy over claim (ii) arises from its application to the case of illusion. When I look at a white wall in circumstances which make it look blue, do I see something blue? And, in general, does something looking F to me entail that I see something F. Most philosophers today take the possibility of illusion to refute any such principle. I will attempt to establish claim (ii) by defending this principle.

Chisholm argues that this principle is false as follows: 'There is no contradiction in saying, "I realise there aren't any centaurs, but that strange animal certainly does *look* centaurian." For the statement "That animal looks centaurian" does not imply that there are any centaurs.'[1]

[1] *Perceiving*, p. 115.

The principle, however, is intended to apply only to phenomenal uses of 'looks', uses characterized (as we noted in chapter 2, §3), by being followed by a term for colour, shape and/or distance; and 'centaurian' is none of these. It seems, in fact, that 'looks centaurian' normally amounts to 'looks like a centaur' or, as there are no centaurs, 'looks like a centaur would'; that is, that it is to be understood comparatively. To say that something looks centaurian is simply to say that it looks the way a centaur would. This means the claim that something looks centaurian is to a certain degree speculative; as there are no centaurs, one must be speculating on how they would look if there were any. And this consequence is surely correct: should it turn out (to our great surprise) that in some remote place there are centaurs, we might well have to revise our conception of what looking centaurian is like.

My defence, therefore, of the principle will be a defence of that principle with 'looks' interpreted in essentially phenomenal terms.

1. One way of describing how things *look* to one is by describing how the coloured expanses in one's visual field *are*. One way of describing how it is when a white wall looks blue to you is by saying that you see a *blue* expanse. One way of describing what is involved in a straight stick in water looking bent is by reference to seeing a *bent* shape. One way of explaining to a person who does not wear glasses what happens when you take them off, is that various coloured shapes *change size* and *become blurred*. One way of describing what happens when you move a pencil towards your nose so that it looks double is that you see *two* images of the pencil.

There is nothing particularly controversial about this. It is simply a reflection of the fact that instead of talking about how something looks, we can talk about how *the look* of something *is*; and instead of saying *X* appears *F*, we can say that the appearance of *X* is *F*; and instead of describing something as looking red in the centre and pinkish towards the edges, we can describe a shape which is red at the centre and pinkish towards the edges. What is important and controversial is how seriously we should take this mode of expression. Current opinion is that it is a mere *façon de parler*, easily and best replaced by modes of expression which make clear that the apparently referential role of 'the look of...', 'the appearance of...', and so on is mere appearance; and the most favoured method of replacement derives from the *Multiple Relation Theory of Appearing* (MRTA).

2. At its simplest, this theory enjoins us to prefer a form like

(1) X looks red to S

to ones like

(2) X presents a red look (appearance) to S

and

(3) S sees a red sense-datum belonging to X.

The theory can take two forms according to whether 'looks –' is taken to be a two-place or three-place relation (not counting a possible additional place for time). C. D. Broad, for example, characterizes it in terms of an unanalysable, three-place relation between persons, properties, and objects.[2] The three-place version, however, faces a serious difficulty.

'The table looks brown to John' certainly contains two singular terms, 'John' and 'the table'; but does not appear to contain a third naming a property, for 'brown' is not a name. It might be suggested that, though 'brown' does not normally serve to designate a property, but rather to ascribe one, it does in this kind of context; just as 'Snow is white', though not normally a name, is, on some views, the name of a proposition in contexts like 'Joe believes that snow is white.' However, 'Snow is white' behaves in a name-like fashion in this latter context. If 'Snow is white' is the proposition most commonly referred to in discussions of truth, and if John believes that snow is white, then John believes the proposition most commonly referred to in discussions of truth. And this fact is a crucial support for the view that 'Snow is white' can be a name. On the other hand, if Brown, the property, is the colour of Caesar's hair and if the table looks brown, it does not follow that the table looks the colour of Caesar's hair. Again, suppose I am looking at a book and a tomato, and they look the same colour to me; then I might say, in slightly strained English, that the book looks the colour of the tomato to me. But if the colour of the tomato is red, it does not follow that the book looks red to me; both the book and the tomato may look (the same) grey to me.

It is, therefore, best to take the MRTA as holding that 'looks red', 'looks round', and so on, are unanalysable, two-place relations between persons (or sighted creatures in general) and objects. This is the interpretation suggested by the practice of writing 'looks red' as 'looks-red' or 'looksred',[3] and will be the interpretation we will assume from now on (though, with appropriate modifications, the

[2] *Scientific Thought*, see p. 237. He did not accept the theory.
[3] Cf., Chisholm, *Perceiving*, p. 116.

objections that follow can be directed at the three-place interpretation also).

The claim that the relevant (two-place) relations are unanalysable is an essential feature of the MRTA in this context. Without it, there is no disagreement with the Sense-datum theory. The sense-datum theorist admits that looking red and looking square are relations between persons and objects, as does everybody. His special claim is that a certain analysis of these relations is possible, an analysis that leads to sense-data. That is, the MRTA contradicts the Sense-datum theory by denying that *any* analysis – and so, *a fortiori*, that advocated by the sense-datum theorist – is possible.

A variant MRTA might be suggested, drawing on the predicate-modifier semantics discussed in the previous chapter. According to such a suggestion, 'looks' in 'looks red', 'looks square', and so on is to be semantically interpreted as a function from one-place to two-place predicates. As a *syntactical* remark, this is beyond dispute but onto-logically uninformative; and as a *semantical* remark, it faces the same difficulty as that which faced the predicate-modifier treatment of adverbs as applied to eliminate mental objects. In brief, 'looks' – viewed as sketched – must be seen as intensional: for it must be allowed that, for example, everything red might be square and vice versa, without everything that looks red looking square and vice versa. The variant MRTA, therefore, avoids sense-data at the unacceptable price of admitting *possibilia*.

I will present three arguments against the MRTA: one drawing on the connexion between meaning and semantic role in relation to what I will call the common-term problem; the second appealing to a distinction between reducible and irreducible relations; and the third deriving from the familiar double-image phenomenon.

3. Sometimes the same word or phrase crops up in different statements in a way that is of no significance as far as meaning is concerned. 'Bach' appears in both 'Bach wrote music' and 'Bachelors are common'; 'bank' appears in both 'The river overflowed its banks' and 'The bank failed': in neither case does the common term signal a meaning connection between the relevant statements. The common term is simply not relevant to the meaning relation between them, though it may be of pragmatic or historical significance.

Usually, however, the appearance of a common term is of considerable semantic significance. Indeed, this is so commonplace it would be pointless to give examples. It can, however, give rise to a problem.

Consider

   (4) Joe is tall

   (5) Joe is tallest

   (6) Joe is taller than Bill.

'Tall' in (4), (5), and (6) is obviously a common term with semantic significance – we have neither a case of ambiguity as with 'bank', nor a lack of semantic import as with 'bach' in 'bachelor' – it is obvious that the appearance of 'tall' in all of (4), (5), and (6) is responsible for their being related in meaning. Yet, equally clearly, 'tall' cannot be said to mean the same in, or to make the same contribution to the meaning of, each of (4), (5), and (6); for its putative semantic role (that is, its explicit syntactic role) is different in each. In (4), 'tall' is a one-place predicate; in (5), it is a part of another, distinct one-place predicate; and in (6) it is part of a two-place predicate expressing a relation.

How, then, can we account for the meaning connection between (4), (5), and (6) consequent upon the appearance of 'tall' in each. We can account for the meaning connection between 'This apple is red' and 'This tomato is red' consequent upon the common term 'red', by saying that 'red' plays the same role and means the same in each. But this simple reply is not available for (4), (5), (6), because of the divergence noted in the role of 'tall'. I will describe a situation of this kind as presenting a common-term problem.

Unless we are to do nothing – that is, give up – in the face of this problem, we must seek some basic expression playing a fixed semantic role in terms of which the various statements can be translated so as to no longer present a common-term problem. In the case of (4), (5), and (6) the solution seems relatively clear. Take the relational expression 'is taller than' as basic and translate each statement so that the only occurrence of 'tall' in each is as a part of 'is taller than'. Thus we might get

   (4)′ Joe is taller than most people

   (5)′ Joe is taller than every person (in the class implicitly in mind)

   (6)′ Joe is taller than Bill.

(As a reflection of current English usage, (4)′ is too simple an account of (4), but the required complexities are not important here.)

A trickier case is that presented by

   (7) *A* is red

and

   (8) *A* is redder than *B*.

We cannot take 'is redder than' as the basic expression in terms of which to understand (7); for (7) is not equivalent to '*A* is redder than most things', or anything like this; as is shown by the fact that there might be just one coloured object which happened to have red as its colour.

A possibility is to take 'red' in (7) as basic and render (8) as

(8)′ *A* is red & (either *B* is not red or *A* is more intense in colour than *B*).

This requires us to acknowledge a new relation, being more intense in colour than, which will, no doubt, figure in corresponding accounts of '*A* is greener than *B*', and so on.

With these illustrations in mind, I now turn to the perceptual case. Consider

(9) This tomato is red

(10) This tomato looks red to me.

It is obvious that (9) and (10) present a common-term problem. Which use of 'red', the monadic in (9) or the relation-forming one in (10), do we take as basic, as that in terms of which we should seek to understand the other?

One approach to this problem is to take the monadic use exemplified in (9) as fundamental, and to seek to construe (10) as equivalent to something like

(11) This tomato produces in me a state of the kind I am in when I see a red object.

This restores a uniform semantic role to 'red', but obviously faces the difficulties raised in chapter 2, §4 to comparative analyses of the phenomenal use of 'looks'. Moreover, it is not open to the multiple relation theorist who holds 'looks red' to be unanalysable. Parallel remarks apply to renditions of (10) in terms of belief or inclination to believe.

The approach this theorist must (and does) adopt to the common-term problem raised by (9) and (10), is to regard the relational use exemplified in (10) as providing the core meaning of colour terms, and to construe (9) along the lines of

(12) This tomato looks red to most people in normal circumstances, with 'looks red' being understood as an unanalysable relation.

While it seems to me entirely reasonable to hold that (9) and (12) are logically equivalent, and though this equivalence is a necessary condition of its being correct that colour terms are to be understood via basic relational expressions of the form 'looks –', it is not a sufficient condition; and there appear to be two decisive objections to a relational view of the kind in question.

Consider, first,

(13) There looks to me to be a red patch in front of me.

(13) is a necessary condition for the truth of (10), and, in general, a statement of the form 'x looks ϕ to S', where 'ϕ' is a colour or shape term, entails the corresponding statement of the form 'There looks to S to be a ϕ somewhere.' When the stick looks bent, there looks to be a bent something somewhere; when the sky looks red at sunset, there looks to be a large red expanse near the horizon; when the penny looks brown and elliptical, there looks to be a brown, elliptical shape; and so on.

Now (13) contains 'red' not 'looks red'. Can we construe (13) so as to bring 'looks' and 'red' together to form a relational expression?

One attempt might follow the lines of (11): translate (13) as 'I am in the kind of state I am normally in when I see a red object', and then, following (12), translate further to 'I am in the kind of state I am normally in when I see an object that looks red in normal circumstances.' In this final version, every (the only) occurrence of 'red' is in 'looks red'. But this procedure is evidently exposed to our earlier objections concerning comparative analyses of 'looks'. Parallel remarks apply against 'I believe (am inclined to believe, have a suppressed inclination to believe) as a result of using my eyes . . . that there is an object which looks red in normal circumstances in front of me' as a translation of (13).

The only other attempt which I can imagine being seriously proposed construes the step from (10) to (13) as Existential Generalization; that is, views (13) as '$(\exists x)$ [x looks red to me]'. (I neglect the 'in front of' part as irrelevant here.) But this suggestion faces a destructive dilemma. One way there may look to me to be something red somewhere, is for me to be appropriately *hallucinating*; say, to make things concrete, I am having a red after-image. Now, either hallucinations – in this case, after-images – are part of what there is (in addition to hallucinating), as we argued in chapter 3; or they are not.

Now if after-images do not exist, then the suggestion that we read (13) existentially must be wrong. For (13) may be true when I am having a red after-image (whether I know it or not), and so when, as there are no after-images, there is nothing to look red to me. On the other hand, if after-images do exist, there will be something to look red, the image, and the existential nature of (13) will no longer be an objection. But what sense can we make of saying that the image looks red, looks square, and so on? After-images do not *look* red or square, they *are* (if they are anything) red and square. I do not intend this merely as a report on ordinary English usage according to which we talk of how after-images are rather than of how they look, but as a reflection of the metaphysical doctrine that what there is is the same as what there is that has properties. If we insisted on construing the redness and squareness of after-images as their bearing the looking-red and looking-square relations to persons, we would be left without an account of *what* stands in these two relations to persons. If after-images exist, they have properties, they cannot merely stand in relations; and the only properties they can plausibly be said to have are colour, shape and, perhaps, position (visual depth).

The upshot is that, whether or not after-images exist, (13) poses an insuperable problem to holding that we understand being red in terms of looking red. If they do not exist, (13) cannot be construed existentially, as it may be true when there is no appropriate relatum. If they do exist, there are cases of being red which are not reducible to looking red, namely the redness of after-images (and the colour and shape of visual hallucinations in general). For if after-images exist, they must have properties, and – unless we countenance unknown and unknowable properties – these must be properties of shape and colour.

Our discussion of the common-term problem for the MRTA has thus far concentrated on the problem raised by common colour terms, in particular, 'red', but 'look' with shape terms also gives trouble. Consider

(14) The stick is bent

and

(15) The stick looks bent to me.

It is particularly clear in this case that the connexion between the two uses of 'bent' cannot be explicated by construing (14) (along the lines of (12), above) as

(16) The stick looks bent to most people in normal circumstances.

For (16) is about human beings and how things appear to them, while (14) is not. Things were various shapes long before there were any sentient creatures and will be long after all such creatures have passed from the scene.

But then there is no question of regarding 'looks bent' in (15) as an *unanalysable primitive*, for to so regard it would be to rule out the possibility of ever explicating the connexion between the meaning of (14) and (15) consequent upon the appearance of 'bent' in both. Hence we cannot suppose that the role of 'looks' in statements concerning the shape things look to have, is to form unanalysable relational expressions. And this conclusion forces an absurd conclusion on one who holds that 'looks' forms unanalysable relational terms in statements concerning the colour things look to have; namely, that 'looks' has a *different meaning* in statements concerning the colour things look to have from that it has in statements concerning the shape they look to have; in the former, 'looks' serves to form an unanalysable relational term, but not in the latter.

This conclusion is absurd because when someone tells you that some object looks some way to him, that is, that he sees it, you do not have to wait to be told whether he is talking about apparent colour or shape, to know what he means. Again, if 'looks' were ambiguous, a statement like 'The penny looks brown and round' would be as absurd as Ryle's example 'She came home in a sedan chair and a flood of tears' – for *both* would be cases of one occurrence of a term in a statement being required to carry two meanings at once.

I should emphasise that I am not arguing that (9) and (12) are not equivalent because (14) and (16) are not. That would be evidently fallacious, and, anyhow, I believe that (9) and (12) are equivalent. My argument concerns the *parts* of (9), (12), (14) and (16), rather than their logical properties considered as wholes. The non-equivalence of (14) with (16) or anything like (16), shows that 'looks bent' cannot be taken to stand for an unanalysable primitive relational expression, for it shows that 'bent' can occur with a meaning evidently related to that of 'looks bent' in a way which cannot be held to be elliptical for occurrences of 'looks bent'. Hence, it shows something about the meaning of 'looks', namely, that it does not serve to form unanalysable relational expressions; which in turn shows that 'looks red' is not such an expression. 'Why not say that "looks" forms such expressions when linked to terms for colour, but not when linked to terms for shape?' Because to hold this is to hold that 'looks' takes a different meaning when linked to colour terms from that it takes when linked to shape terms, a view already noted to be very implausible.

4. I now come to the second objection to the MRTA, the objection which draws on the distinction between reducible and irreducible relations. I will be arguing that 'looks *F*' is reducible.

A relation is reducible if a statement that *A* bears the relation to *B* can be translated into a statement which asserts that A bears some more basic relation to B and asserts something about one or both of A and B which is not itself a relation of one to the other. A relation is irreducible if it is not reducible. Evidently, any unanalysable relation is *ipso facto* irreducible.

An example of a reducible relation is 'is taller at seven feet than'. The statement 'A is taller at seven feet than B' is equivalent to 'A is taller than B and A is seven feet tall', where 'is taller than' is a more basic relation and being seven feet tall is not a relation between A and B (though it is, on most views, a relation). Likewise, 'is a brighter red than' is reducible: 'A is a brighter red than B' means that A is brighter in colour than B and A is red and B is red.

It is more difficult (because it is philosophically controversial) to give examples of irreducible relations. A plausible example, though, is 'is the same colour as'. It is hard to see how 'A is the same colour as B' could be analysed in terms of a simpler relation *between A and B*. Of course, many who countenance colour universals would translate this statement as 'The colour of A is identical with the colour of B.' Here we have a simpler relation, identity, but not one between A and B; hence, 'is the same colour as' may be analysable, but does not appear to be reducible. A clear case of an irreducible relation is strict identity. It is always impossible to analyse assertions of strict identity between A and B in terms of a simpler relation between A and B.

A number of reducible relations involve the causal relation. For example, 'I am being warmed by the stove' just says that I am warm, which is not a matter of bearing a certain relation to the stove, and that the stove is causally responsible for maintaining my state of being warm. Another example is 'I painted the wall red', this just says that certain actions of mine caused the wall to become red. Of course, someone might advance a 'multiple relation theory of wall painting', insisting that our statement should be written 'I paint-red the wall', and pointing out that, as well as painting-red, we have painting-blue, painting-green, and so on, as possible relations between persons and walls.

These relations, however, cannot be regarded as unanalysable. Because, first, it is clearly a necessary condition of the truth of 'I paint-red the wall' that there is an appropriate causal link between my actions and the wall's colour; unless the wall is red *because* of things I do, I did not paint it red. And, second, it is also a necessary condition that the wall be red – a state of the wall produced by me but not constituted by a relation to me. (The wall's being red is not a matter of its bearing a certain relation to me, for it might have been in the very same state of being red even though I had never existed.) Now if we say merely that painting-red is a relation between persons and walls, these two necessary conditions are forever left unexplained. But clearly they are amenable to explanation by reference to the reducibility we have already noted. To say that the painting-red relation holds between a person and a wall is just to say that the wall is red as a result of a certain causal relation between the person and the wall. (The spelling out of this causal relation will involve questions in the philosophy of action not relevant here, and also questions of English usage – does throwing the paint on count as painting, etc.)

Now the same two considerations that apply to painting-red apply to looking red. A necessary condition of the truth of 'The orange looks red to me' is that there be a causal connexion between the orange and me; this causal link is essential to its being *the orange* and not something else which looks red to me. If it should turn out that the orange played no causal role in producing in me the state I report by saying that the orange looks red to me, then it may be true that it was *as if* the orange looked red to me, or that I *believed* the orange looked red; but it cannot be true that the orange looked red to me.[4]

A second necessary condition is that the orange not only causally act on me, but that it act on me to produce a certain kind of state. And this state might have existed in the absence of the orange or any other material object looking red to me. For I can be in exactly the state I am in when the orange looks red to me without there being any appropriate material object looking red to me. For instance, I might be suffering a total hallucination indistinguishable from the orange looking red. An actual example of this kind of thing is the phosphene mentioned in chapter 3, §19. A phosphene can be subjectively indistinguishable from an actual light flash.

This state of affairs of some material thing looking so-and-so being indistinguishable from a totally hallucinatory experience, is not just abstractly possible; we can, in broad outline, specify how to bring such a state of affairs about. We know enough about the physiological processes involved in seeing to be certain that the immediate or proximate cause of the state corresponding to something's looking so-and-so is

---

[4] My defence of this point is brief as it is widely accepted, due, e.g., to H. P. Grice, 'The Causal Theory of Perception', see §4. The matter is referred to again in chapter 7.

an event in the brain. Hence, to bring about the requisite state, what is needed is just the duplication of the appropriate brain event.

Therefore, the considerations suggesting that painting-red is reducible apply equally to looking red, and, in general, to looking F, and so suggest that X looking F to S is a matter of X causing (in a way to be detailed in chapter 7) a state in S which is itself not a relation between S and X. This is in no way a proof. The argument is designed to make the contention that looking F is reducible a plausible one. The essence of it is that being warmed by and painting-red are evidently reducible in the way indicated, and that the considerations that apply in their case appear to apply also in the perceptual one.

5. My final objection is independent of the analysability issue. It concerns whether the MRTA succeeds as a device for systematically eliminating substantival phrases like 'the look of . . .' and 'a red appearance' which invite a sense-datum ontology in favour of relational expressions like 'looks square' and 'appears red'.

There is no question but that the statements of §2

(1) X looks red to S

and

(2) X presents a red look to S

are equivalent, and hence that the relevant substantives can be eliminated in *some* cases. But the crucial issue is whether this can always be done. We all know that expressions putatively designating events can sometimes be eliminated. 'Mary's birth preceded John's' can be rephrased as 'Mary was born before John'. But to eliminate the need for events, this must be shown possible for all cases, including notoriously difficult ones like 'Mary's birth caused great rejoicing.'[5] Similarly, the MRTA needs to show that it can handle *all* cases in a plausible way; that is, the theory needs to show that it affords a *systematic* way of eliminating the substantives in question.

One case that gives an MRTA theorist trouble is the double-image phenomenon. He urges that we describe the two images we get when looking at, say, a pencil held near one's nose, in terms of the pencil *looking double*. But all this gives us is a translation of a statement like

(17) The pencil presents two images to me

as

(18) The pencil looks double to me.

It gives us no idea about what to do with familiar, sometimes true statements about double images like

[5] The causal case is discussed in D. Davidson, 'Causal Relations'.

(19) The left-hand image is fuzzier than the right-hand image

and

(20) The images are further apart now than they were a moment ago.

There seems no way to eliminate 'image' in (19) and (20) in favour of a relational idiom. I suppose that (19), for instance, could be written as

(21) The pencil looks left-hand image fuzzier than right-hand image to me.

But (21) still contains 'image', and it would be absurd to suggest that 'looks left-hand image fuzzier than right-hand image' is an unanalysable relational expression. Because our theorist is going to need to postulate 'looks left-hand image . . . than right-hand image', for a whole range of substitutions for the dots in order to handle other statements like (19) except with 'fuzzier' replaced by 'redder', 'sharper', and so on. And it is obvious that the meanings of all these are intimately related and interconnected.

When we talk about things looking double to us, we talk not just of their looking double, but also of the differences and relations between the images. The sense-datum theorist has no difficulty with this fact. He interprets all this talk at face value. The only way the MRTA theorist appears able to even start on explicating this fact is by a grossly implausible multiplication of unanalysable relations.

6. I think we must conclude that the MRTA faces very considerable difficulties, that is, that it does not show that when we say things like, 'When I put on blue glasses, the white patch turns blue', 'When I press my eyeball I see two images of the pen', or 'That bent, brown shape is the stick', or, generally, talk of the look or appearance of physical things as if the look or appearance *really* had the properties the physical things look to have, we are indulging in a mere *façon de parler*, easily reconstruable relationally in a way that eliminates looks and appearances from our ontology.

This does not, in itself, show that the Sense-datum theory is correct. The main thrust of the arguments just given is that looking so-and-so is analysable; and why should this fact in itself lead us to sense-data, in particular, why should this force us to say that when something looks so-and-so, something seen is so-and-so? The case for sense-data arises from the fact that if looking so-and-so is analysable, there must be *some* analysis it has; and there seems no alternative to the Sense-datum analysis in the offing.

In chapter 2, we saw that comparative and belief analyses fail.

Nevertheless, if we had been able to accept an adverbial theory (or a state one) in chapter 3, statements about how things look could be analysed in terms of those things causing us to sense redly, roundly, or whatever[6] – an analysis which does not commit us to sense-data. But, obviously, we might sense F-ly without an object having caused us to do so in a manner which would count as that thing looking F to us.[7] Such cases will count as hallucinations, and we saw in chapter 3 that the adverbial theory fails for hallucinations.

This is the negative side of the case for sense-data: the failure of the MRTA establishes the need for an analysis, and the Sense-datum theory (SDT) seems to be the only viable candidate – a candidate, moreover, which is not plucked out of thin air but simply takes seriously how we find it natural to describe what it is for things to look so-and-so. The positive side of the case is that the SDT allows us to give plausible accounts of various inter-connexions between perceptual statements. (In giving this case, I will sometimes for completeness repeat points more or less explicit in earlier chapters.)

8. Before detailing this positive case, let us be more explicit about the SDT. From §0, we have that two essential clauses are that (i) whenever seeing occurs, there is a coloured patch which is the immediate object of perception, and (ii) this coloured patch bears the apparent properties. The SDT calls the coloured patch in question a sense-datum; and, on the conception of Moore and Price and on that being defended here, so calling it is entirely neutral on the question of whether sense-data are physical or mental.

In chapter 1, we noted that opaque physical objects of reasonable volume are not immediate objects of perception. They are seen in virtue of seeing something else, and we analysed this situation in terms of a relation between the physical object and the something else. We called this relation that of belonging to and the position can be summed up, using our definition of a sense-datum, by saying that seeing something physical may be analysed as immediately seeing a sense-datum which belongs to that physical object. That is, where X is a physical object, 'S sees X' is analysed as 'S immediately sees a sense-datum which belongs to X.' Moreover, on the SDT, the immediate object bears the apparent properties, so that 'X looks F to S' is analysed as 'S immediately sees a sense-datum which is F and which belongs to X.'

---

[6] The details of an approach of this kind are spelt out in Chisholm, *op. cit.*, ch. 10, §2.

[7] As Chisholm himself notes, *op. cit.*, ch. 10, §2.

Finally, translating the conclusion of chapter 3 using the terminology of the SDT, the analysis of hallucination is in terms of seeing a (mental) sense-datum which does not belong to any physical object.

This leaves two matters unresolved. First, the relation of belonging to has not been specified. The specification is postponed to chapter 7. In view of the remarks on the necessity of causal links in §4, it will, of course, involve a causal connexion between the object and the sense-datum. Secondly, the question of 'visual depth' has not been dealt with. Are sense-data two-dimensional or three-dimensional?

It is sometimes thought that sense-data are essentially linked to attempts to give a purely two-dimensional account of visual sensory experience, an account in terms of coloured shapes projected on to a flat (or perhaps slightly concave) plane at right-angles to the line of vision. But this is certainly not true of the sense-datum theories of Broad and Price. For example, in the preface to the 1954 reprint of *Perception*, Price says

> it is a strange misunderstanding to assume, as some eminent thinkers have, that visual sense-data must be 'flat', i.e. two-dimensional. It is a plain phenomenological fact that visual fields have the property of depth. And why should the sense-datum philosophers, of all people, be supposed to deny this obvious fact? On the contrary, they have usually been careful to emphasise it; and in this book it is emphasised *ad nauseam*.[8]

I am committed to this view that sense-data are at various distances from perceivers and at various angles to their line of sight. For my approach to sense-data has been via the analysis of the phenomenal use of 'looks', and we noted that this use takes terms for distance as well as colour and shape – as in 'This object *looks closer than* that one.' Moreover, such a use of 'looks closer than' cannot be analysed comparatively or epistemically any more than the corresponding use of, for instance, 'looks red'. Briefly – as the points are familiar from chapter 2 – '*X* looks closer to me than *Y*' does not mean something like '*X* and *Y* look, respectively, the way closer and further away things normally look.' Because it is a commonplace that we are sometimes visually deceived about how far away things are, and it seems clearly possible that there might be subjects who were so deceived more often than not. These subjects would have things looking closer than other things just when it was not the case that things were looking to them the way

8 *Perception*, pp. vii–viii.

closer and further away things, respectively, normally do look to them. Likewise, 'X looks closer than Y to me' does not mean anything like 'I am inclined to believe that X is closer than Y.' For I might not only be a subject of the kind just referred to – visually deceived about how far away things are more often than not – I might be *aware* that I was such a subject, and so not be even inclined to believe.

Therefore, I must hold that sense-data are various distances away as well as various colours and shapes. Just as when something looks red, there is something (a sense-datum) which is red; so when X looks further away than Y, there are sense-data which actually are different distances away. Similarly, when an object looks at an angle, there is a sense-datum which is at an angle.

Of course, many philosophers have found the idea of sense-data actually *in* space mysterious (particularly if the sense-data are mental, as I argue in the next chapter). But the point is rarely *argued*. And when it is, the arguments parallel those against locating bodily sensations in space which we rejected in §20 of the previous chapter. I am sometimes asked why I do not follow the lead of those who locate mental objects in a special, private space. To me, this is like saying 'I find it mysterious that mental objects are in normal space, so I will locate them in mysterious space.'

Allowing that the world of sense-data is three-dimensional, enables a simple treatment of the point emphasised by Gilbert Ryle that 'round plates, however steeply tilted, do not usually look elliptical'.[9] A two-dimensional sense-datum theorist faces a dilemma over this case. A round plate held at a reasonably steep angle does *not* look the same as one held at right-angles to the line of vision. But one held at right-angles manifestly looks round. Therefore, the plate at an angle cannot be said to look round *simpliciter*. But it is also true that the plate held at an angle does *not* look the same as an elliptical plate held at right-angles to the line of vision. The latter, however, manifestly *does* look elliptical. Therefore, the round plate at an angle cannot be said to look elliptical *simpliciter*. The dilemma facing the two-dimensional theorist is now clear: Is the sense-datum belonging to the round plate held at an angle, round or elliptical? If he opts for it being round, he fails to adequately reflect in his theory the difference between seeing the round plate straight on and seeing it at an angle; if he opts for it being elliptical, he fails to reflect the difference between seeing the round plate at any angle and seeing an elliptical plate straight on.

[9] *Concept of Mind*, p. 216.

The three-dimensional theorist has an extra dimension in which to resolve this dilemma. The sense-datum belonging to the round plate held at an angle is round *and at an angle*. Hence, it differs from the sense-datum belonging to the round plate seen straight on in not being at right-angles to the line of vision, and differs from the sense-datum belonging to an elliptical plate in being round, not elliptical.

It is, therefore, unfortunate that the 'elliptical penny' case has been so often used in presentations of the argument from illusion. In most cases, the sense-datum belonging to a round penny viewed at an angle is round, like the penny, and so the usual argument for it being distinct from the penny proceeds from a false premise.

In the light of this account of the SDT, even though it is incomplete, we can look at the positive case for it.

(i) We noted in §3 that a statement like

(22) *X* looks blue to *S*

entails something like

(23) There looks to *S* to be something blue.

On the Sense-datum theory, the explanation for this is that (22) is equivalent to

(24) *S* immediately sees a blue sense-datum belonging to *X*.

While (23) is equivalent to

(25) *S* immediately sees a blue sense-datum.

And the entailment from (24) to (25) is a simple, formal one.

(ii) It is evident that

(26) *X* looks yellow to *S*

conjoined with

(27) *X* looks yellow to *T*

entails

(28) *X* looks the same colour to *S* and *T*.

It is evident that

(29) *X* looks the same shape to *S* and *T*

conjoined with

(30) *X* looks square to *T*.

entails

(31) *X* looks square to *S*.

It is evident that

(32) *X* looks bright red to *S*

entails

(33) *X* looks red to *S*.

On the Sense-datum theory, these entailments are all simple, formal consequences of such entailments as that from '*x* is bright red' to '*x* is red' and that from '*x* and *y* are both yellow' to '*x* and *y* are the same colour'.

(iii) We have noted that hallucination and perception of something physical may be indistinguishable as far as the subject is concerned. This suggests, as we noted in §4, that we seek an analysis which reflects this fact. The SDT does this in the simplest way possible, by analysing seeing something physical as a conjunction, one conjunct (the one pertaining to the immediate perception of a sense-datum) being a necessary condition both of seeing something physical and of hallucinating, the other conjunct (the one relating to the sense-datum belonging to the physical object) being a necessary condition of seeing something physical. The situation where the subject cannot tell whether or not he is under a hallucination or seeing something physical is simply one where he knows the first conjunct is true, but does not know if the second is. And the common element in perceiving something physical and hallucinatory is explained by the fact of the shared conjunct.

(iv) Finally, the SDT provides a simple account of the role of 'red', 'square', 'circular', 'double', and so on in 'looks-' statements. These words play their standard role in such statements, that of characterizing things, these things being sense-data.

9. I want now to make some general remarks about the case we have put forward for sense-data, particularly *vis à vis* the literature, and to try and anticipate some objections. The major objection to sense-data, that they lead to Idealism or Representationalism, both of which are unacceptable, will be dealt with in chapter 6 by arguing that Representationalism is not unacceptable.

What we have been seeking is an understanding of certain statements about our visual experience. One way of understanding these statements, the way of the SDT, is to take substantives like 'image', 'look', 'appearance', 'the look of'[10] seriously, as actually designating something, generically named a (visual) sense-datum. This may properly be described as reifying appearances (as it commonly is) but it is not inventing them, and, more generally, the sense-data of the SDT are not

---

[10] More precisely, 'the look of', 'the appearance of' do not, even putatively, designate. They are functors from things to their looks, and it is instances like 'the look of that tomato' which putatively (and actually on the SDT) designate.

inventions. Sense-data are commonly attacked as outrageous philosophical inventions foisted on the common man. But they are not inventions any more than events or propositions. To accept events or propositions as part of what there is, is to take expressions like 'John's birth' and 'what Bill believes', respectively, as genuinely naming. Now these expressions putatively naming events and propositions, and those putatively naming appearances and images are not inventions and are not foisted on the common man. They are a familiar part of the way we seek to say how things are. Of course, the *term* 'sense-datum' is an invention, just as 'sibling' is, but neither sense-data nor siblings are inventions.

By these lights, the more usual approaches to sense-data are to be rejected. The conception of sense-data as the subjects of those fundamental judgements which form the foundations of our knowledge of the world around us is irrelevant for us, as our case for sense-data has derived from analytical considerations, not epistemological ones: perhaps sense-data do have an important epistemological role to play, but on our approach that will be a discovery about them, not a matter of definition.

The other main approach to sense-data in the literature, the phenomenological one, according to which sense-data are discovered by careful, disinterested examination of one's perceptual experience, is, by our lights, also beside the point at issue. Careful, disinterested examination of one's perceptual experience can reveal a great many truths of the form '*X* looks red', 'There is a green, round patch in my visual field', and so on. But, after all, careful examination of families can reveal truths of the form 'The average family is . . .'; but that does not show that the average family exists. Sense-data are not to be discovered by introspection any more than the average family is to be discovered by careful examination of families.

This does not mean phenomenology is irrelevant to our case for sense-data. It is a phenomenological fact that, in the well-known circumstances, a straight stick looks bent; and it is the nature of one's experience which leads one to describe this situation as there being a bent, brown outline in one's visual field. But this, *in itself*, no more shows that the bent, brown outline exists than does the fact that the nature of Smith's dancing may lead one to say that there is a dance Smith cannot do, shows that dances exist. The position appears to be this. Attention to the phenomenology of visual perception, to how it is natural to describe how things look, leads to *truths*; truths we all acknowledge concerning bent shapes, double images, mirages, converging railway lines, and so on; but the question of the existence of sense-data turns not just on what is true, but also on how we should understand these truths – that is, on their ontic commitments.

This is why the questions 'Are there foveas?' and 'Are there sense-data?' are so different.[11] There is no controversy about how to understand statements concerning foveas, and hence the issue over their existence boils down to whether the appropriate statements are true. On the other hand, the appropriate statements concerning sense-data, that is, concerning looks and images, are, without dispute, true; the controversy is over how to understand them.

This is also why I do not discuss the possibility of what is sometimes called *a sense-datum language*: a language for perceptual experience completely independent of languages for physical reality. Considerations grouped under the heading *The Private Language Argument* are often thought to show that a purely sense-datum language is impossible. But this is a thesis in the philosophy of language which is separate from the ontological thesis I have been urging; it bears on whether our talk about sense-data is conceptually independent of our talk about physical objects; while my concern has been simply to urge that our talk putatively about sense-data really is *about* them – be it conceptually independent of physical-object talk or not.

10. It is time to mention the notorious arguments from illusion, variation, perceptual relativity, and so on and so forth. And let me say straight away that I think these arguments prove nothing, and, consequently, nothing in what follows depends on them. I believe that the current opposition to sense-data derives in large measure from their unfortunate historical association with these arguments.

These notorious arguments sometimes play a categorical, and sometimes a hypothetical role. Sometimes they are deployed to show that there are sense-data, and sometimes to show that *if* there are sense-data, then they are not identical with the surfaces of material objects. Normally, when they are given the former, categorical role, they are also given the latter, hypothetical one, as well. To take a recent example, T. L. S. Sprigge argues as follows:

> If I look at a white wall without sunglasses on, and then look again with sunglasses on, while all will admit that there has been no change in the character of the wall, there has been a

---

[11] Cf., G. A. Paul, 'Is There a Problem About Sense-Data?'.

change in the appearance of the wall ... the appearance has
changed, and ... the wall has not, at least not in any way relevant
to the perceptual situation. If one thing has changed in a thus
relevant way and another thing has not, it is a logical inference that
the two are not identical.[12]

Here we have an argument for the existence of appearances (and
so, of sense-data) in the step from 'the appearance has changed' to
'*one thing* has changed'; and also an argument concerning the nature of
the appearance, the one thing that has changed, to the effect that it is
not the wall, on the ground that the wall has not changed.

On the existence point, the obvious reply is to point out that the
average family has changed in size in the last three years, but no one
thinks that this entails that something, one thing, has changed size; and
no one would go on to argue that, moreover, the average family is
not identical with my family because my family has not changed size in
the last three years. What is crucial is not the fact Sprigge emphasises,
namely the truth of 'The appearance has changed', but, rather, how
we should understand this undoubted truth. What we must do is consider all the reasonable theories about the meaning of such statements,
decide which is the best (and if our arguments above succeed, the
SDT is), and then see whether on that theory there is an appearance
which changes colour (as there is on the SDT). *As it stands*, I think
Sprigge's argument for the existence of appearances or sense-data can
only be regarded as a *petitio principii*.

The same point applies to appeals to the facts of illusion. The fact
that straight sticks can look bent, round pennies can look elliptical,
and so on cannot, in itself, show that a certain analysis, in this case the
SDT, is correct. Generally speaking, the arguments from illusion,
variation, and so on, intended as arguments for the existence of sense-
data as well as for conclusions about their nature, beg the question. For
they presuppose readings of statements about how things look which
take 'the look of the tomato' and the like to actually name something,
and so presuppose what is at issue.

In fairness, it should be noted that it is not only advocates of these
arguments who overlook the need to explicitly defend their reading of
'looks-' statements. Opponents of sense-data sometimes do the same.
Many opponents content themselves with saying that 'X looks F to S'

<hr />

[12] *Facts, Words and Beliefs*, pp. 4–5.

does not entail that anything F is seen by S, and *that is that*.[13] But, of course, 'X looks F to S' is equivalent to 'The look of X to S is F'; so that to deny that there is an F is to adopt a position about 'the look of X to S', namely, that it is a *merely nominal* singular term. Thus, the denial of sense-data requires a theory about 'looks-' statements as much as the entertainment of sense-data does. And, therefore, the denial of sense-data must be backed up by a theory – the MRTA, or a belief analysis, or whatever. Of course, a great many philosophers have seen this and have stuck their necks out by offering a theory which dispenses with sense-data, but I think that there have also been a great many philosophers who have thought you could rationally deny that there are sense-data without sticking your neck out at all.

Likewise, sense-data cannot be avoided by merely translating 'Something looks red to S' as 'S seems to see a red thing' and then pointing out that it is obvious that one may *seem* to see a red thing without there being anything red. It is obvious that one can seem to see a red thing without anything *physical* being red. But this is beside the point. The issue is whether there need be anything red – be it physical or not. And this is just the point on which the suggestion is silent. It gives 'S seems to see a red thing' as the translation of 'Something looks red to S' without telling us how to construe 'seems to see'. 'Seems to see' functions syntactically as a relation, but clearly the suggestion cannot allow that it functions semantically as a relation. For then 'S seems to see a red thing' could only be true if there were a red thing, which is precisely the conclusion of the SDT that the suggestion is seeking to avoid.

Similar remarks apply to appeals to sentential operators like 'It is just as if . . .' Sense-data cannot be eliminated just by writing 'Something looks red to S' as 'It is just as if S were seeing something red.' For precisely what is the reading to be given to 'It is just as if' as an operator on sentences? The obvious reading to give 'It is just as if p' is that it asserts that, in all crucial respects, things are as they are when p is true. But the crucial point about seeing something red is that one is appropriately related to something red. Hence, on the obvious reading, 'It is just as if S were seeing something red' requires something red for its truth – again, precisely the conclusion that is not wanted.

[13] See, e.g., W. H. F. Barnes, 'The Myth of Sense-Data'; and, as Chisholm says in 'The Theory of Appearing' commenting on the kind of view Barnes puts forward, 'There are many philosophers, I suspect, who are content to leave the matter here.'

There is, I think, no escape from the point made two paragraphs back: sense-data can only be avoided by offering a *worked-out theory* to replace the SDT. (And we have seen that the SDT appears to be superior to the currently available replacements.)

The arguments from illusion, variation, and so on are more defensible when restricted to their hypothetical role, but, nevertheless, even when we grant that there are sense-data, it does not seem to me that these arguments show sufficiently definitely that sense-data are not parts of material things.

For example, Sprigge's argument that the appearance has changed while the wall has not (and no doubt he would argue the same for the facing surface of the wall) invites the response that the president of America changed in 1973 while Richard Nixon and Gerald Ford did not (in the relevant sense), yet no-one would conclude from this that neither Richard Nixon nor Gerald Ford was president in 1973. That is, why not say that 'The appearance changes' is misleading in the same way that 'The president changes' is: in neither case is there *one* thing with different properties at different times, rather, in both cases, there are *two* things. This would enable one to say that one appearance anyway, presumably the one before putting on the sunglasses, was identical with a part of the wall. Generally speaking, if one accepts the existence of sense-data, then illusion, hallucination, and the like certainly show that some sense-data are not material things or parts thereof, but they do not show that *all* sense-data are not.

Though the issues are more than familiar, it is perhaps worth putting them briefly by means of a simple example. Take a white wall which is illuminated by a white light which is slowly turning red. The sense-datum changes from white to pink, the wall does not. (I will leave the references to wall-parts and surfaces out.) Hence, Sprigge would argue, the sense-datum is not the wall. But one who accepts the existence of sense-data, can urge that there are many sense-data in this case, and that Direct Realism can be salvaged by insisting that the first, white sense-datum is identical with the wall, even if the others are not. Two objections, which are sometimes run together, are commonly made to this reply. One is that the white sense-datum is subjectively similar to the pink and red ones. But, as J. L. Austin in particular urges,[14] it is not obvious that we must accept the principle underlying this reply – why not subjective similarity with ontological difference? The other is that it would be *arbitrary* to pick on just one

[14] In *Sense and Sensibilia*, see p. 50.

sense-datum as the wall. But a choice is arbitrary if there is no reason for it rather than an alternative one; and in this case there is a good reason for picking the white sense-datum – it's the only one whose colour is the same as the wall's.

The argument from illusion and those arguments associated with it seem to me, therefore, insufficient to establish that all sense-data are mental, even if it is granted that the existence of sense-data has been shown by other, independent arguments.[15] To establish that all sense-data are mental we need the conclusion of the next chapter. Before we proceed to this chapter, I want to discuss a final objection to our argument for sense-data and an attempt by Armstrong to show that sense-data give rise to difficulties over similarity and indeterminacy.

11. I suspect that some will feel that the notion of an intensional verb and the corresponding notion of an intensional object enables the following objection to our argument for sense-data. (I put the objection into the mouth of an imaginary objector.) 'Can't I grant your objections to the MRTA, the adverbial theory, and so on by agreeing that looking F is to be analysed (in the phenomenal case) in terms of seeing an F, without going to the sense-datum extreme of saying that there is an F seen. For I can say that "see" is an intensional verb like "believes" or "worships", or, better, that it is like "desire" and "look for" in having an intensional and a material use. There is a use of "desire", the intensional, on which "I desire a sloop" may be true without there being a sloop I desire; and a use, the material, on which there must be.[16] Likewise, can't I say that there is a material use of "see", as in "I see a chair", which entails that the object – in this case, the chair – exists; and an intensional use, as in "I see a red shape", which does not. In the latter case, we say that the object is merely an intensional one.'[17]

The essential point to make in reply here is that to say that a verb is intensional in the sense of taking an intensional object is not to ex-*plain* anything, it is not to put forward a *theory*. It is, rather, to draw attention to the need for one. To say that 'desire' in 'I desire a sloop' is intensional (or may be) is to say that the statement is not to be taken

---

[15] Likewise, the time-gap argument seems to me to fail. I do not discuss the point as my reasons are familiar from, e.g., A. J. Ayer, *Problem of Knowledge*, ch. 3, §(ii), and W. A. Suchting, 'Perception and the Time-Gap Argument'.

[16] For more on this duality see W. V. Quine, *Word and Object*, ch. IV, §30.

[17] The terms and possibility of this objection derive, of course, from G. E. M. Anscombe, 'The Intentionality of Sensation: Some Grammatical Features'.

at face value. 'A sloop' in the statement does not designate something which is related to me as desired to desirer: rather, 'desire a sloop' ought to be regarded as a whole, best written 'desire-a-sloop'; or, perhaps, 'a sloop' should be taken as indicating a mode of desiring – I desire sloopily; or . . .

Likewise, to say that 'see' is intensional in 'I see a red shape' (or to say that 'a red shape' is an intensional object) is to take this statement at other than face value, and so to embark on questions such as whether it should be rendered as 'I see redly', or with an unanalysable relational term 'looks-red', or . . . In other words, one cannot repudiate sense-data and the SDT without embracing an alternative theory: one cannot have one's cake and eat it.

There is a more local difficulty as well. The most natural and common way of bringing out the distinction between the two uses of 'desire' (and similar remarks apply to 'look for', 'hunt', and so on) does not apply to the case of seeing. The intensional use of 'desire' is that on which I desire *a* sloop without desiring a particular sloop – I desire a red sloop with blue sails, but not that sloop moored out there. The non-intensional use is that on which I desire a given sloop – *that* sloop moored out there. But if I see a red shape, I see a *particular* red shape – the triangular one, to the left of that green shape. There is a sense of 'desire' on which I can desire a sloop without it making sense to ask whether I desire *that* sloop rather than *this* one. There is no such sense of 'see'; if I see a red shape, there must be an answer to whether it is that one, this one, or . . .

12.* In *A Materialist Theory of the Mind*, D. M. Armstrong puts forward an argument, based on what is known in psychology texts as a j.n.d. (just noticeable difference), against theories of perception which hold that the nature of perceptual experience requires the postulation of sense-impressions or sensory items (sense-data). This argument can be generalised in such a way that it would, if successful against sensory item theories of perception, be equally successful against any act–object, as opposed to adverbial, style of analysis of sensations in general. I will argue that the argument fails.

Armstrong argues

> If *A* is exactly similar to *B* in respect *X*, and *B* is exactly similar to *C* in respect *X*, then it follows of logical necessity, that *A* is

---

* The material in this section derives from F. C. Jackson and R. J. Pinkerton, 'On An Argument Against Sensory Items'.

exactly similar to C in respect X. 'Exact similarity in a particular respect' is necessarily a transitive relation. Now suppose that we have three samples of cloth, A, B and C, which are exactly alike except that they differ very slightly in colour. Suppose further, however, that A and B are *perceptually* completely indistinguishable in respect of colour, and B and C are perceptually completely indistinguishable in respect of colour. Suppose, however, that A and C can be perceptually distinguished from each other in this respect.

Now consider the situation if we hold a 'sensory item' view of perception. If the pieces of cloth A and B are perceptually indistinguishable in colour, it will seem to follow that the two sensory items A_1 and B_1 that we have when we look at the two pieces *actually are identical in colour.* For the sensory items are what are supposed to make a perception the perception it is, and here, by hypothesis, the *perceptions* are identical. In the same way B_1 and C_1 will be sensory items that are identical in colour. Yet, by hypothesis, sensory items A_1 and C_1 are not identical in colour.[18]

In my view, the crucial mistake in this argument is the re-iterated use of 'B_1' in the second paragraph of the above quotation. The first occurrence of 'B_1' refers to the sensory item corresponding to B which we have when we look at A and B together. The second occurrence of 'B_1' refers to the sensory item corresponding to B which we have when we look at B and C together. The mistake is the assumption that the sensory item corresponding to B which we have when we look at A and B is identical in colour to the sensory item corresponding to B which we have when we look at B and C. This assumption is crucial to Armstrong's argument, because without it there is no 'middle' term to make transitivity applicable. But Armstrong gives no reason why a sensory item theorist should accept such an assumption, and, in view of the familiar fact of perceptual relativity, it is hard to see what reason could be given. That is, my argument against Armstrong's first argument is that, (i) though it may be true that the sensory items we have when we look at A and B are identical in colour and that the sensory items we have when we look at B and C are identical in colour, it does *not* follow from this, or anything else given, that the sensory items we have when we look at B in the two cases are identical in colour; and, (ii), that it is necessary to Armstrong's argument that this should

---

[18] Armstrong, *A Materialist Theory of the Mind*, p. 218.

follow. Because if the sensory items associated with B in the two cases are different in colour, then the fact that the sensory item associated with A (A_1) is identical in colour with the sensory item associated with B in one case and the sensory item associated with C (C_1) is identical in colour with the sensory item associated with B in the other case, will have no bearing on whether A_1 and C_1 are identical in colour. But if this is the case there will be no inconsistency with the fact that A and C may be distinguished in respect of colour.

The difficulty just raised for Armstrong's first argument turns on the point that, on sensory item theories, there will be *two* sensory items associated with B in the case on which Armstrong's argument relies. Therefore, the obvious repair to the argument is to base it on a case involving just *one* occasion of looking at B, and so just *one* sensory item associated with B. Thus, it might be suggested that we take the case where A, B and C are looked at together (that is, by the one person at the one time), and where A and B are indistinguishable (in colour), B and C are indistinguishable, while A and C are distinguishable. The trouble with this suggestion is that the case is *logically impossible*. It is logically impossible to have A, B and C all *together*, and be unable to tell A from B in colour, and B from C in colour, while able to tell A from C in colour. This is impossible, because, for example, if one can tell A from C but cannot tell B from C, then one can tell A from B simply by reference to the fact that one can tell A from C but cannot tell B from C.

The obvious reply for Armstrong to make here is to point out that the colour-discrimination of A from B just described is by reference to a *third party*, C. He might then use this as a basis for arguing that – despite the impossibility of being unable to colour-discriminate A from B, and B from C, while being able to colour-discriminate A from C, when A, B and C are viewed together – it is possible, even when A, B and C are viewed together, that A looks to be identical in colour with B and B looks to be identical in colour with C, while A looks to be different in colour from C. However, the suggestion that A might look to be the same colour as B, B might look to be the same colour as C, while A looks to be a different colour from C, *to one and the same person at one and the same time*, is *inconsistent*. As A and C *ex hypothesi* look to be different colours, looking to be the same colour as A will be distinct from looking to be the same colour as C; therefore, the suggestion involves one object, B, looking to have two different colours at the same time to the same person, which is impossible.

And, moreover, anyone who thought that the latter was not impossible could not use Armstrong's argument anyhow. For the argument rests on the principle of the transitivity of exact similarity: if x and y are exactly similar in respect ϕ, and y and z are exactly similar in respect ϕ, then x and z are exactly similar in respect ϕ. And this principle cannot be accepted by one who holds that one thing may look different colours to one person at one time. For let ϕ be looking a certain colour to a certain person at a certain time, and let a_1 and a_2 be two distinct instances of same; then our imagined denier of the impossibility holds that y may be a_1 and a_2. But, clearly, x may be a_1 and not a_2, and z may be a_2 and not a_1; and we have a counter-example to transitivity. And, moreover, anyone who holds that it is possible for one thing to look two different colours to one person at the same time, can hardly insist that it is impossible for one thing to *be* two different colours at the one time; so he leaves it open to the sensory item theorist to meet the alleged problem case by saying that the sensory items may have two colours at the one time.

Armstrong has a second argument against sensory items which can be dealt with more briefly. It concerns the indeterminacy of our perceptions, a matter often thought to give the SDT trouble. He says

> The classical case is that of the speckled hen. I may be able to see that it has quite a number of speckles, but unable to see exactly how many speckles it has. The hen has a definite number of speckles, but the perception is a perception of an indeterminate number of speckles. However, this indeterminacy is present in perception generally ... when I see or feel that one object is larger than another, I do not perceive exactly how much larger the first object is.
>
> ... the difficulty that this indeterminacy of perception creates for a theory of sensory items is that it seems to imply that the items will have to be indeterminate in nature. The non-physical item that exists when we perceive the physical speckled hen will have to have an indeterminate number of speckles.[19]

Armstrong is right to object to the implication that sensory items are indeterminate in nature. In the case of the speckled hen a sensory item theorist must concede that the item has a definite number of speckles – in the words of the slogan Armstrong quotes later, 'To be is to be determinate.' On the other hand, Armstrong seems to me to

[19] *Ibid.*, pp. 219–220. This kind of objection is perhaps best known from Barnes, *op. cit.*, §II.

be wrong when he says that the concession that the sensory item has a definite number of speckles poses a difficulty for the sensory item theory. A sensory item theorist needs merely to say that the item has a definite number of speckles, but that we are not perceptually aware of what this definite number is.

Now Armstrong is perfectly well aware that this reply is available to the sensory item theorist, for he says, near the bottom of p. 220, 'The alternative reply would be to say that the sensory items do have perfectly determinate characteristics, but that we are only *aware* of something less.' His argument against this reply is, quoting from the bottom of p. 220 and the top of p. 221, 'This [reply] has the paradoxical consequence that objects [sensory items] specially postulated to do phenomenological justice to perception are now credited with characteristics that lie quite outside perceptual awareness.' It seems to me that Armstrong is here confusing a matter of *sufficiency* with one of *necessity*. If the rationale for postulating sensory items lies in the need to do phenomenological justice to perceiving, then it is clear that being perceptually aware of some characteristic will be a *sufficient* condition for attributing that characteristic to a sensory item. However, it is not clear at all that being perceptually aware of some characteristic will be a *necessary* condition for attributing that characteristic to a sensory item. That is to say, it is clear that every feature of which we are immediately perceptually aware, must, on sensory item theories, be a feature of a sensory item. But it is not at all clear that every feature of sensory item must be a feature of which we are perceptually aware.

To put our objection (to Armstrong's reply to our reply to his second argument) another way, if sensory items are postulated to do justice to the phenomenological side of perception then we must give them *enough* properties to do this. However, this does not prevent us giving sensory items *more* than enough properties to do this, if these extra properties are required by considerations other than that of doing justice to the phenomenology of perceiving. Thus, to take the case in question, a sensory item theorist must, on phenomenological grounds, attribute the property of having many speckles to the sensory item associated with a speckled hen. But also he must, on the *metaphysical* ground that to be is to be determinate, attribute the property of having some definite number of speckles to this sensory item. Likewise, when explaining what happens when a pillar box is seen in normal conditions, a sensory item theorist attributes the property of being red to a sensory item for phenomenological reasons. But he must also attribute to this item either the property of being the same colour as, or the property of being different in colour from, Julius Caesar's fourth visual sensory item. He must do this, not for phenomenological reasons (because whether or not a thing is the same colour as Caesar's fourth visual sensory item is not something of which we are perceptually aware) but for the *logical* reason that *any* two coloured things either have the same colour or a different colour.

To put the matter in terms of the particular sensory item theory advocated here – the SDT; looking *F*, in the *phenomenal* usage, is analysed in terms of seeing an *F*, and looking to have the same colour as Caesar's fourth sensory item and looking to have 274 speckles are not phenomenal uses.

13. Finally, I want to comment on a difficulty commonly felt concerning the identity conditions for sense-data. Here is how Barnes put it (he uses Broad's 'sensum' instead of 'sense-datum');

> how do we determine the duration of a sensum? If I blink my eyes while looking at a red patch are there two sensa separated in time, or is there only one interrupted in its career? If a change occurs in my visual field has the sensum changed or been replaced by another? If the latter, is there any reason why, when no change is observed, a sensum should not be replaced by another exactly like it?[20]

and later

> A sense field may appear as one single variegated sensum. If one part moves in relation to the rest, we can say (i) the whole sensum is changing, (ii) the parts of the sensum are re-arranging their relative positions, or . . . (iii) a sensum is moving across a visual field. There seems no good reason for adopting one explanation rather than another. Similarly, if I have a visual field, half red and half blue, I can at pleasure treat this as one sensum or as two.[21]

Most of what Barnes says in these two passages is entirely correct, but does not constitute an objection to sense-data; because the points apply equally to physical objects. For example, if I have a piece of paper, one half of which is red, the other half of which is blue, I can 'at pleasure' treat this as one physical object or two attached ones. But no one thinks this is a significant objection to physical objects.

It is generally recognised that 'How many?' asked of a group of physical objects requires (demands) supplication with what P. T.

[20] Barnes, *op. cit.*, p. 150.   [21] *Ibid.*, p. 151.

Geach[22] calls a *sortal*. 'How many *molecules*?', 'How many *medium sized pieces of furniture*?', 'How many *book types*?', 'How many *book tokens*?' all make sense only inasmuch as they have been provided with the italicized sortals or *count-nouns*. The same is true of sense-data. There is no answer to how many sense-data are in a person's visual field at a given time. There are only answers relative to a specification such as: of medium size, belonging to spatially separated material things, and of uniform colour. And, once such a specification is provided, there is no particular problem about counting sense-data.

Barnes also mentions the point that a sense-datum theorist may be unable to choose between saying that a (large) sense-datum is changing, that parts of this sense-datum are re-arranging their relative positions, and that a sense-datum is moving across a visual field. But this point is not an objection. All we have are three different but consistent ways of describing the same situation. And precisely the same kind of thing can happen with physical objects. Take a railway signal whose arm is falling: we can describe this either by saying that the signal is changing, that parts of it are re-arranging their relative positions, or that the arm is moving. This fact does not cast doubt on the existence of the signal.

Some philosophers who favour sense-data have wanted to hold that sense-data cannot change over time, and so would not allow one of the descriptions mentioned by Barnes. But this, again, is not a substantive point of difference from physical existents. There are two approaches current to change over time: one based on a four-dimensional conception of non-abstract things, the other on the 'common sense' three-dimensional conception of things enduring through time. J. J. C. Smart, an advocate of the first conception, puts it thus

> It is perfectly possible to think of things and processes as four-dimensional space–time entities. The instantaneous state of such a four-dimensional space–time solid will be a three-dimensional 'time-slice' of the four-dimensional solid. Then instead of talking of things or processes changing or not changing we can now talk of one time slice of a four-dimensional entity *being* different or not different from some other time slice ... therefore, we replace the notions of change and staying the same by the notions of the similarity or dissimilarity of time-slices of four-dimensional solids.[23]

---

[22] In, e.g., *Reference and Generality*.
[23] *Philosophy and Scientific Realism*, p. 133.

In the same way, there are two positions over sense-data and change. We can regard sense-data as instantaneous and hold that when an after-image, for instance, fades, there is a succession of sense-data, each one lighter in colour than the preceding one. Or else we can regard sense-data as enduring through time and so as subject to real change; that is, that in our example there is one thing in many states, rather than many things each in a slightly different state. The choice between these two positions, both as applied to sense-data and material things, is a difficult one pertaining to the philosophy of time. Nothing in what follows requires us to make it in this work. We can, however, note that the surprisingly common position which allows a sense-datum to remain the same over time but not to change over time,[24] is to be rejected. This position is an unacceptable blend of the two possible ones.

Finally, there is Barnes' point about blinking: 'are there two sensa separated in time, or is there only one interrupted in its career?' What puzzles me is why this should be thought a problem *for sense-data*. We are all familiar with the issue of whether if this chair were to disappear and then apparently re-appear in just the same place with just the same properties, it would be right to say the very same chair re-appeared, or whether we ought to say that a numerically different but qualitatively identical one had appeared. Again, it seems that no special problem for sense-data has been identified by Barnes. (As it happens, I think the correct response is to say that there are *two* chairs and *two* sense-data in the cases described, but the matter is not important for what follows.)

14. To conclude, we now have before us the case for sense-data, and are thus in a position to say that the immediate objects of perception are sense-data. We have seen that it is clear that not all sense-data (and so, not all immediate objects of perception) are physical. But, for all that has been said so far, perhaps some are. The next step is to argue that no sense-data are physical, that is, that all are mental. (I am assuming that there is no third possibility, intermediate between being mental and being physical.) This step is the business of the next chapter, and with its completion we will have completed our argument for the most controversial claim of the Representative theory of perception.

[24] See, e.g., Price, *Perception*, p. 115.

5
Colour and science*

0. It is a commonplace that there is an apparent clash between the picture Science gives of the world around us and the picture our senses give us. We *sense* the world as made up of coloured, materially continuous, macroscopic, stable objects; Science and, in particular, Physics, tells us that the material world is constituted of clouds of minute, colourless, highly-mobile particles.

The precise relationship between these two pictures has been a matter of considerable debate, and we will at the end of this chapter be able to give a simple and intuitively plausible account of it (namely, what I take to be Locke's account); but what I want to focus on to begin with is just one aspect of the question, namely, the implications of what Science says about the world for whether or not material things have the property of being coloured. Does Science imply, contrary to what we seem to see, that the pen I am now writing with does not have the property of being blue? I will argue that it does, that Science forces us to acknowledge that physical or material things are not coloured (which, as we will see, is not at all the same as saying that Science shows that every statement like 'My pen is blue' is false). This will enable us to conclude that sense-data are all mental, for they are coloured.

1. I might be expected to argue for this conclusion in the following, familiar way: 'Physics shows that objects are collections of minute, widely-separated, *colourless* particles. Therefore, they are not coloured.'[1] But there are difficulties with this attractively simple argument.

First, at most, Physics shows that material things are *at least* collections of widely-separated, colourless particles; it does not show that they are *at most* such collections – it is not an essential part of any current physical theory that objects do not have additional characteris-

---

* §2–§5 of this chapter derive from my 'Do Material Things Have Non-Physical Properties?'

[1] For a detailed recent development of this kind of approach see B. Aune, *Knowledge, Mind, and Nature,* esp. ch. VII.

tics. And it must be remembered that wholes may have properties markedly different from those of the parts that make them up: a heavy object may be made up of many light parts, and so on.

Further, and most importantly, there is no formal, demonstrable inconsistency between the 'commonsense' picture of material things and that of Modern Physics, all we have is a commonsense intuition that both pictures cannot be true together. Now I do not deny the force of this intuition, or the relevance of such intuitions to philosophical inquiry; the trouble here is that, at the level of commonsense intuition, the picture of Modern Physics is itself inconsistent. The paradoxes of Quantum Mechanics show that. This means that we must either reject our normal intuitions in these contexts, and so ignore the intuitive feel that there is a clash between Modern Physics and our senses, or else we must anticipate a future, radical revision in Modern Physics, a revision which may, for all we know, remove the appearance of a clash. Another way of putting essentially the same point is that there is currently no such thing as *the picture* of ultimate reality associated with Modern Physics to clash with our everyday conception of the world. (Anyone who holds a phenomenalist or 'convenient fiction' theory of the fundamental particles of physics agrees with this conclusion, though for very different reasons. I do not hold such a theory, but it is worth noting that the argument that follows is independent of this.)

2. My argument for the conclusion that material things are not coloured derives from science in general rather than from Modern Physics in particular. Whether or not Modern Physics gives us an acceptable picture of the ultimate nature of the material world, it is clear that scientific inquiry (in all the sciences) has made enormous progress in providing causal explanations of what goes on in the world around us. The Molecular theory of gases and the laws associated with it really do explain why gases diffuse, why increase in pressure leads to decrease in volume, why increasing the temperature of a fixed volume of gas increases its pressure, and so on; the Oxidation theory of combustion really does explain (as the Phlogisten theory does not) what happens when something burns; the Newtonian theory of gravitation really does explain aspects of planetary motion; and so on and so forth.

These various causal explanations differ in respect of how fundamental they are; and, perhaps, as physicalists claim, the most fundamental explanations are those offered in Physics, and all the others can in principle be reduced to those offered in Physics. But all I need for my argument is the truth of certain scientific causal explanations, and, in particular, the truth of certain accounts of how the material things around us cause changes in our brains. We need not enquire into which, if any, are the most fundamental.

I will start by arguing for the intermediate conclusion that either colour is a scientific property or it is not a property of material things.

3. First we need an account of what a scientific property is. A scientific property is a property appealed to by current science in explaining the causal effect of one material thing on another material thing, or a logical consequence of such a property or properties. Thus having mass and charge are scientific properties, and so is having a property in common with something, for the latter is a logical consequence of having the same mass as that thing. This definition explicitly ties being a scientific property to current explanations of causal interactions; having a certain amount of calorific fluid is thus not a scientific property, and nor are any new properties which may be invoked by scientists in the future. This definition is sketchy, but sufficient for our needs.

Now consider the following argument:

pr. 1. Our reason for believing that material things are coloured is (certain of) the perceptual experiences we have.[2]

pr. 2. When material things cause perceptual experiences in us, the immediate causes of these experiences are certain events in our brains.

pr. 3. The causal effect a material thing has on our brain is, as far as it is concerned, a function solely of its scientific properties.

pr. 4. If premises 2 and 3 are true, then our perceptual experiences provide no reason for believing that material things have non-scientific properties.

∴   Either colour is a scientific property, or we have no reason to believe that material things are coloured.

The argument is valid. Premises 2, 3 and 4 together entail the consequent of premise 4 – that our perceptual experiences provide no reason for believing that material things have non-scientific properties; and this with premise 1 entails that only if colour were a scientific property would we have reason to believe that material things were coloured, and so, entails the conclusion. Further, the conclusion makes

---

[2] This is to be understood as equivalent to 'What, if anything, makes it rational to believe that material things are coloured is (certain of) the perceptual experiences we have'.

it totally reasonable to assert that either colour is a scientific property or it is not a property of material things. For though the precise status of Occam's razor is a matter of dispute, it seems clear enough here that properties we have no reason to believe are possessed by material things are properties we ought not ascribe to them. I claim that premises 1 and 4 are true on essentially conceptual or philosophical grounds, and that premises 2 and 3 are empirically well-supported. I will consider the premises in turn.

4. (i) Premise 1 is clearly true. The reason we have for believing that material things are coloured is certain of the experiences we have, in particular, the kind most people have when their eyes are open and suitably illuminated objects are before them. In short, we believe material things are coloured because they *look* coloured. By contrast, we believe things are shaped because, in addition to looking so, they *feel* so and behave so; and we believe some things have magnetic fields because this supposition *explains* observed phenomena; but with colour it is essentially the look of things and nothing more. This is why there would be no reason to believe that things are coloured in 'the country of the blind'.

Some behaviourists may object that our reason for believing that material things are coloured is the sorting behaviour of human beings in daylight.[3] However, human beings do not believe that things are coloured because they sort things in certain ways; they sort them in certain ways because they believe them to be (differently) coloured. Indeed, in cases where the objects have all properties other than colour in common, the only way they can sort them is on the basis of colour. Moreover, we have already looked askance at Behaviourism, and surely Behaviourism applied to colour is one of the least plausible manifestations of that doctrine. (I return to this point in §9.)

(ii) Premise 2 employs the notion of an immediate cause, which may be defined in the usual way via the notion of a mediate (remote) cause. A is a *mediate* cause of B if A caused B, and there is a C such that A caused C and C caused B; A is an *immediate* cause of B if it is a cause, but not a mediate one, of B. A familiar example of mediate causation is the movement of a train causing the brake van to move. The engine causes the van to move by causing the intermediate carriages to move, and the movement of those carriages then causes the van to move. In the same way, premise 2 asserts that when material objects cause perceptual experiences in humans, they do so by causing certain events in

[3] Cf., J. J. C. Smart, 'Colours', and *Philosophy and Scientific Realism*, ch. 4.

the brain which then cause the experiences. (Obviously, premise 2 presupposes the falsity of Parallelism.)

This account of how to construe premise 2 makes it clear how we show that it is true. With the train we show that the movement of the carriage next to the brake van (or, more precisely, the movement of the connecting coupling) is the immediate cause, rather than the engine's movement, by showing that (*a*) if the engine moves, but for some reason the relevant carriage does not, the van does not move, and that, (*b*) if the relevant carriage does move, although the engine does not, the van moves. In the same way, showing premise 2 true is a matter of showing that, (*a*), if the appropriate brain events occur, the experiences occur, regardless of changes in material things around us, and that, (*b*), if the brain events do not occur, neither do the experiences, regardless of changes in the world around us. All neuro-physiologists accept both contentions, and they are in the best position to judge. Everything we know about how the objects around us cause sense experiences in us points to the causal chain going through the brain and central nervous system. The hypothesis that physical things act *directly* in causing sense-experiences may once have been plausible, but it is no longer.

(iii) Premise 3 asserts that the effect of the action of a material object on our brains is, as far as the object is concerned, just a (causal) function of certain of its scientific properties. What this means is that, whether or not objects have non-scientific properties, the effect they have on human brains (via light rays, contact, or whatever) depends, as far as they are concerned, solely on certain of their scientific properties. A simplified illustration of this kind of situation is when a piece of litmus paper is inserted in a liquid. Whether or not it turns red is solely a function of whether the liquid is acid or not: the density of the liquid, its temperature, and so on are all irrelevant. The property of the liquid relevant to whether the paper turns red is its degree of acidity. Likewise, according to premise 3, the properties of material objects relevant to the kind of brain event their action produces are all scientific.

Now it is known in broad outline how a material thing causes the brain events relevant to sensory experience. For those experiences particularly relevant to our perception of colour, the process involves the action of light reflected from the object into the eye. And the role of the object is essentially that of modifying the wave-length composition of the light, and the properties of the object which effect this modification are scientific ones like the texture and the molecular structure of its surface.[4] The details of this account will, of course, be modified by future research on the sense organs and how they are affected by external objects, but the present approach gives every indication of being along the right lines. There is, in particular, no reason to expect that future research will uncover the need to add a brand new property to the stock of scientific properties in order to effect a satisfactory explanation of just what happens when external objects cause changes in our brains and central nervous system. In other words, we do not yet know the (operative) necessary and sufficient conditions in full detail, but we are far enough along the road to knowing them to be able to predict with fair confidence that they will not require us to invoke properties over and above those countenanced by current science.

It might reasonably be urged that premise 3 goes too far in that it supposes we have, at the present stage of scientific knowledge, sufficient reason to reject certain forms of dualist attribute theories of the person. If persons are merely their material bodies plus appropriate, *causally efficacious*, irreducibly psychological properties, it may be that certain material bodies – those belonging to sentient creatures – sometimes affect human brains in ways not fully explicable without attributing non-scientific properties to these bodies. But we can admit this possibility by restricting premise 3 in a way which does not impair our argument.

If we take premise 3 to apply just to *inanimate* material things, and make the corresponding changes throughout the argument, we will end up with the conclusion that colour is not a property of *inanimate* material things. But no one thinks that the bodies of persons are coloured in a different sense to that in which, for example, flowers are; so that we will still be able to draw the conclusion that colour is not a property of material things in general. (Alternatively, premise 3 could be restricted to those causal effects of material things on our brains *relevant to judging that they are coloured*.)

(iv) The case for premise 4 is that if premises 2 and 3 are true, then the occurrence of (perceptual) experiences, any experiences at all, will be irrelevant to whether or not material things possess non-scientific properties. Because if our experiences are immediately dependent on certain of our brain events and if the only properties of material things relevant to their effect on our brains are scientific, then our experiences

---

[4] For something more than this schematic outline see, Wyburn, Pickford, and Hirst, *Human Senses and Perception*, part 1.

would be exactly the same regardless of whether or not material things had non-scientific properties in addition to their scientific ones.

The point is that, if premises 2 and 3 are true, it is unnecessary to suppose that material things have non-scientific properties in order to explain the occurrence of the relevant perceptual experiences. Indeed, the supposition that material things have non-scientific properties will not only be unnecessary, it will be quite useless. Premise 2 asserts that, when material things produce perceptual experiences in us, it is the nature of certain brain events which determines the kind of experiences produced, because these brain events are the immediate cause. And premise 2 asserts that the properties of material things relevant to the nature of the brain events they may cause, are all scientific. Therefore, if premises 2 and 3 are true, the non-scientific properties of material things, supposing there are such for the purposes of argument, have no causal role to play in the production of experiences. And so, our perceptual experiences cannot be any sort of evidence for material things having non-scientific properties. These experiences cannot be regarded as *reflecting* or *registering* the instantiation of any non-scientific properties, for they would be just the same whether or not material things had such properties.

In order to make the reasoning being advanced in support of premise 4 clearer, let us apply it in a different case.[5] Suppose I have a barometer which is normally a good indicator of approaching rain. When the reading drops sharply, it nearly always rains soon after. Now suppose the reading drops sharply on some particular occasion, but that I happen to know that the cause of this drop is a mechanical failure. Surely it is clear that, despite the past correlation between the reading dropping sharply and subsequent rain, I have no evidence whatever on this occasion for impending rain. And the reason is that, because the drop is caused by a mechanical failure and not a drop in atmospheric pressure, it would have occurred whether or not the pressure had dropped, and so, whether or not rain were in the offing.

Thus it appears a valid epistemological principle that if I know that p would obtain whether or not q were the case, I cannot regard p as evidence for q. This is just the principle which lies behind premise 4.

This completes my argument for the conclusion that either colour is a scientific property or it is not a property of material things. It is not intended to be apodeictic. Premises 2 and 3 might conceivably

[5] A similar example is used to different purpose by B. Skyrms, 'The Explication of "*X* knows that p"'.

turn out to be false. Future research might show that material things act directly to produce perceptual experiences, or that we need to add some radically new properties to the present stock of scientific properties to explain certain interactions between material things. Either is possible, but neither is likely. And, moreover, we must believe at *t* the best theories available at *t*; and the best theories presently available favour both premises. If we do not like the conclusion, we may *hope* future research shows one or both premises are false, but we have, I think, no choice at the present time but to accept them both.

5. The final step from the intermediate conclusion that either colour is a scientific property or it is not a property of material things to the desired conclusion that colour is not a property of material things, is via Disjunctive Syllogism: for colour is not a scientific property.

The colour of things does not appear in any currently accepted (or even recent) scientific causal explanations of the interactions between objects. A chemist may remark that acids turn litmus paper red, but his *explanation* of this will not mention colour at all. It will be in terms of free hydrogen ions combining with certain chemicals in the paper to form new compounds with different responses to incident light waves etc., etc. There is not one causal law in which 'is red', 'is blue', and so on appear.

Despite this, it has been recently suggested that colour is a scientific property (to put the matter in our terminology). For instance, in chapter 6 of *A Materialist Theory of the Mind*, Armstrong suggests that colour can be (contingently) identified with a scientific property of the surface of objects like their having a certain surface 'grid' or their reflecting a certain wave-length distribution (simplifying the scientific details for the purposes of illustration). (A similar view has been expressed by David Lewis and J. J. C. Smart.)[6]

This suggestion, however, runs foul of conclusions of earlier chapters. The criteria governing the identity of properties is a matter of considerable controversy. But at least it is clear that a necessary condition for property X to be identical with property Y is that X and Y have the same extension. Now, from earlier chapters, we have it that certain mental objects, for instance, red after-images, belong to the extension of redness. These mental objects do not, though, belong to the extension of properties like having a certain surface grid or reflecting a certain distribution of wave-lengths. Therefore,

---

[6] J. J. C. Smart, 'On Some Criticisms of a Physicalist Theory of Colours'. Smart reports Lewis as sharing this view.

redness is not any such scientific property, and likewise for colours in general.

When I say that colour is not a property of material things I am not, of course, saying that every statement that some material thing is a certain colour is false. I am saying, rather, that the truth conditions of a statement like 'That material thing is red' are not to be given in terms of that material thing having the property of being red, but in some quite different way, in particular, in terms of the sense-data normally belonging to that thing having the property of being red. Our old friend, 'The average family has 0·9 pets', again provides a parallel: one who says, as we all do, that there is no average family, is not (necessarily) denying the truth of the statement, he is instead denying that its truth conditions are to be given in terms of *something*, the average family, having 0·9 pets.

6. We are now, finally, in a position to obtain the major conclusion of this work – that the immediate objects of (visual) perception are always mental. I have argued in previous chapters that the immediate objects of perception are always visual sense-data, and that such sense-data have colour properties. But material things do not have colour properties (and this applies also to their parts of course); therefore, sense-data are not material, and so, must be mental. This gives us our conclusion.

I should, perhaps, emphasise the crucial role of sense-data and the rejection of the MRTA. It might be thought we could have obtained the major conclusion directly from the conclusion of chapter 1 without reference to sense-data. In chapter 1 we concluded that the immediate objects of perception are coloured shapes, hence, as material things are not coloured, it might be thought we could have concluded directly that the immediate objects of perception are mental. But without chapter 4 on sense-data, we would be unable to meet the following argument: 'The immediate objects of perception are only loosely describable as coloured shapes. Strictly, they are things with shape properties and certain unanalysable *relations* to persons, such as *looking red* and *looking yellow*. Hence, the failure of material things and parts thereof to have colour *properties* does not rule them out as immediate objects of perception, for it is consistent with their having these *relations*.' We can, however, meet this line of objection by referring back to the objections to the MRTA.

7. Finally, I think it is worth noting how the account of colour that emerges from this chapter resolves the uneasy tension between sub-

jectivism and objectivism about colour. Many writers have observed how very hard it is to be a full-scale objectivist about colour. Colour seems *too* variable relative to conditions of observation and of sense-organs to be an objective feature of the world.[7] But it has often been thought that in order to maintain a subjectivist stance about colour it is necessary to take a *relational* view of colour, to treat colour as a relation between things and persons, and this fits ill with the 'out-thereness' of colour. Red, green and so on appear to qualify objects distinct from us; the colour of an object looks to be very obviously on the surface of it; and, as Berkeley observed, shape and colour seem to be inextricably intertwined (try finding an instance of colour without an instance of shape or extension), and, yet, shape is clearly an *intrinsic* property (there might be one solitary *sphere* in the universe).

The account of colour that emerges from this chapter makes sense of all this. Colour is subjective in that it qualifies mental items, while being an *intrinsic* quality of those items. And the Berkeleyan point that every instance of colour is equally an instance of shape and extension follows from the nature of the latter mental items – sense-data have colour, shape and extension.

8. I will conclude by considering two objections to the argument of this chapter. The first is that the discussion of premise 1 assumed the falsity of behaviourist theories of colour and that there is an adequate behaviourist theory – that of J. J. C. Smart and G. Pitcher. My argument against this objection will be that this theory is not adequate.

The second objection is that a thesis of Hume and Berkeley – recently revived by D. M. Armstrong – is inconsistent with the conclusion of this chapter. I will deal with the second objection first.

In the *Principles of Human Knowledge*, Berkeley claims 'that it is not in my power to frame an idea of a body extended and moving, but I must withal give it some colour or other sensible quality, which is acknowledged to exist only in the mind. In short, extension, figure, and motion, abstracted from all other qualities, are inconceivable.'[8]

Hume, likewise, claims that an object cannot have the primary qualities alone, that every object must have some secondary qualities.[9] Clearly, if Hume and Berkeley are right, there must be something badly wrong with the argument of this chapter. The argument was

---

[7] This variability and its import is forcefully spelt out in K. Campbell, 'Colours', in *Contemporary Philosophy in Australia*.
[8] *Principles of Human Knowledge*, §10.
[9] *Treatise of Human Nature*, book I, part IV, §4, 7th par. onwards.

developed in terms of colour, but might equally have been developed for any of the secondary qualities; hence I am committed to holding that it is strictly sense-data rather than material things that have the secondary qualities. Moreover, I obviously must (and do) allow that material things might exist without sense-data existing, therefore, I must allow the possibility that an object should have only the primary qualities.

Berkeley's argument is more an intuition than an argument, and at the level of intuition Hume's and Berkeley's claim is implausible. There are objects – for example, those made of clear glass – which have practically no colour, taste, or smell, and surely such objects might have failed to have any colour, taste, or smell at all. Hence, Hume and Berkeley must hold that it is a logically necessary truth that objects which fail to have colour, taste, or smell, either emit a sound when struck or have a temperature. It is very hard to believe this. Surely it is a contingent feature of our world that things emit sounds when struck and are hot or cold.

Hume, however, has a sustained argument to offer, an argument revived and restated by Armstrong, which I will now consider in the form given by Armstrong.[10]

Armstrong raises the question of how we should define *material thing* or *physical object*, and suggests that if we attempt a definition in terms of primary qualities alone we find that each primary quality either fails to distinguish a material thing from empty space or involves us in circularity. From this, he concludes that we must appeal to properties outside the class of primary qualities, that is, to the secondary qualities (unless we are prepared to countenance unknown and unknowable properties akin to the notorious substratum of Locke to mark off the material).

Suppose, for instance, appeal was made to shape, size, and duration to mark off the material, then Armstrong's objection is that 'we can speak of the shape, size and duration of an empty space or vacuum just as much as that of a physical object, so there is no differentiating mark there'.[11] While if appeal is made to solidity or impenetrability,

---

[10] In *Perception and the Physical World*, ch. 12. He rejects the conclusion of the argument in his later *A Materialist Theory of the Mind*, p. 282, but for a reason I do not find compelling. The argument has also been discussed in M. C. Bradley, 'A Note on a Circularity Argument'; N. Fleming, 'The Idea of a Solid'; and J. J. C. Smart, *Philosophy and Scientific Realism*, pp. 74–5.

[11] *Perception and the Physical World*, p. 185.

his objection is that 'impenetrability is a relation, and a relation that one physical object has to another physical object. But if this is so, we cannot make it a differentiating mark of a physical object, or part of a differentiating mark, on pain of circularity.'[12]

I will look first at Armstrong's argument concerning shape, size, and duration.[13] He points out that we can talk of the shape, size, and duration of an empty space. This is true but is not immediately to the point. What is at issue is whether appeal to the *properties* of shape, etc. serves to distinguish objects from empty space. Armstrong needs to show that empty spaces *have* certain properties, including shape, etc., not just that we can make sense of a statement like 'The space between those two cars is oblong.' For consider an event E which has no cause, then it will be true that nothing caused E. But no one will infer from this[14] that nothing has the property of causing E and so that E does, after all, have a cause, namely, nothing.

The crucial issue which needs to be considered is whether an empty space is part of what there is. If it is, then it may have properties, including, presumably, shape, size, and duration: if it is not, then there is no 'it' to have any properties at all; and a statement like 'The space between those two cars is oblong' will have to be reconstrued in such a way that it no longer appears to sustain the inference to 'There is something oblong, a space, between those two cars.'

The issue, then, is: 'Are there holes, do they exist?' David and Stephanie Lewis point out[15] that we certainly say things which suggest that there are – for example, 'There are many holes in that piece of cheese.' Can we either avoid this apparent ontic commitment or render it palatable? For surely, as it stands, to say that there are holes, empty spaces etc., is to take paradigm examples of *nothings* and make them into *somethings*.

One way of trying to avoid the apparent ontic commitment is to reconstrue 'There are holes in A' as 'A is perforated', but, as the Lewises observe, this kind of manoeuvre cannot handle statements like 'There are the same number of holes in A as in B' and 'The number of

---

[12] *Ibid.*, p. 187.
[13] It is here that Armstrong's argument differs most fom Hume's. Hume argues concerning such properties as these (he concentrates on extension and motion) that they presuppose either colour or solidity. He then argues concerning solidity in the same way as Armstrong.
[14] Especially after reading Hume, *Treatise*, book I, part III, §3, from which the example is taken.
[15] in 'Holes'.

people in this room is the same as the number of holes in that piece of cheese.'

One way of trying to render this apparent ontic commitment palatable is to *identify* holes with *hole-surrounds* or *hole-linings*, that is, with the bit of matter around the hole, and so make holes non-controversial, material somethings. But the Lewises give good reasons against this that I will not repeat here.

There is, fortunately, a third response available (not discussed by the Lewises). Holes are not hole-surrounds, for they are nothing at all; nor can statements 'about' holes in things be translated in terms of unstructured one-place predicates like 'is perforated' or 'has four holes'; but what can be done is to translate statements putatively about holes in terms of statements about hole-surrounds. 'There are many holes in that piece of cheese' just says that it contains many hole-surrounds; 'There are the same number of holes in *A* as in *B*' just says that *A* and *B* have the same number of hole-surrounds; and so on and so forth. To offer these translations is not to identify holes and hole-surrounds anymore than to translate statements about the average family in the usual way is to identify the average family with the families that there are.

It is, therefore, mistaken to hold that size, duration, and shape are properties of holes, empty spaces, vacuums, and so forth, because nothing can be a property of nothing. Can we, then, appeal to such properties to differentiate material things? No. Because after-images, for example, are not material things but have shape, etc. Moreover, unlike Armstrong, I am committed (by chapter 2) to allowing after-images as part of what there is. We can, however, appeal to size, shape, and duration (with the possible addition, depending on one's views about space, of position) to mark off *non-abstract things in general*, and so take the task of delimiting the class of material or physical things in general as that of appropriately adding to size, shape, duration, and position to exclude after-images and the like.

Locke added *solidity* or *impenetrability* to this list (preferring the first term for reasons not relevant here), and characterized it as 'that which . . . hinders the approach of two bodies, when they are moved one towards the other'.[16] Armstrong's already noted objection to this addition is circularity, on the ground that impenetrability is a relation between material things. But having three sides is a property of triangles; nevertheless, specifying a triangle in terms of its having

[16] *An Essay Concerning Human Understanding*, book II, ch. 4, § 'Idea of Solidity'.

three sides is not circular. In order to sustain the charge of circularity, it must be shown that impenetrability cannot be defined without reference to materiality: it is not sufficient just to observe that impenetrability is a relation between material things – of course it is, if it were not Locke's definition could be ruled out immediately on simple extensional grounds.

It seems, though, that impenetrability can be defined without reference to materiality, as follows. It is a fact about this world that some non-abstract things tend to spatially exclude each other – as Locke puts it, they hinder each other's (too near) approach. Let's call this relation 'resistance'. We can now define the class of impenetrable things as the class of non-abstract things that resist some other non-abstract thing. This class is, as a matter of fact in our world, near enough to the class of non-abstract things which resist *every* other non-abstract thing. So that in our world we can talk simply of being impenetrable; but, in other possible worlds, we would need to talk of being impenetrable relative to *this* class or *that* class of things. Now the definition just given is not circular. For we have already seen how to define non-abstract things in terms of size, etc., and resistance is evidently definable in terms of causal relations between non-abstract things; therefore, a definition of material things in terms of impenetrability cannot be convicted of circularity.

It seems to me, thus, that Armstrong's argument against defining material things in terms of such primary qualities as size, duration, shape, and impenetrability fails. And so, the case for saying that material things must have some secondary qualities fails.

In *A Materialist Theory of the Mind*, Armstrong's presentation of the argument just discussed is rather different, for he there emphasises the role of the doctrine that things cannot have only relational properties rather than the circularity charge. Here is the relevant passage:

I put the argument in the form [in *Perception and The Physicaι World*] 'How can we differentiate a physical object from empty space?' Mere spatial properties are insufficient, because physical objects share these with empty space. But if we look at the properties of physical objects that physicists are prepared to allow them, such as mass, electric charge, or momentum, these show a distressing tendency to dissolve into *relations* that one object has to another. What, then, are the things that have these relations to each other? Must they not have a non-relational nature if they are to sustain relations? But what is this nature? Physics does not tell us. It is here that the secondary qualities, conceived of as irreducible properties, are thrown into the breach to provide the stuffing for matter. [p. 282]

My reply to this argument will (I hope) be clear from what has been said above. 'Mere spatial properties' *are* sufficient to differentiate an object from empty space, and so the principle that every object must have some intrinsic property is satisfied by noting that shape is intrinsic. (It makes perfectly good sense to talk of the shape of the Universe as a whole, and so shape is not a relation.) It may be the case that the properties distinctive of physical and material objects, by contrast with non-abstract objects in general, are relational, but this is not objectionable. It just means that *physical* and *material* are relational notions.

It is also worth noting that the conclusion that mass and charge are relations is sometimes accepted too quickly. What is obvious and should be accepted quickly is that specifications of mass and charge *in units* are relational. To say that an object has a charge of so many *coulombs* or a mass of so many *grammes* is to assert a (highly complex) relationship between that object and the other objects in the Universe. This is clear from the way these units are specified in Physics' texts in terms of relations between objects.

(It might be thought that G. Schlesinger's, 'it is false that overnight everything has doubled in size', shows that this relational view is wrong. In this paper, Schlesinger argues that the supposition that *everything* doubled in size overnight makes perfect sense. And his style of argument could easily be directed to showing that the idea that everything doubled in mass or charge overnight makes perfect sense, and an overnight doubling in mass or charge is a doubling in mass or charge *in units* (from ten grammes to twenty grammes, etc.) Hence, it might appear that a fully relational view of the latter cannot be taken. But the possibility of an overnight doubling (granting for argument's sake that a Schlesinger-type argument can show this possible) shows not that a relational view is mistaken, but only that a relational view assuming the relata are objects *as they currently are* is mistaken. If Schlesinger is right, the relata of the mass-in-grammes and charge-in-coulombs relations are not merely present time-slices, but also past and future time-slices of objects; when I say that all objects have doubled their mass in grammes, I cannot mean that they have altered their masses relative to objects as they now are, but they will have altered their mass-in-grammes relationships with objects as they *were*, to *past* time-slices.)

However, although mass-in-grammes and charge-in-coulombs, for instance, are relations, it does not follow that having a mass and having a charge are relations. Why not say that having a charge of two coulombs is a relation, but having a charge *simpliciter* is not? This seems the right kind of thing to say for length. If there were, had been and would be only one (non-abstract) object, there would be no sense to saying it was two metres long. But it is clear that there might be such an isolated object, and that it would have to have *some* length: an object couldn't fail to have any length whatever. Thus, having length *simpliciter* is not a relation, though having a certain length in a certain unit is.

9. In 'Colours' and again in *Philosophy and Scientific Realism*, chapter 4, J. J. C. Smart puts forward a behaviourist theory of colour. He no longer accepts this theory, but some still do, for example, G. Pitcher in *A Theory Of Perception*,[17] and, as noted already, we are committed to denying it.

Here is Smart's statement of the theory.

> First of all it is necessary to introduce the notion of a *normal human percipient*. This must be done indirectly by means of a simpler notion, that of 'being more normal in a certain respect than . . .' I shall say that a person *A* is more normal than a person *B* with respect to a certain type of colour discrimination if he can discriminate things of a certain sort with respect to colour while *B* cannot do so.[18]

Smart claims that this definition of normal human percipient in terms of discrimination with respect to colour is non-circular on the ground that discrimination with respect to colour can be elucidated independently of colour. I do not accept this claim, but will accept it for the purpose at hand.

Smart then defines 'a normal percipient' as 'one who is at least as normal in respect of any colour discrimination as is any other percipient'.[19]

---

[17] See ch. 4, pp. 198–216.
[18] *Philosophy and Scientific Realism*, p. 76.
[19] *Ibid.*, p. 77.

This enables Smart to analyse '*x* is red' as: 'a normal human percipient would not easily pick this thing [*x*] out of a heap of geranium
petals, though he would easily pick it out of a heap of lettuce leaves.'[20]

It is not clear just how much of an *analysis* this, call it (*A*), is intended to be. Some of the things Smart says about it suggest that it is
merely intended to serve as a *recipe* for the introduction of the meaning
of the word 'red' in English to a non-speaker of English. Smart
acknowledges, for instance, that what he has offered is not an 'explicit
definition or translation of "red"', but, nevertheless, 'it is a perfectly
good *instruction* for . . . [e.g.] a foreigner learning English'.[21]

Construed as a recipe and with appropriate empirical details added
(by linguistics, not philosophy) there seems no real objection to what
Smart says. Equally, so construed, there is no threat to premise 1 of
§3. Premise 1 is not any kind of thesis about how to teach colour
words. It is only if construed as an analysis that there is any threat to
premise 1. However, construed as an analysis, there are grave objections to Smart's claim.

The usual objection to Smart's claim involves reference to the possibility of inverting the colour spectrum, of mapping each colour into
its complement on the colour wheel (red to green, blue to yellow, and
so on). I will not pursue it here: it's well enough known already, and it
involves complexities which we can, I believe, avoid.[22]

I will offer one, very simple, objection to Smart's theory (construed
as an analysis). As it stands, (*A*) entails the existence of geraniums
(and of lettuces, but let's leave this to one side), for *x* cannot be hard
to pick from the non-existent; while '*x* is red' does not. Is there any
way this quite disastrous consequence can be avoided?

It might be suggested that the reference to geranium petals be replaced by one to red things, thus making the account of '*x* is red' as
that *x* cannot be easily picked from red things (omitting details un-
important here). But this is blatantly circular.

It is also unsatisfactory to extend the number of paradigmatically
red things in (*A*) so that, for example, '*x* is red' is analysed in terms of
being hard to pick from geranium petals, pillar boxes, ripe tomatoes,
blood, and so on and so forth. For it is evident that the truth of '*x* is
red' does not entail the existence of *any* of these things: things might

[20] *Ibid.*, p. 79.

[21] *Ibid.*, p. 79, my emphasis.

[22] See, e.g., Smart's own discussion of the objection in *Philosophy and Scientific
Realism*, pp. 81–2, and Pitcher, *A Theory of Perception*, pp. 206ff.

have been red although the world contained no pillar boxes, no blood, no geraniums, no ripe tomatoes, and so on and so forth. Indeed, as we noted in chapter 2, it is logically possible that there should have been only *one* red thing.

The obvious reply at this point is to suggest a different reading of (*A*): instead of reading it so that it is existentially committed to geraniums, read it as asserting that *x* is hard to pick from geranium petals *if there are any such*. That is, in the possible case where there are no geranium petals (or blood, ripe tomatoes, etc. – the remarks that follow apply equally to all), we construe (*A*) as saying that *x* is red if it *would* be hard to pick from geranium petals if there were any. But *x* will be hard to pick from geranium petals in this case just if they are red. So the claim amounts to that in the possible worlds where there are no geranium petals (ripe tomatoes, etc.) but are red things, if there were geraniums, then they would be red. And, of course, this claim is absurdly strong. No doubt, in *some* possible worlds where there are no geraniums, if there were some, they would be red; but in other possible worlds where there are no geraniums, if there were some, they would be some colour other than red.

We have been concerned with Smart's behaviourist theory of colour. Obviously other behaviourist theories are possible: but it seems that they will all need to attempt an elucidation of '*x* is red' (to stick with this example) in terms of some behaviouristically elucidated relationship between *x* and other objects. Now if these other objects are designated as red, then the theory will be circular; while if they are specified via examples of well-known red things (well-known, that is, to persons employed in philosophy departments in the West), such as blood and geranium petals, the difficulties recently detailed will apply. Hence, I think we are entitled to reject behaviourist theories of colour in general.

10. This concludes my defence of the claim that colour is not a property of material things, and so completes the somewhat extended argument for the claim that the immediate objects of visual perception are always mental.

6

The objections to representationalism

o. Having now given what seems to me to be the case for holding that the immediate objects of visual perception are always mental sense-data, I turn to certain questions arising from this conclusion.

Many would reject our conclusion as follows: 'Your conclusion amounts to a denial of Direct Realism. This leaves you committed to one of Idealism (presumably of a phenomenalist variety) or Representationalism, and both face decisive objections.' My reply to this argument is that Representationalism does not face decisive objections. In this chapter I consider some of the very many objections that have been brought against Representationalism and argue that they all fail.

The principal objection to the Representative theory of perception is, of course, the epistemological one. And the main part of this chapter is devoted to it. But I want first to consider a number of lesser objections, as they serve, I think, to illustrate the way in which the Representative theory of perception has not been given the consideration due to it. For they are all characterized by their attributing to the theory some claim which simply is not part of it.

1. In *The Nature of Things*, A. Quinton argues that the Representative theory 'destroys the conditions of its own intelligibility. How can any theory about the nature of objects or their relation to impressions be understood if the only words we can understand are those which refer to impressions and it is assumed that words for objects cannot be defined in terms of them?' (p. 174)

Here Quinton is attributing two doctrines to Representationalism which are not part of it, (i), that 'the only words we can understand are those which refer to impressions', and, (ii), that words for objects cannot be defined in terms of words for impressions.

As far as the first attribution goes, the most one could say is that *some* representationalists have held certain views about the meaning of some (*not* all) words – examples being 'red' and 'square' – to the effect that we can understand them only by abstracting from experience, which – when combined with their representationalism – leads to the view that our understanding of these words derives from (*not* is limited to) their application to sense-impressions. This meaning doctrine may or may not be true, but it is in any case not an essential part of Representationalism.

The second attribution appears to be a misunderstanding of the representationalist's claim that sense-impressions and (material) objects are contingently (in particular, causally) related. This does not entail that the words for objects and those for sense-impressions are not interdefinable. The Representative theory is not a two-meaning theory, a theory that every term applied to both impressions and objects is radically ambiguous. The theory does deny the inter-translatability of *statements* about impressions and objects; but this is no more to the point than the impossibility of translating statements about the existence of oranges as ones about tomatoes, is relevant to whether 'is round' means the same applied to oranges and tomatoes. And it has, of course, been a prominent feature of our defence of sense-data that terms applied both to them and to objects are not equivocal. (This is not inconsistent with the conclusion of chapter 5: 'Colour and Science'. According to that conclusion, 'red' stands for the *same* property when it is applied to material things and when it is applied to sense-data, and so, it means the same – it is just that when applied to material things it stands for a property of sense-data as a matter of *empirical* fact.)

2. Likewise, consider Armstrong's objection that
> on the Representative theory the only thing that it is logically possible to perceive immediately is a sense-impression, while physical objects are things quite other than sense-impressions. So it is logically impossible to perceive physical objects immediately. But this means that any characteristic that sense-impressions have is a characteristic that physical objects cannot have. For consider the characteristic X which is a characteristic of a certain sense-impression. It must be an immediately perceivable characteristic, because sense-impressions are immediately perceivable. Now, by hypothesis, no characteristics of physical objects are immediately perceivable, therefore no physical object can have the characteristic X.[1]

This attributes to the Representative theory a doctrine which is not part of it.

---

[1] *Perception and the Physical World*, p. 31. For present purposes, Armstrong's sense-impressions may be taken to be our sense-data.

The theory holds that physical objects are *in fact* never immediately perceived, not that it is logically impossible for them to be immediately perceived. This is clear from the fact that the evidence for the claim is nearly always (and is in this work) avowedly *empirical*. It is, according to the theory, an empirical fact that sense-data are mental.

It might be thought that Armstrong's objection could be sustained in a form not exposed to this objection, namely, by urging that if X is a characteristic of physical objects it is a characteristic which *is not* (as a matter of fact) immediately perceived, according to the Representative theory; while if it is a characteristic of sense-data, it *is* immediately perceived (again, as a matter of fact). Hence, no characteristic, X, can belong to both physical objects and sense-data according to Representationalism.

But there is a further mis-attribution. The Representative theory does not hold that all characteristics of physical objects are not immediately perceived. It holds that the objects themselves, not their characteristics, are not immediately perceived. And all this implies concerning some characteristic, X, of a physical object is that it is not immediately perceived *when it qualifies a physical object*; and this does not contradict X being immediately perceived *when it qualifies a sense-datum*, anymore than Joe's being happy when at the races contradicts his being unhappy when at work.

The mistake of supposing Representationalism asserts the logical impossibility of immediately perceiving physical objects also lies behind Armstrong's final argument against the theory.

> Immediate perception and mediate perception are correlative terms. We can understand talking of the one only if it makes sense to talk about the other. Now if physical objects are mediately perceived, as the Representative theory asserts, then we can only understand this assertion if it makes sense to talk of their being immediately perceived . . . So it cannot be true, as the Representative theory asserts, that *it is logically impossible to perceive physical objects immediately*.[2]

Apart from the italicized mis-attribution, the argument is surely highly dubious. 'Material' and 'immaterial' are correlative terms, but no one supposes the (correct) doctrine that numbers are immaterial is in trouble because it is logically impossible that they be material. The most the observation that two terms are correlative can yield is

[2] *Ibid.*, p. 34, my italics.

that if one applies to something, it must be possible that the other apply to something, but not necessarily the same something.

3. I now come to the most widely canvassed objection to Representationalism, that it makes the external world it posits unknowable: if Representationalism were true, it is argued, we could not rationally believe that there are external objects or that they are of such and such a character. Despite the frequency with which this objection is regarded as decisive, it seems to me very hard to find any force in it.

The classic reference is Berkeley. For example, he argues:

> Suppose, what no-one can deny possible, an intelligence, without the help of external bodies, to be affected with the same train of sensations or ideas that you are, imprinted in the same order and with like vividness in his mind. I ask whether that intelligence hath not all the reason to believe the existence of Corporal Substances, represented by his ideas, and exciting them in his mind, that you can possibly have for believing the same thing? Of this there can be no doubt; which one consideration is enough to make any reasonable person suspect the strength of whatever arguments he may think himself to have for the existence of bodies without the mind.[3]

It is strange how often this passage is referred to by direct realists when presenting their case against Representationalism, for, as the last sentence makes quite clear, Berkeley regards himself as refuting 'the existence of bodies without the mind' – that is, *any* non-idealist theory of perception, not just Representationalism. It is also worth noting that what Berkeley claims 'no one can deny possible' would be denied by many philosophers today. For they would claim that *a priori* considerations show that it does not make sense to suppose that all, or even most, of our perceptions are illusory; they claim, for example, that the notion of an illusion presupposes that most of our perceptions are veridical.[4] If this is right, Berkeley's argument proceeds from a false premise. But let's suppose (as I must confess seems to me plausible) that Berkeley is right about the logical possibility of total illusion, for the purposes of our discussion.

The principal difficulty with the passage as an argument against Representationalism is that all it establishes is that our evidence for believing in external bodies cannot be regarded as *deductive*, it does

---

[3] *Principles of Human Knowledge*, §20.
[4] See, e.g. G. Ryle, *Dilemmas*, Ch. VII.

not *logically entail* the existence of external bodies. But, of course, there are many cases of (very) good reasons which are not deductive – indeed, most good reasons are not. Hence, without additional argument to show that the representationalist cannot hold that the evidence of our senses provides good reason for believing in external objects, Berkeley's argument can appeal only to the sceptic about induction.

Is there such additional argument available? Berkeley's main attempt to provide it rests on an implausible doctrine about cause which virtually no one now accepts.[5] But contemporary writers have attempted to provide it by arguing that a certain general principle governs non-deductive support of the relevant kind, and that Representationalism entails the violation of this principle.

4. This principle is that in order to argue inductively from the characteristics of Xs to the existence and/or characteristics of Ys, it is necessary that sometimes both Xs and Ys be observed directly. If this principle is correct, Representationalism is in trouble for its adherents will be unable to argue inductively from the characteristics of sense-data to external objects.

Now there is a general difficulty facing discussion of this principle. It would be nice to be able to expound the standard, accepted theory of inductive inference, and then assess the principle by reference to that theory. But there is no standard, accepted theory. The problem of induction is one of the major, unsolved problems in philosophy. The best we can do is to assess the principle by reference to the many examples of inductive practices that we all grant to be rational.

A great many of these examples can be seen as instances of the pattern: As which have been directly observed have been observed to be B; therefore, all (many, most, etc.) As are B. And it is clear that this pattern will yield the principle in question – or near enough for Representationalism to be in trouble. But it is also true that a great many examples of inductive practice we all take to be rational fall under a quite different pattern, that known as Hypothetico-deductive method or as argument to the best explanation; and many such examples violate the principle in question.

Consider a familiar example, the Molecular theory of gases. The Molecular theory of gases explained the various experimentally observed properties of gases embodied in gas laws like Boyle's, Charles' and Dalton's, and enabled the prediction of new properties which were

---

[5] See, e.g. *Principles of Human Knowledge*, §19. The doctrine is that matter cannot act on spirit.

subsequently experimentally verified. On this basis and *prior* to the direct observation of molecules, it became universally accepted that gases are made up of sub-microscopic particles (molecules). And similar remarks apply to the whole development of the atomic theory of matter in all its forms.

The moral for the Representative theory is clear: construe the external world as like the molecules of the Molecular theory of gases, that is, as things which we may justifiably believe in, and believe to have various properties, on the basis of their explanatory power, without their ever being directly observed.

Once we view the matter in this way, we can see how to reply to Quinton's objection (further to the one already discussed) that 'Any representative theory requires us to accept some contingent proposition asserting relations of causation, and perhaps resemblance, between objects and impressions [sense-data]. In requiring this proposition to be accepted prior to the justification of any beliefs about objects it rules out its own justification.'[6] Quinton's claim is that in order to justify *any* belief about objects, the representationalist needs to establish *first* a relation between objects and sense-data, but the latter involves, of course, beliefs about objects; so to justify any belief about objects, we need to have already justified some beliefs about objects. This is the essence of Quinton's charge against Representationalism.

Suppose, however, someone argued in the same way against the Molecular theory of gases, namely, that it requires us to accept certain contingent propositions relating gas molecules to gas phenomena; and in requiring these propositions to be accepted prior to the justification of any beliefs about molecules, it rules out its own justification. The reply in this case is clear. The hypothetico-deductive mode of inductive argument is *not hierarchical*. One does not first establish one part of the explanatory hypothesis and then build from that; one formulates (guesses, divines, . . .) the hypothesis as near complete as possible, and then works back to the phenomena to see whether assuming the hypothesis provides a good explanation of them.

Likewise, the representationalist can reply to Quinton that one does not *first* establish causal links between objects and sense-data and *then* use them to establish beliefs about objects. Our beliefs about objects, *all* of them (including the ones about causal links between sense-data and objects), form a theory, 'the theory of the external world', which

[6] *The Nature of Things*, p. 174.

is then justified by its explanatory and predictive power with respect to our sense-data.

I will now consider four objections to the attempt to appeal to the Hypothetico-deductive method to justify the external world theory of the representationalist.

5. In *Perception*, Price urges that, instead of the hypothesis of an external world much as we suppose it to be, there are a 'thousand and one others which we might have thought of, most of them so much simpler'.[7] But are there? Price mentions only Berkeley's God hypothesis, and *that* hypothesis is certainly not simpler.

Broadly, there are two ways we can conceive of the God hypothesis. We can take it as holding that God produces each sense-impression we have in a separate act, quite unrelated to any other act; or we can suppose that God proceeds according to some general plan. If the former, the God hypothesis can be ruled out straight away, because it will lack any predictive power. It merely tells us that God produces the sense-impressions he does produce. This is no explanation, it is only an elaboration of what is to be explained.

On the other hand, if we understand the God hypothesis as asserting that God proceeds according to some plan (as Berkeley certainly did), the hypothesis will no longer be simpler than that of the external world. The problem of our knowledge of the external world is just being replaced by the problem of our knowledge of God's plan. Spelling out God's plan will be just as complicated a business as spelling out our conception of the external world.

Moreover, no one (including Price) would dream of reading a paper to a scientific society arguing that the God hypothesis is superior to the Molecular theory of gases. It seems, therefore, that the *onus probandi* lies with Price to show that there is some crucial difference between the Molecular theory of gases and the theory of an external world.

Generally it seems to me that the correct response to one who claims against the representationalist that there are many hypotheses simpler and better than the external world hypothesis is the same as that to one who claims that there are many hypotheses simpler and better than the Molecular theory of gases, namely, that such a claim must be backed by actually giving in detail an alternative hypothesis. And this no one has ever been able to do in either case. Price asks, for instance, 'Why should the cause of the sense-data be in space at all?'[8] But this

7 Price, *Perception*, p. 89.   8 *Ibid.*, p. 90.

is an objection only if allied with an *articulated theory* which has the causes non-located; what is required is not a rhetorical question but an alternative theory.

6. In the same section, Price also argues against the hypothetico-deductive approach (to the epistemological objection to Representationalism) as follows:

> how do we come to think of this hypothesis? Do we just invent it out of the blue? And if we do, how have we been clever enough to think of just this hypothesis, with just these particular details (such complex detail too) ... Of course we do not invent it. We have already on other grounds formed a conception of the physical world, and moreover of this particular physical world containing just this square table in front of me. And we must note that the difficulty arises not once only but many times over. We must modify our assumption to keep pace with what we call scientific discovery, or indeed with the continual growth of our own experience. Something new is always happening, and whether we like it or not we are always coming across fresh sense-data whose determinate characteristics and relations are new to us, though their generic characteristics are not.[9]

As far as the first point concerning the origin of the hypothesis goes, there is a misunderstanding of the nature of hypothetico-deduction. It matters not whether an apple caused Newton to think of the theory of Gravitation or whether having a bath caused Archimedes to think of Archimedes' principle; what matters is the explanatory and predictive power of these theories regardless of how they came to be thought of in the first place.

The second point – the one introduced by 'And we must note ...' – is difficult to grasp at first reading, but I *think* it can be best understood if taken in conjunction with Price's concluding remarks on the Method of Hypothesis (his name for the hypothetico-deductive approach):

> the so-called justification of the hypothesis does not consist (as it should) in showing that from the assumption certain conclusions follow which are identical with the observed facts; what we really do is to argue the other way about – from the observed facts, the characteristics and correlations of our sense-data, and the so-called assumption is our conclusion, not our premise.[10]

[9] *Ibid.,* p. 89.   [10] *Ibid.,* p. 91.

I think Price's essential point here is that we go from sense-data to physical objects, not the other way around; and that this is particularly clear if we bear in mind the difficulty of anticipating nature. We frequently don't know what is going to happen, and in such cases we don't first form a set of competing hypotheses and then test them against our future sense-data. Rather, we wait for the future sense-data and *then* form the hypothesis.

All this is true, but not an objection. The hypothesis of the Method of Hypothesis is *not* that there is a square table in that room, a red tomato on that mantelpiece, and so on; it is not, that is, a set of *particular* hypotheses. It is, rather, a *general* hypothesis to the effect that there are external objects existing independently of us whose properties bear a systematic relationship to those of our sense-data (the spelling out of this relationship involving the best current theories in optics, the physiology of sense-organs, etc.). It is this general hypothesis which is tested against particular cases. The more particular hypothesis that there is a square table in that room, and so on are, as Price observes, derived *from* the nature of our sense-data together with the general hypothesis. Hence, Price's observation immediately above that 'we argue the other way about – from the observed facts, the characteristics and correlations of our sense-data' is no objection, for it is true of the various particular hypotheses, not the general one. Likewise, Price's remark in the first quotation of this section that 'we must modify our assumption to keep pace with what we call scientific discovery, or indeed with the continual growth of our own experience' applies to the various particular hypotheses only (and, hence, is misleading in its use of the singular 'assumption').

7. Armstrong has a quite different objection to the hypothetico-deductive approach, which runs thus:

> surely we are not prepared to degrade bodies into hypotheses? We want to say that our assurance of the existence of the physical world is far stronger than any assurance we could obtain by indirectly [hypothetico-deductively] confirming a theory. If the Representative theory were true, it would be proper to have a lurking doubt about the existence of the physical world. Yet such a doubt does not seem proper.[11]

I think Armstrong is trading here on an equivocation on the word

---

[11] *Perception and the Physical World*, p. 30. Armstrong does not take this objection to be apodeictic.

'hypothesis'. On one common meaning, an hypothesis is little better than an informed guess. And it is clear that 'we are not prepared to degrade bodies into hypotheses' on this meaning. But this is not the meaning of 'hypothesis' relevant to the hypothetico-deductive method. One can be absolutely certain of something on hypothetico-deductive grounds, as, for example, we are of the theory of Gravitation and of the Molecular theory of gases. More precisely, we are absolutely certain that the theory of Gravitation and the Molecular theory of gases are correct in outline, while allowing the possibility of considerable change concerning more detailed parts of the theories. It is not 'proper to have a lurking doubt' about the correctness in outline of the Molecular theory of gases. Hence, the representationalist can maintain that it is not proper to have a lurking doubt about the existence of the external world, though he must allow that many matters of detail (and important ones) are unclear. And this latter concession seems right. Surely there is much concerning the fundamental nature of the world and its causal links with our senses that remains to be discovered.

8. Now for a more general objection. It might be objected that our comments in defence of Representationalism against the epistemological objection have been excessively negative. We have shown, perhaps, that the usual arguments to the conclusion that Representationalism makes the external world unknowable are not decisive. But, it might be argued, this is not enough. Our knowledge that there is an external world is as secure as anything we know, and so the best theory of perception is the theory that makes our knowledge as secure as possible, namely, Direct Realism.

What lies behind this objection is the very common assumption that Direct Realism is epistemologically superior to Representationalism. I think this assumption is mistaken and that the two theories are on a par regarding our knowledge of the external world.

It helps to introduce the issue by reference to a related one concerning our knowledge of other minds. It is often suggested that a principal source of the other minds problem is the impossibility of being directly aware of another's pain (say).[12] But suppose (*per impossible?*) that I was on some occasion directly aware of someone else's pain, that a pain of his was not just qualitatively similar but numerically identical with one of mine. Would this really help? Surely, in addition to having his pain, I would need to know that I was having it. But this would

[12] For a classic statement of this view see A. J. Ayer, 'One's Knowledge of Other Minds'.

require me to know at least that he was in pain, and so, it appears, nothing would have been gained. We need, that is, not just direct awareness but also knowledge of direct awareness.

Likewise, the direct realist cannot answer the question of how we know that an object, *A*, exists and has certain properties merely by pointing out that he allows that we may immediately perceive *A*. Immediate perception of *A* is not sufficient. We need also, (i), to know that we are immediately perceiving *A*, and, (ii), to know whether or not *A* is looking as it really is. Take the ubiquitous red tomato. Even if we grant the direct realist's claim that we immediately perceive it, in order to know that it exists, we need to know that we are so perceiving it; and in order to know that it is red, we need to know that it is looking the colour it really is.

The point emerges very clearly from the kind of examples used to discredit Representationalism. G. J. Warnock remarks, for instance, that 'To decide that a protrait is a good likeness of a man, I must look both at the portrait and at the man',[13] in the course of urging that the representationalist cannot justify taking sense-data to represent physical objects. We have already argued that the possibility of a hypothetico-deductive justification shows that looking at the man (object) is not a necessary condition. It is, moreover, not sufficient. Looking at the man is of no help in deciding whether the portrait is a good likeness unless I know that I am looking at him, and know that the way he looks to me is the way he actually is. Looking at the President will not help me to decide if a certain portrait is a good likeness if I do not know that it's the President I'm looking at; or if I do, but do not know that he is heavily disguised.

I will concentrate first on the point that an object may look other than it is. Suppose that I am looking at a tomato and that (somehow) I know that I am. How can the direct realist explain how I can be justified in believing that it is, say, red.[14] We have already noted that he cannot simply refer to the fact that the tomato looks red, for things do not always look as they are. Clearly, he will have to construct some kind of inductive argument from the way things look to the way they are. But in doing this he will face the same general problem that besets the representationalist. We have already noted the familiar point that

---

[13] *Berkeley*, p. 102.
[14] I'm assuming a Direct Realism which treats colour as an objective property of external objects. The same point could be made with shape if other forms of Direct Realism were at issue.

the representationalist cannot argue from sense-data to objects on the pattern: *A*s which have been directly observed have been observed to be *B*; therefore, all (many, etc.) *A*s are *B*. The same applies to the direct realist.

Just as the representationalist cannot establish *observationally* a correlation between sense-data of certain kinds and objects of certain kinds, because he cannot allow that objects may be observed independently of observing sense-data; equally the direct realist cannot establish *observationally* a correlation between the colour something looks to have and the colour it actually has, because he cannot allow that the colour something has may be observed independently of observing the colour it *looks* to have. Observing the colour an object actually has is observing the colour it looks to have in the case where the two are the same: there are not *two* ways of observing an object – one giving the colour it looks to have, the other the real colour. Observation just gives, necessarily, the apparent colour, which may or may not be the real colour.

What the direct realist must do is justify his beliefs about the colours of objects hypothetico-deductively, by noting that an object's *having* a certain colour or shape or distance away from one would *explain* its *looking* the colours, shapes, etc. it does and would lead to predictions which may be checked. So we see that the direct realist is committed to a hypothetico-deductive approach in the same way as the representationalist.

The general position is this. The representationalist and the direct realist differ profoundly over the ontology of the looks–is distinction, but are in the same situation regarding the epistemology of the distinction. The representationalist insists that *there is* something bearing the apparent properties, and his epistemic problem is to justify going from this something – the sense-datum – and its properties, to the object. The direct realist avoids the additional *entity* by giving objects an additional *characteristic* – of the looking so-and-so kind, but still has an epistemic problem, that of going from these characteristics to the actual properties of the object. And it appears that, despite the difference in ontology, the basic approach to the epistemic problem has to be the same in both cases.

The epistemological problem for Representationalism has two aspects: one concerns whether the theory can allow that we know that external objects *exist*; the other concerns whether the theory can allow that we know what these external objects are *like*, their nature as well as their existence. It might be granted that the argument just given shows that Representationalism and Direct Realism are on a par concerning the second aspect, while being urged that Direct Realism is definitely superior concerning the first.

We noted, however, that immediate perception of A doesn't settle all epistemological problems concerning object A; we need, in addition, to know, (i), that one is immediately perceiving A, and, (ii), whether A is looking as it is. The argument just given centered on (ii); I will now argue that reference to (i) shows that Direct Realism is not epistemologically superior concerning the existence of external objects any more than it is concerning their nature.

'How can it be suggested for a moment that Direct Realism faces any kind of problem over the existence of external objects? The direct realist holds that we sometimes immediately perceive these objects, and this *entails* that they exist!' But, of course, the representationalist holds that we sometimes immediately perceive sense-data which belong to external objects, and that entails logically that these external objects exist – 'x belongs to y' entails 'y exists'.

No one is going to be satisfied with this reply on behalf of Representationalism on the (correct) ground that in holding that we sometimes immediately perceive sense-data which belong to external objects, he is assuming that we are not always hallucinating – which is the essential point at issue. But, equally, the direct realist who urges that we sometimes immediately perceive external objects is assuming that we are not always under an hallucination. How can he justify this assumption?

He cannot refer to the arguments for Direct Realism, because they are of an essentially negative character. They are, for example, to the effect that the Arguments from Illusion and Time-gap fail to show we are not immediately aware of external objects. These arguments do not show that there are external objects, only that certain arguments which *assume* that there are and attempt to show that, even so, we are not immediately aware of them, fail. He may, perhaps, attempt some kind of *a priori* argument like that adverted to earlier from the concept of a hallucination to the logical impossibility of total, universal hallucination; but, as noted, this kind of argument is equally available to a representationalist.

This leaves only the possibility of an inductive justification: now one such justification that comes to mind straight away is in terms of the manifest ability of the hypothesis of external objects to explain and predict our sense-experience. But this is to justify the assumption that we are not always under hallucination by a hypothetico-deductive argument in just the way the representationalist does.

The alternative would be to attempt an argument on the pattern: *A*s which have been directly observed have been observed to be *B*; therefore, all (many, etc.) *A*s are *B*. But this is no more available to the direct realist than it is to the representationalist. For there is no *intrinsic* mark of the non-hallucinatory. As noted in chapter 4, any sense-experience might be hallucinatory: on any occasion where I am perceiving some physical object, I might have exactly the same experience and yet be perceiving nothing. This means that there is no such thing as *observing* that an experience is veridical – one cannot (and does not) look for the special 'glow of the veridical' about one's experiences to establish that they derive from external objects. Instead, what one must do, and what one does do, is obtain *other* sense-experiences and see what sense can be made of the corpus – that is, one argues hypothetico-deductively. In other words, one cannot argue from a correlation between sense-experiences and objects to a sense-experience on a given occasion corresponding to an object, because there is no *independent* way of observing objects: one can't observe an object without having a sense-experience.

9. The discussion thus far has been traditional in the following sense. It has taken the problem of justifying our belief in an external world to be the problem of justifying an *inference* based on *sense-experience* or '*the evidence of our senses*'.

This traditional empiricist assumption at least appears to be denied in some recent writings on perception, notably in those of Quinton and J. L. Austin.[15] It is, notoriously, very hard to fruitfully discuss assumptions as fundamental as this one. It is – like the Quinean one that 'there is' equals 'exists', and the non-Quinean one that there is an analytic–synthetic distinction – the kind of assumption in terms of which philosophical discussion proceeds rather than to which it is directed. I suspect that assumptions as fundamental as these are finally to be judged not in themselves, but in terms of the edifices erected upon them – they are a case where the proof of the pudding is in the eating. And, in the case of the assumption concerning 'the evidence of our senses', it is certainly true that one major ground for rejecting it has been the belief that it leads to nothing but trouble, for example, sense-data and Representationalism. Hence, if our defence of sense-data and

[15] Quinton, 'The Problem of Perception'; Austin, *Sense and Sensibilia*.

Representationalism has been successful, we have undermined this ground and, to this extent, defended the assumption.

The other main ground given for rejecting the assumption has been that, as a matter of evident psychological fact, we don't usually first form beliefs about how things look and feel and then form beliefs about how they are. We have already endorsed this claim of psychological fact in chapter 1, §10. It seems to me, however, to carry little epistemological weight. What is at issue is how we *justify* our perceptual beliefs, not how we *arrive* at them. Moreover, when there is some kind of difficulty, we *do* refer to our sense-experience. 'Surely they are too *shiny* to be real flowers, they must be plastic'; 'It was too *vivid* to have been a dream'; 'The outline is too *indistinct* for me to tell'; and so on and so forth.

There is another reason which might be offered deriving from recent work on knowledge. Prompted in part by E. Gettier's argument that true justified belief may not be knowledge,[16] causal theories of knowledge have been advanced which essentially take a belief that *p* to constitute knowledge if it bears the appropriate causal relation to *p*.[17] Now someone who accepted such an approach might argue that the key issue is whether we *know* that there is an external world of a certain kind, and the answer to this question has nothing to do with inferences from sense-experience but has to do with the existence of causal links. I don't wish to discuss whether such theories are true. I just want to note the obvious points that, first, such theories cannot threaten Representationalism for it explicitly asserts causal links between minds and the external world, and, secondly, that such theories do not negate the significance of the hypothetico-deductive approach: they merely re-locate its target; it will bear on whether we are justified in taking ourselves to know rather than on whether we know *simpliciter*.[18]

There is a final, overriding reason why challenges to the traditional empiricist assumption cannot threaten our defence of Representationalism against the epistemological objection, namely, that *the objection makes the assumption*. The objection consists in urging that Representationalism cannot justify the inference from sense-data to external

---

[16] 'Is Justified True Belief Knowledge?'

[17] See, e.g., A. Goldman, 'A Causal Theory of Knowing'; what follows applies generally to what Armstrong calls 'Externalist Theories' in *Belief, Truth and Knowledge*, ch. 11.

[18] I am indebted here to J. B. Maund and Chris Mortensen.

objects, and such an inference is in point only if the traditional assumption is correct. This reply would not be available to us if we had drawn the mediate–immediate distinction in the usual epistemological way, because this way appeals to the assumption in question – that is, we would already have been committed to the assumption. But we drew the distinction analytically and so are in a position to say: either the traditional empiricist assumption is true, in which case our hypothetico-deductive reply to the epistemological objection to Representationalism stands; or else it is false, in which case the epistemological objection is mistaken from the very beginning.

10. I should emphasise in conclusion that the aim of this chapter is *not* to expound and defend a representative theory of perception. It is, rather, to defend the Sense-datum theory from the objection that it leads to either Idealism or Representationalism, and that both of these face decisive objections. My case has been that Representationalism does not face decisive objections; that is, I have argued that a representative style of theory is defensible; I have not argued which *particular* representative theory should be preferred. The choice of a particular representative theory depends on the precise analysis of the belonging-to relation between external objects and sense-data. I offer and defend an analysis of this relation in the second half of the next, final chapter.

7

Seeing things and seeing that

0. In the first part of this chapter I honour the undertaking made in chapter 1, §1, to show that seeing things is more basic than seeing-that. I attempt to do this by arguing (i) that seeing things cannot be analysed in terms of seeing-that, and (ii) that seeing-that can be analysed in terms of seeing things. In the second part of this chapter I comment further on the analysis of seeing things. In particular, I offer, by way of completing my defence of Representationalism, an account of the belonging-to relation between sense-data and material objects.

1. One good reason for doubting that seeing things can be analysed in terms of seeing-that is the extreme complexity of attempts at such.[1] But we can, I think, avoid these complexities because the general lines that any such attempt must follow are sufficiently clear for the objections I wish to press.

In the spirit of keeping things simple in order to keep them as clear as possible, I will usually consider cases of seeing-that where S sees that something, A, is F, rather than more complex cases like S seeing that A is R to B, or S seeing that A is F or G, or S seeing that an A will F soon. Also, I will for the next few sections confine myself to what Fred I. Dretske calls cases of *primary epistemic seeing*.[2]

Dretske refers to cases where S sees that ... as cases of epistemic seeing, and points out that sometimes S may see A is F because (in some sense) he sees A, while other times he does not see A at all. He refers to the former as primary, the latter as secondary. I can, for instance, see that the desk I am writing on is brown because (in part) I can see the desk; this is thus a case of primary epistemic seeing. But I can also see that the petrol in my car is running low, although I cannot see the petrol – what I can see, rather, is the gauge; this is thus a secondary case.

In confining myself to the primary case, I am obviously making

---

[1] See, e.g., §3 of J. W. Roxbee-Cox's, 'An Analysis of Perceiving in Terms of the Causation of Beliefs I'.

[2] *Seeing and Knowing*, pp. 78ff.

things simpler for advocates of analysing seeing things in terms of seeing-that. So, in the context of an argument against such advocates, there is no objection to this procedure.

2. It is clear that 'S sees A' cannot be analysed as 'S sees that A is F.' This follows immediately from the fact that, while 'A' in 'S sees A' is subject to substitutivity (of co-referential terms), it is not in 'S sees that A is F'. As we noted in the introduction

$(A = B)$ & S sees A. $\supset$ S sees B

is valid. While, on the other hand,

$(A = B)$ & S sees that A is F. $\supset$ S sees that B is F.

is not valid. For instance, if the pleasant looking man in plain clothes is a policeman, then the financier absconding to Brazil who sees the pleasant looking man in plain clothes sees the policeman – even though he is, we may suppose, unaware of the fact. But he may see *that* the pleasant looking man in plain clothes is approaching him, without seeing that the policeman is approaching him. Again, the poisoner's victim may see that his coffee is being poured without seeing that the coffee containing arsenic is being poured.

The obvious way to try and circumvent this difference in the logic of 'S sees A' and 'S sees that A is F', this difference which prevents a simple analysis of the former in terms of the latter, is to consider certain substitution instances of 'S sees that – is F' got by replacing the blank by a term designating A (one, but only one, of which is 'A'). Thus one might try to analyse 'S sees A' in terms of the truth of 'S sees – is F' for at least one substitution instance got by replacing the blank by a term designating A.[3] (I have left the interpretation of the 'is F' part to one side as the points that follow do not depend on it.)

There are, however, as we will now see, fundamental problems with this approach. They arise from the consideration that some things lack (proper) names. I have a name, you have a name, numbers have names; but very many things do not. For example, most blades of grass and most molecules do not.

This means that we cannot, in general, give an account of S seeing something in terms of the truth of 'S sees that – is F' for some name of it substituted in the blank. For the thing seen may have no name. It might be suggested that we handle cases where there are no names conditionally: if the thing had a name, then 'S sees that – is F' would be true when the name was substituted. But it should be obvious from

[3] This is the general approach favoured by Roxbee-Cox, *op. cit.*

earlier arguments that this will not do. Briefly, imagine a variant on Rumpelstiltskin who has no name and is determined to vanish should he be given one, and suppose I see him. Obviously it is not the case that if he had a name, N, I would see that N is F.

What, then, of definite descriptions? Because of the truth (be it necessary or contingent) of the Identity of Indiscernibles, everything is designated by some definite description. The problem here is rather that the person seeing something may not have any idea at all of what definite descriptions apply to it. Suppose I am looking at a large brick wall, then I will see a great many bricks, including, say, the seventy-first from the left. But it is very unlikely that I will see that the seventy-first brick from the left is, say, red; I will not see that the seventy-first brick from the left is anything. Likewise, someone watching wheat grains pouring from a silo may see the ten millionth one without seeing that the ten millionth one is so-and-so. Again, when I watch people pouring from a football ground after the game, I do not see that the fifteen thousandth to leave is a Richmond supporter, or that the fifteen thousand and first person to leave the ground is a Carlton supporter, though I may see both the fifteen thousandth and the fifteen thousand and first persons to leave.

Therefore, though everything I see has a definite description designating it, many things I see lack a definite description which yields a truth when substituted in a statement of the form 'I see that – is F.'

At this point, it might be suggested that we turn to indefinite descriptions. In the wall case, it may be granted that I do not see that the seventy-first brick from the left is red (let us suppose the wall both is and looks red), but – it may (correctly) be pointed out – I will see that a brick in the general region is red, indeed I may well see that all of them are red. It may, thus, be suggested that 'S sees A' counts as true if 'S sees that – is F' is true for at least one indefinite singular term true of A substituted in the blank.

This final suggestion, however, makes it far too easy for 'S sees A' to be true. Looking out the window, I can see that a brick in the wall opposite is red. The indefinite description 'a brick in the wall opposite' is true of *every* brick in the wall opposite, but it need not be true that I see every brick in the wall opposite. Again, I see that a drawing pin has fallen to the floor. 'A drawing pin' is true of every drawing pin, but I do not see every drawing pin.

It seems, therefore, that attempts to analyse seeing things in terms of seeing-that face a destructive dilemma. In view of the noted difference in logical behaviour under substitution, the account must proceed in terms of selected substitution instances of 'seeing-that' schemas; and either these instances are formed by substituting definite singular terms or indefinite ones. If definite, be they names or definite descriptions, it becomes too hard for statements about seeing things to be true; if indefinite, it becomes too easy for them to be true.

3. The preceding line of argument rests heavily on the point that constructions of the form 'S sees that A is F' are opaque. In order to reinforce this point, it is important to distinguish this construction from 'S sees A is F' (without the 'that'). And the discussion of this distinction will lead to an important qualification.

A construction of the form 'S sees A is F' is ambiguous. It can be taken opaquely as 'S sees that A is F', or transparently as 'S sees of A that it is F'. (More precisely, it is 'S sees of – that it is F' which is a transparent mode of containment for singular terms, in Quine's sense, *Word and Object*, §30. 'S sees of A that it is –' is still an opaque mode of containment for general terms.)

Consider again our financier absconding to Brazil. We noted the obvious point that he may see that the pleasant-looking man is approaching him without seeing that the detective is. But, nevertheless, surely we want to acknowledge that there is someone that he sees is approaching him, and this someone cannot be the pleasant-looking man without being the detective; so there is someone – who *is* the detective – that he sees is approaching him, without it being the case that he sees that the detective is approaching him. The only way to make sense of all this is to acknowledge two readings for 'The financier sees the detective approaching him.' On one it is false: the financier does not see that the detective is approaching him. On the other it is true: the detective does see of the detective that he is approaching him. It is this duality of readings which enables the detective to report at the subsequent court hearing that the accused saw *him* approaching without, fortunately, seeing that the detective on his trail was approaching.

Quine's dictum[4] – which I accept – against quantifying into opaque contexts is to the point here. For we have a contrast between seeing that there is something which is F, and there being something which is seen to be F. A distant wheat field has a sufficient tinge of green for me to see that some of the ears are unripe, without there being any ear of wheat such that I see that it is unripe: 'I see that $(\exists x)$ x is unripe' is

[4] See, e.g., his 'Three Grades of Modal Involvement'.

true, while '$(\exists x)$ I see that x is unripe' is false. Again, I look at two very similar paintings and see that one is a copy of the other, but I cannot tell which is the copy and which is the original: I see that there is an x such that x is a copy, but there is no x such that I see that x is a copy. We must, therefore, allow a transparent locution in addition to the familiar opaque one.

What I am suggesting, then, is an extension of Quine's distinction between transparent and opaque belief-locutions[5] to seeing-that. Moreover, the distinction in the case of belief will be important later, so it may be as well to briefly rehearse it.

The statement 'I believe (that) George Blake is a spy' is most naturally taken to be about a certain proposition, namely, that George Blake is a spy. It is not about George Blake, but about the proposition; for if it were about Blake, the man, then 'George Blake' in 'I believe that George Blake is a spy' would be subject to substitutivity.

This is because George Blake does not alter with the mode of reference to him. Suppose the man next to me in the bus is George Blake, then the man next to me and Blake share all characteristics. Hence, if 'I believe that George Blake is a spy' were about George Blake, what it said about him would be equally true of the man next to me in the bus: it could make no truth-value difference whether he was referred to one way or the other. But, notoriously, it may. I may believe that George Blake is a spy without believing that the man next to me in the bus is a spy, even though they are one and the same. (For many years the British Secret Service did not believe that Kim Philby was a spy, though they did believe that 'the third man' was a spy, and Kim Philby was the third man. Hence, their belief was about a proposition, not about the third man. For everything true of the third man was true of Kim Philby.)

Hence, belief statements are normally about propositions, not about persons, trees, ships, and so on. But it would be absurd to refuse to allow that beliefs about persons (or trees, and so on) are possible. We obviously sometimes do believe things about people. Contrast, for instance, the case where I believe that the tallest spy is a spy because of my knowledge of elementary logic and the fact that no two people are exactly the same height, with the case where the tallest spy is pointed out to me as a spy. In the first case it is clear that my belief

---

[5] See, e.g., *Word and Object*, §30. Though the remarks about this distinction that follow derive from Quine, he should not, of course, be held in any way responsible for my way of putting the matter.

is about a proposition, but, in the second, surely my belief is (or at least may be) about a person – the person pointed out to me.

It is in the second case that it might well be true not just that I believed – like most of us – that someone is a spy, but also – unlike most of us – that there was someone whom I believed to be a spy.

Moreover, sometimes we do wish to allow substitutivity in belief-contexts. We all want to assert that the CIA believed its greatest failure (the Bay of Pigs invasion) would be a success, but no one thinks that the CIA believed the proposition that its greatest failure would be a success. Its belief was, rather, *about* its greatest failure.

It, therefore, seems that we must distinguish between the opaque, propositional construction '*S* believes that *A* is *F*', and the transparent construction '*S* believes of *A* that it is *F*.' (To confine ourselves to the simplest case of a one-place predicate with singular term following 'believes'; extensions to *n*-place predicates and so on are dealt with by Quine in *Word and Object*, §31–5.)

Now for the important qualification heralded at the beginning of this section. My arguments against analysing seeing things in terms of seeing-that apply only to the opaque seeing-that locution. I do not think that seeing *A* can be in any way analysed in terms of seeing that *A* is *F*, or in terms of seeing that *B* is *F*, where *A* = *B*; but it may be the case that seeing *A* can be analysed in terms of seeing of *A* that it is *F*. But if this is the case (I do not know if it is), it is not any kind of objection to the approach of this work. For '*S* sees of *A* that it is *F*' may be taken to express a relation between *A* and *S*, because '*A*' in it is subject to substitutivity. Hence it accords with the approach of this work: the attempt to analyse seeing in terms of relations between persons and things.

4. I now turn to the positive task of providing an analysis of seeing-that (henceforth understood opaquely) in terms of seeing things. I will start by tackling primary seeing-that and later define the secondary sense in terms of the primary one. I will again largely restrict the discussion to the case where the sentence following 'sees that' is of the form '*A* is *F*.'

First, I need to be more restrictive than Dretske about what counts as a primary case of epistemic seeing. Sometimes we see that *A* is *F* because *A looks F*. For example, I may see that the sky is blue because it looks blue, or that the stick is straight because it looks straight. These are the most characteristically *visual* cases of seeing-that, and henceforth I will mean by 'the primary case', cases of seeing that A is F where A is seen *and* looks F.

There are two relatively non-controversial necessary conditions for the truth of 'S sees that A is F'; namely, (i) A is F, (ii) S believes that A is F, to which, as we are starting with the primary sense, we can add (iii) S sees A, and (iv) A looks F to S. Should we add clauses concerning justification and grounds to this list? G. J. Warnock claims that seeing that p involves '(i) that p is the case; (ii) that the claimant knows that p is the case; (iii) that there are in what he sees sufficient grounds for concluding that p; and (iv) that he so concludes on those grounds'.[6]

It is clear that Warnock's (iv) is too strong. I can see that the vase on the mantelpiece is orange even if I know already that it is on *other* grounds. In such a case, I do not conclude that the vase is orange because of seeing it. Likewise, if I were to look out of the window I would see that the sky is blue, but I would not then conclude that it is on the basis of what I see. I already know it. It might be suggested that (iv) be weakened to something like 'that he so concludes on those grounds *or* – if he has already done so on other grounds – would have so concluded on those grounds if he had not had the other grounds'.[7] But we have already seen a number of times that such 'conditional way-outs' fail. Suppose I know that mischief is afoot and that some of the objects in the room look some colour other than their own, and suppose that there is no way of telling *visually* which objects these are; and further suppose that a reliable friend tells me before I go into the room that the vase is orange and I take his word for this. When I go into the room I see the vase and that it looks orange, and so know that it is not one of the objects which looks a colour other than it is. It is clear that I see that the vase is orange; but I do not conclude that it is orange because of what I see, for I have already concluded this on the ground of what my friend has told me. And, further, it is *not* the case that if I had not had this latter ground, I would have concluded on the basis of what I can see that the vase is orange. Rather, if I had not had the latter ground – that is, if I had not been told that the vase is orange by my friend – I would not have held any belief one way or the other about the colour of the vase, because I knew that mischief was afoot.

[6] 'Seeing', p. 214.
[7] Don Locke makes essentially this suggestion in *Perception and Our Knowledge of the External World*, p. 33.

The position is not as clear with Warnock's (ii) and (iii). But I am inclined to think that they are not necessary conditions for seeing-that. Consider a child at her first conjuring show, who – ignorant of the ways of magicians – takes the magician's hat to be empty because it looks empty when he shows it to the audience. And suppose she just happens to be right – the hat is empty. Surely she saw that the hat was empty, although she neither knew it nor had sufficient grounds in what she saw for concluding it.

I will, therefore, omit claims like Warnock's (ii) and (iii) from the analysis to be offered below. But they can be tacked on to this analysis by anyone unconvinced by the case for omitting them, as they do not contradict anything in the analysis.

5. Thus far we have four necessary conditions for S (primarily) sees that A is F:

(i) A is F.
(ii) S believes that A is F.
(iii) S sees A.
(iv) A looks F to S.

Do we need to add any further conditions to (i)–(iv). Dretske suggests that

(A) The conditions under which S sees A are such that A would not look the way it now looks to S unless it was F.[8]

is a necessary condition. But consider the following case. I know that an object next door is either white or black. I am asked to go and see which it is. I know that the lighting next door is such that *any* dark-coloured object looks black in it, but light-coloured objects look grey. I go next door and the object looks black, and so I report that it is black.

Now (A) is violated. It is not true that the object is seen under conditions such that it would not have looked the way it now looks unless it were black. It would have looked black if it had been any dark colour. But surely I am correctly said to have seen that it is black. Again, surely I can correctly be said to see that a glass contains water, although I know it would look the same if it contained gin or vodka instead – I just know that the latter are unlikely in the circumstances.

6. Can we, then, simply add (i)–(iv) together to obtain a sufficient

---

[8] Dretske, *Seeing and Knowing*, p. 82; he has a further condition (p. 88) which I will not discuss, but the counter-examples to be given to (A) can be applied to it also.

condition for, and so an analysis of, '*S* sees that *A* is *F*'? Perhaps surprisingly, the answer is no. The problem is, to put it metaphorically to start with, that (i)–(iv) can all be satisfied but in an insufficiently *unified* way.

Suppose, for example, that I know that Smith owns an Ethiopian artefact which is red, and suppose that I am at Smith's house, am seeing the artefact, and it looks red to me. All this is quite compatible with my not seeing that the Ethiopian artefact is red; for I may have *no idea at all* that I am seeing the Ethiopian artefact; I may, for instance, think that I am seeing a Syrian artefact of Smith's which happens to be the same colour, red. In this case – although I am seeing the Ethiopian artefact, it is and looks red, and I believe that it is red – I, clearly, do not *see* that it is red.

Or consider a case where I see the tallest spy without having any idea that I am. Then I will be seeing the tallest spy, he will (we may suppose) look tall to me, and I will, on general logical grounds, truly believe that the tallest spy is tall; but I will not be seeing that the tallest spy is tall.

An obvious moral to draw from these cases is that

(v) *S* believes that he sees *A*

must be added to our list of necessary conditions for *S* seeing that *A* is *F*. But the enlarged set of necessary conditions, (i)–(v), are still not together sufficient. For suppose Smith's artefacts are all kept in one room. Then when I go into this room I may be (justifiably) quite certain that I am seeing the Ethiopian artefact, because I know that it is one of the many artefacts before me; and I may know that it is red and it may be looking red to me, without it being the case that I see that it is red. Because there may be a number of red artefacts before me, and I may have either no idea, or a quite mistaken idea, which is the Ethiopian one.

Or, again, suppose I am addressing a large audience which is so arranged that I can see every member's hair colour; and suppose that I have been told that John Doe is one of the brown-haired members of the audience, but I have no idea which one is John Doe. Clearly, I may see John Doe, believe that I am seeing him, and he may both have and look to me to have brown hair, without it being true that I see that John Doe has brown hair.

It is tempting to suggest at this point that the reason the cases just given do not count as appropriate cases of seeing-that, is that my seeing does not cause, in the one case, my belief that Ethiopian artefact is red and, in the other, my belief that John Doe has brown hair. It is, that is, tempting to add to (i)–(v) something like '*S*'s belief that *A* is *F* is caused by his seeing *A*.'

However, the difficulties we found for Warnock's (iv) in §4 obviously apply to this suggestion. I may already believe that *A* is *F* for other reasons. Hence, the condition is not necessary. It is not sufficient either. Suppose I go into the room containing Smith's artefacts. And suppose that I know that the room contains the Ethiopian artefact and that I am seeing it; but I know the latter only because I know that I can see every artefact in the room – I have, that is, no idea which artefact is the Ethiopian one. And suppose that, unlike the earlier cases I do not know the colour of the Ethiopian artefact, but I do believe (whether truly or falsely does not matter) that it is the same colour as the Syrian artefact. And, finally, suppose that I mistakenly take the large, red and red-looking, artefact in the centre of the room to be the Syrian artefact when it is in fact the Ethiopian one, and, *consequently*, I believe that the Ethiopian artefact is red because of my belief that the two are the same colour.

In the case just described, I do not see that the Ethiopian artefact is red despite the fact that (i) the Ethiopian artefact is red, (ii) I believe that it is red, (iii) I see it, (iv) it looks red to me, (v) I believe that I see the Ethiopian artefact, and, finally, my belief is caused by my seeing the Ethiopian artefact.

This rejection of the causal condition does not imply that cause has no part to play in the analysis of seeing-that. We have already acknowledged seeing *A* and *A*'s looking *F* as necessary conditions, and – as we noted in chapter four, §4 and will expand on shortly – both of these essentially involve causality.

7. At this point, we appear to have run out of plausible necessary conditions to add to (i)–(v) to give, when conjoined, a sufficient condition for '*S* sees that *A* is *F*'; and yet we have noted that (i)–(v) are insufficient in themselves. The solution is, I think, to combine (i)–(v) in a slightly different way.

The cases which showed that simply conjoining (i)–(v) was inadequate were cases where I failed to correctly *identify* the objects in question. In one case I did not know which artefact was the Ethiopian artefact; in the other, I did not know who in the audience was John Doe; and, similarly, in the subsequent case entertained in connexion with whether a causal condition should be introduced, I took the Ethiopian artefact to be the Syrian one.

Now, identification pertains to the transparent belief locution. We all know enough elementary logic to know *that* $A = A$ (provided A exists). But we commonly do not know which thing is A; that is, we do not know *of* A that it is A. Thus, in the cases involving the Ethiopian artefact, I knew that the Ethiopian artefact was the Ethiopian artefact, but I did not believe of the Ethiopian artefact that it was the Ethiopian artefact: in one case, I believed of the Syrian artefact that it was the Ethiopian one, and in the other I did not believe of anything that it was the Ethiopian artefact.

I suggest, therefore, that the belief element in seeing-that is not so much a matter of having the appropriate beliefs-that, but a matter of believing about or of the thing in question the appropriate things. Thus, when S sees that A is F, what is crucial is not whether S believes that A is F or that he is seeing A, but that he believes of A that it is A and F and seen by him.

The 'success grammar' of 'sees that' requires, moreover, that these beliefs be true. We get, therefore, as our analysis of 'S sees that A is F' (I label the clauses in a way that emphasises their connexion with (i)–(v)) the conjunction of

(i)' A is F.
(ii)' S believes of A that it is A and F.
(iii)' S sees A.
(iv)' A looks F to S.
(v)' S believes of A that it is seen by him.[9]

Or, more briefly as (iv)' entails (iii)', S sees that A is F if and only if S truly believes of A that it is A and F and looks F to him. The latter can be expressed perspicuously by exploiting the fact that quantification into belief-contexts demands the transparent reading, as: $\exists x$ (S truly believes x is A and F and looks F to him).

This account preserves the already noted opacity of seeing-that. For although the singular term following the 'of' in the transparent belief-locution is subject to substitutivity, the predicate following the 'that' cannot always be replaced by a co-extensive predicate. Thus, even when $A = B$, S may believe of x that it is A, without believing of x that it is B. It also preserves: 'S sees that A is F' entails 'S believes that A is F'. Because (ii)' entails 'S believes that A is F', though not conversely.

8. We have so far been concerned with primary epistemic seeing,

[9] Not 'S believes of A that it is seen by S'; for S might be under a misapprehension about what singular terms apply to him.

and it is now time to complete the account of seeing-that in terms of seeing things by giving an account of secondary epistemic seeing in terms of primary epistemic seeing.

We noted in §1 as a case of secondary seeing-that, seeing that the petrol tank is empty because the gauge reads empty. Other obvious cases are: seeing that the burglar forced the front door; seeing that the wind is freshening; and seeing, by looking at the stove timer, that the pie is done. In these cases – though we do not see the fuel tank, the burglar, the wind or the pie – we do see something else; the gauge, the scratch marks on the front door, the trees bending in the wind, and the stove timer. Moreover, the something else will look some way to us and we will (primarily) see that it does. For example, I might (secondarily) see that the petrol tank is empty by (primarily) seeing that the gauge points left, for I see the gauge and it looks to point left. Thus it seems that when one secondarily sees that A is F, one primarily sees that B is G.

We can, therefore, set down three conditions for 'S secondarily sees that A is F' (taking for granted the condition definitive of the secondary case, namely, that either S does not see A or A does not look F to S).

(*a*) A is F.

(*b*) S believes that A is F.

(*c*) For some B and G, S primarily sees that B is G.

(The use-mention confusion in (*c*) can be removed.)

The outstanding difficulty is to appropriately elucidate in a further condition the connexion between B's being G and A's being F – the connexion, for instance, between the gauge pointing left and the fuel tank being empty; between the trees' bending and the wind's freshening; and so on.

Sometimes the connexion is causal. For example, the wind's freshening causes the trees' bending. But the pie being cooked does not (in most stoves) cause the relevant reading on the timer. Dretske suggests (*Seeing and Knowing*, p. 153) that part of the connexion is that conditions are such that B would not be G unless A were F; but surely it need not be the case that the conditions are such that the stove timer would not read as it does unless the pie were cooked. Suppose the timer is of a variety which stops when it reaches the relevant reading, so that it may have the reading in question although the pie is hopelessly burnt (due to being left in the stove too long after the timer has stopped). Yet I may still see that the pie is ready by looking at the timer and seeing that it has stopped at the relevant reading, because I may know that the timer stopped very recently.

I think the best we can do is add to (*a*), (*b*) and (*c*) something like

(*d*) The circumstances are such that *S*'s belief that *B* is *G* is a sufficient ground for the knowledge claim (by *S*) that *A* is *F*, and *S* believes this.

The conjunction of (*a*), (*b*), (*c*) and (*d*) seem to me to constitute an analysis of '*S* secondarily sees that *A* is *F*'.

In (*d*), it is required that *S*'s belief that *B* is *G* (that *S* so believes follows, of course, from (*c*)) be a sufficient ground rather than the actual ground, to cater for cases where *S* already knows on other grounds that *A* is *F*. What is essential is only that *B* being *G* (the timer reading as it does, the gauge pointing left, etc.) be a potential ground for *S*'s belief that *A* is *F* (that the pie is done, that the tank is empty) which is sufficient for knowledge, without it necessarily being the operative ground.

Moreover, it is required in (*d*) that *S* believe that his belief that *B* is *G* is sufficient for knowledge. For in those cases where *S* believes on other grounds that *A* is *F*, we will not allow that *S* sees that *A* is *F* if he is unaware that his belief that *B* is *G* is a sufficient ground for a knowledge claim that *A* is *F*. Not only must *B* being *G* be connected to *A* being *F*, *S* must be aware of this connexion.

The reason I have expressed (*d*) in terms of sufficiency for knowledge rather than simply requiring that, in the circumstances, *B* being *G* is good evidence for *A* being *F*, relates to Gettier's paper 'Is Justified True Belief Knowledge?'.

Suppose the gauge points left because it is broken, but that I have good reason to believe that it is operating normally (it looks alright and I had it fixed last week); and suppose that I primarily see that the gauge points left. And, finally, suppose that, by chance, the tank is empty. It is quite clear in this case that I do *not* see that the tank is empty; yet the tank is empty, I believe that it is, I primarily see that the gauge points left, and the gauge pointing left is, in the circumstances, good evidence for the tank being empty.

I do not, however, in this case *know* that the tank is empty; I have true, justified belief, but not knowledge. In particular, the gauge pointing left provides good evidence without being a sufficient ground for a knowledge claim that the tank is empty. Hence, our formulation of (*d*) enables us to avoid mistakenly classifying this case (and the *multitude* of others anyone familiar with the literature prompted by

Gettier's paper will be able to construct) as a case of secondarily seeing-that.

9. I now come to the final concern of this chapter: the analysis of *belonging-to*. What account should be given of the relation between a sense-datum and a material object in virtue of which seeing the sense datum constitutes seeing the material object? It has been argued in this work that whenever one sees a material thing, M, one immediately sees a sense-datum, D; what is the essential relation between M and D for which we have used Moore's label, 'belongs to'?

When I see a material thing, M, there is a causal transaction between M and a state of mine – an event involving M effects a change in my sensory states. It is now widely acknowledged, as we noted in chapter 4, §4, that this is not merely a contingent fact, but, rather, an essential part of the concept of seeing something. H. P. Grice illustrates this point as follows:

> it might be that it looked to me as if there were a certain sort of pillar in a certain direction at a certain distance, and there might actually be such a pillar in that place; but if, unknown to me, there were a mirror interposed between myself and the pillar, which reflected a numerically different though similar pillar, it would certainly be incorrect to say that I saw the first pillar, and correct to say that I saw the second; and it is extremely tempting to explain this linguistic fact by saying that the first pillar was, and the second was not, causally irrelevant to the way things looked to me.[10]

Put in terms of sense-data, this means that a necessary condition of a sense-datum, D, belonging to material things, M, is that there be a causal link between M and D. Now causal links putatively between objects are analysable in terms of the causal relation between events (some would replace 'events' here by 'states of affairs'). 'The stone broke the window' is true because something like 'The *impact* of the stone caused the *breaking* of the window' is true. Hence, the necessary condition is that an *event* involving M cause, not D, but an event such as the having by me of D.

It is, therefore, a necessary condition for 'D belongs to M' that an M-event caused the having of D (by whoever it may be). But it is not a sufficient condition. We know that there is a whole chain of events involved in seeing an external object. An event on the surface of the object causes light of a certain composition to be reflected, this light

[10] Grice, 'The Causal Theory of Perception', §v.

enters the eye and causes changes in the optic nerve, these changes affect the brain, and so on. Yet, the sense-datum does not belong to, for example, the optic nerve or the light.

In order to obtain a sufficient condition, we must single out the essential feature of the M-event which distinguishes it from all the other events. In *Perception*, H. H. Price suggests that a distinction between *standing* and *differential* causal conditions helps here.

> There are certain conditions which condition *all* the sense-data of any one sense, conditions in the absence of which none of them can come into being: in the case of visual sense-data, there must be a source of light, an eye, a retina, an optic nerve, etc., and these must be in a certain state . . . But these standing conditions, just because they are necessary to all the visual sense-data alike, do not wholly determine any one of them. For that, something more is wanted, a varying or differential condition which accounts for the difference between this red sense-datum and that blue one, between this square one and that elliptical one. Obviously it is absurd to identify M with any or all of the standing conditions . . . but it is quite plausible to identify it with the *differential* condition. [*op. cit.*, p. 70]

There is, however, an ambiguity in this passage, the resolution of which faces Price with a destructive dilemma.[11] Are the standing and differential conditions objects or events (or states)? If events, then the claim that conditions involving the optic nerve, for example, do not wholly determine one's sense-data in the absence of M is simply false. If appropriate events occur in this nerve, the appropriate sense-data will be had, whether or not M produced these events. If the conditions are objects, as the passage most naturally suggests, then the crucial point is, presumably, that the existence of the optic nerve, for example, is necessary for the having of any visual sense-data at all, while M's existence is only necessary for having certain kinds of sense-data.

But this second reading leads to a quite unacceptable conclusion, namely, that it is impossible to see one's own optic nerve. Autocerebroscopes are rare but possible; so that one may in certain circumstances see one's own optic nerve despite its being – in Price's terminology on the second reading – a standing condition.

10. What, then, is the crucial feature of the M-event (which in special cases may, as we have just noted, be an event involving the optic nerve)? I suggest that we look for the answer in terms of the

[11] For a different objection, see *ibid.*

relation between M and the sense-datum the M-event causes. A simple suggestion along these lines would be: a sense-datum, D, belongs to an object, M, if an M-event caused the having of D and D closely resembles M. On this suggestion, seeing M would be a matter of M causing a closely representative sense-datum.

There are obvious difficulties with this suggestion; indeed, it is both too strong and too weak. It is too strong because there are many cases of seeing material things where there is no resemblance between the material thing and the sense-datum. Seeing the stars in the night sky is an obvious example of this, another example is seeing something with coloured, distorting glasses on.

An example which shows it is too weak is the following. A neurologist is taking an electrograph of my brain waves with my eyes masked. A sudden flash of light startles him and causes him to jolt his equipment in such a way as to send a very mild current through the electrodes strapped to my head. This current causes a phosphene which, by chance, corresponds exactly to the flash of light (same position, same intensity, same colour, same duration, and so on). It is clear that I do not see the light flash despite its causal role and despite the similarity that obtains between flash and sense-datum.

The feature of the last case which stands out is the *abnormality* of the causal chain between material thing and sense-experience; and it might, therefore, be thought that a simple account of the following kind suffices: a sense-datum, D, belongs to an object, M, if an M-event caused – in the *normal way, whatever that way may be* – the having of D.[12]

This account is *topic-neutral* in that the precise, intrinsic nature of the causal chain is not specified. Material things might have been seen via some quite different causal mechanism from that which in fact operates in our world; the latter was, after all, discovered by laborious empirical investigation rather than by reflection on the concept of seeing. What matters according to the suggestion in question is that the causal chain, whatever its detailed nature may be, is the normal one – the one involved, for instance, when I see my hand, or the orange on the mantelpiece, or . . .

There are two problems with this approach. The first is that it requires us to pick out certain cases of seeing as paradigm cases (just as the topic-neutral approach to pain requires that one pick out certain behaviour and/or stimuli as paradigmatic of pain). It requires,

[12] *Ibid.*, mentions this approach with approval.

for instance, nominating seeing an orange and seeing one's hand as paradigms. And it is *absolutely contingent* what things one sees: that we see oranges and hands is an exemplar of a contingent fact.

The second problem is that abnormality of the causal chain between object seen and sense-impression does not entail not seeing. The (I believe Russian) claim that some people can see with their fingers may be empirically implausible, but it cannot be refuted *a priori*. Likewise, there is no inconsistency in supposing that 'Martians' see objects, but by causal means quite distinct from our own.

11. I believe that an adequate account of the belonging-to relation can be obtained by concentrating on the spatial-property relations between the material object and the sense-datum.

I am clearly committed to holding that colour similarities between sense-data and material objects are irrelevant. For, in chapter 5, I argued that material objects do not, whereas sense-data do, have colour properties. But even a full-blown objectivist about colour must grant that colour similarities are irrelevant. This is because an objectivist must allow that material objects can (for example, by the totally colour-blind) be seen in 'black-and-white'. This means he must allow that material objects can be seen although the sense-data belonging to them differ markedly from them in colour.

We must, thus, look to spatial-property relationships for our analysis of belonging-to. Simple spatial similarities are clearly not to the point. The fact that we see stars and see objects through distorting glasses shows that similarity of shape is not crucial; the fact that we see stars and see objects through telescopes shows that distance is not crucial; and, finally, the fact that we see objects in mirrors and through periscopes shows that relative position is not crucial. What, then, is crucial? I suggest that it is what I call the *functional spatial dependence* of the sense-datum on the object, a dependence which is consequent on the causal connexion between the object and the sense-datum.

Suppose, to illustrate, that I am looking at an orange. There are four spatial properties at issue: shape, size, distance (away), and (relative) direction. If, say, all of these except size are kept fixed, what happens? Well, if the orange doubles in size, the sense-datum doubles in size (approximately); if the orange halves, the sense-datum halves; and so on. Thus, the size of the sense-datum is a function of that of the material object. Likewise, if the orange changes direction while remaining constant in the other spatial respects, a similar dependence will be exhibited: as the orange moves to the left, the sense-datum will move to the left; as the orange moves upward, so will the sense-datum; and so on. Thus, the direction of the sense-datum is a function of that of the material object. In some cases, the functional relation will not be so simple. For example, when an object seen through an inverting lens goes up, the sense-datum goes down. But there is still a functional relationship, and that is the important point.

Similar remarks apply to shape and distance. And in each case the functional interdependence is, of course, a consequence of the kind of causal connexion that obtains between material object and perceiver. It is because of the way the orange causes me to have the sense-datum of it that when the orange gets bigger, so does the sense-datum, and likewise for the other spatial properties. Therefore, the case I have just described is one where the sense-datum is functionally spatially dependent on the object, and this dependence is consequent on the kind of causal connexion that holds between the object and the sense-datum.

It is this which seems to me crucial to seeing a material object. That is, in my view, a sense-datum, D, belongs to a material object, M, just if (i) an M-event causes the having of D, and (ii) the spatial properties of D are functionally dependent on those of M as a consequence of the manner in which M causes the having of D.

This formula appears to cover the intuitively clear cases of seeing something. We have already seen how it covers the case of seeing a medium-sized, nearby, opaque material object. It also covers the cases of seeing planets and stars, for the position and size of the bright speck 'in the night sky' is a function of the position, size and distance of the corresponding planet or star.

The formula also excludes the cases we want to exclude. Take the case of the phosphene caused by the startled neurologist. We noted that even if the phosphene and the causally responsible flash of light correspond exactly, the flash may not be seen. This is because the causal connexion does not sustain a functional correspondence in spatial properties. The causal path is via the startled neurologist, and there will be a totally erratic connexion between the spatial properties of the flash and the phosphene.

12. Finally, I want to comment on a possible objection to the formula of §11.

I am, on occasion, correctly said to see the university when I can see only, say, one building. Now, obviously, if the university doubles in size due to the parts I cannot see doubling in size, it may well be that the sense-datum belonging to the university remains unaltered. Again, I am correctly said to see someone in a tent dress, though my sense-datum may be invariant to considerable changes in that person's shape.

In reply, we need to distinguish three entities seen and two relations. When I see a reasonably sized opaque material thing, I see: (i) the sense-datum, (ii) the thing's facing surface, and (iii) the thing. Now, the relation between the facing surface and the thing is common ground in the philosophy of perception. The formula of §11 is designed to elucidate only the controversial relationship – that between sense-data and the surfaces of material things. Now when I see the university by seeing a certain facing surface of it, though the university may double without the sense-datum doubling, the facing surface cannot (as a matter of empirical fact, given the nature of the causal link). If the particular building-face I see increases in size, so will my sense-datum. Likewise, when I see a person in a tent dress, the relation the formula of §11 is intended to capture is not that between the person's body and the dress, but that between the facing surface of the dress and the sense-datum. And it will be the case that the shape of the sense-datum will be a function of the shape of this facing surface.

13. This completes my case for a Lockean Representative theory of visual perception. The first four chapters present my case for a Sense-datum theory of perception. Chapter 5 gives the reason for holding that all sense-data are mental. This forces a choice between Idealism and Representationalism. In chapter 6 I argue that there is no good reason for not choosing Representationalism. And, finally, in this chapter, I have, first, attempted to justify my taking the perception of things as basic throughout; and, secondly, I have tried to make more precise, by giving an analysis of the belonging-to relation, the particular kind of Representationalism that should be chosen.

Bibliography

Anscombe, G. E. M., 'The Intentionality of Sensation: Some Grammatical Features', in *Analytical Philosophy*, second series, ed. R. J. Butler, Oxford: Blackwell, 1965, pp. 158–80.

Armstrong, D. M., *Perception and the Physical World*, London: Routledge and Kegan Paul, 1961.

Armstrong, D. M., *Bodily Sensations*, London: Routledge and Kegan Paul, 1962.

Armstrong, D. M., *A Materialist Theory of the Mind*, London: Routledge and Kegan Paul, 1968.

Armstrong, D. M., 'Colour-Realism and The Argument From Microscopes', in *Contemporary Philosophy in Australia*, ed. R. Brown and C. D. Rollins, London: Allen and Unwin, 1969, pp. 119–31.

Armstrong, D. M., *Belief, Truth and Knowledge*, Cambridge: Cambridge University Press, 1973.

Aune, Bruce, *Knowledge, Mind, and Nature*, New York: Random House, 1967.

Austin, J. L., *Sense and Sensibilia*, London: Oxford University Press, 1962.

Ayer, A. J., *The Foundations of Empirical Knowledge*, London: Macmillan, 1940.

Ayer, A. J., 'One's Knowledge of Other Minds', *Theoria*, xix (1953); reprinted in his *Philosophical Essays*, London: Macmillan, 1959, pp. 191–214.

Ayer, A. J., *The Problem of Knowledge*, Harmondsworth: Penguin, 1956.

Baier, Kurt, 'The Place of a Pain', *Philosophical Quarterly*, 14 (1964), 138–50.

Barnes, W. H. F., 'The Myth of Sense-Data', in *Perceiving, Sensing, and Knowing*, ed. R. J. Swartz, New York: Doubleday Anchor, 1965, pp. 138–67.

Bennett, Jonathan, *Locke, Berkeley, Hume: Central Themes*, Oxford: Oxford University Press, 1971.

Berkeley, George, *Principles of Human Knowledge*, in *The Works of George Berkeley*, Bishop of Cloyne, ed. A. A. Luce and T. E. Jessop, 9 vols., Edinburgh: Nelson and Sons, 1948–57.

Bouwsma, O. K., 'Moore's Theory of Sense-Data', in *Philosophy of G. E. Moore*, ed. P. A. Schillp, Illinois: Northwestern University Press, 1942, pp. 201–22.

Bradley, M. C., 'Sensations, Brain-Processes, and Colours', *Australasian Journal of Philosophy*, 41 (1963), 385–93.

Bradley, M. C., 'A Note On a Circularity Argument', *Australasian Journal of Philosophy*, 44 (1966), 91–4.

Bradley, M. C., 'Two Arguments Against the Identity Thesis', in *Contemporary Philosophy in Australia*, London: Allen and Unwin, 1969, pp. 173–89.

Broad, C. D., *Scientific Thought*, London: Routledge and Kegan Paul, 1923.

Broad, C. D., 'Some Elementary Reflections on Sense-Perception', in *Perceiving, Sensing, and Knowing*, ed. R. J. Swartz, New York: Doubleday Anchor, 1965, pp. 29–48.

Brown, N., 'Sense-Data and Physical Objects', *Mind*, 66 (1957), 173–94.

Campbell, Keith, *Body and Mind*, London: Macmillan, 1971.

Chisholm, Roderick M., *Perceiving: A Philosophical Study*, Ithaca, N.Y.: Cornell University Press, 1957.

Chisholm, Roderick M., 'The Theory of Appèaring', in *Philosophical Analysis*, ed. Max Black, New York: Books for Libraries, 1971, pp. 97–112.

Davidson, Donald, 'Theories of Meaning and Learnable Languages', in *Logic, Methodology and Philosophy of Science*, ed. Y. Bar-Hillel, Holland: Reidel, 1965, pp. 383–94.

Davidson, Donald, 'The Logical Form of Action Sentences', in *Logic of Action and Preference*, ed. N. Rescher, Pittsburgh: Pittsburgh University Press, 1966.

Davidson, Donald, 'Causal Relations', *Journal of Philosophy*, 64 (1967), 691–703.

Descartes, Rene, *Descartes: Philosophical Writings*, trans. G. E. M. Anscombe and P. T. Geach, Edinburgh: Thomas Nelson, 1954.

Deutscher, Max, 'A Causal Account of Inferring', in *Contemporary Philosophy in Australia*, ed. R. Brown and C. D. Rollins, London: Allen and Unwin, 1969, pp. 97–118.

Dretske, Fred I., *Seeing and Knowing*, London: Routledge and Kegan Paul, 1969.

Ducasse, C. J., *Nature, Mind and Death*, Illinois: Open Court, 1951.

Firth, Roderick, 'Sense-Data and The Percept Theory', in *Perceiving, Sensing, And Knowing*, ed. R. J. Swartz, New York: Anchor Books, 1965, pp. 204–70.

Fleming, Brice Noel, 'The Idea of a Solid', *Australasian Journal of Philosophy*, 43 (1965), 131–43.

Geach, P. T., *Mental Acts*, London: Routledge and Kegan Paul, 1957.

Geach, P. T., *Reference and Generality*, Ithaca, N.Y.: Cornell University Press, 1962.

Gettier, E., 'Is Justified True Belief Knowledge?', *Analysis*, 23 (1963), 121–3.

Goldman, Alvin I., 'A Causal Theory of Knowing', *Jornal of Philosophy*, 64 (1967), 365–72.

Goldman, Alvin I., *A Theory of Human Action*, Englewood Cliffs: Prentice-Hall, 1970.

Grice, H. P., 'The Causal Theory of Perception', *Proc. Aristotelian Society*, supp. vol. 35 (1961), 121–68.

Grice, H. P., 'Some Remarks about the Senses', in *Analytical Philosophy*, ed. R. Butler, Oxford: Blackwell, 1962, pp. 133–53.

Hume, David, *A Treatise of Human Nature*, ed. L. A. Selby-Bigge, Oxford: Oxford University Press, 1955.

Jackson, Frank, 'Do Material Things Have Non-Physical Properties?', *Personalist*, 54 (1973), 105–10.

Jackson, Frank and R. J. Pinkerton, 'On An Argument Against Sensory Items', *Mind*, 82 (1973), 269–72.

Jackson, Frank, 'On The Adverbial Analysis of Visual Experience', *Metaphilosophy*, 6 (1975), 127–35.

Jackson, Frank, 'The Existence of Mental Objects', *American Philosophical Quarterly*, 13 (1976), 33–40.

James, William, *Principles of Psychology*, New York: Henry Holt, 1890.

Kim, Jaegwon, 'On the Psycho-Physical Identity Theory', *American Philosophical Quarterly*, 3 (1966), 227–35.

Kim, Jaegwon, 'Properties, Laws and the Identity Theory', *Monist*, 56 (1972), 177–92.

Lewis, David, 'General Semantics', *Synthese*, 22 (1970), 18–67.

Lewis, David and Stephanie, 'Holes', *Australasian Journal of Philosophy*, 48 (1970), 206–12.

Locke, Don, *Perception and Our Knowledge of the External World*, London: Allen and Unwin, 1967.

Locke, John, *An Essay Concerning Human Understanding*, ed. J. W. Yolton, 2 vols., London: J. M. Dent, 1961.

Lotze, R. H., *Outlines of Psychology*, trans. and ed. by G. T. Ladd, Boston: Ginn, Heath, 1886.

Mates, Benson, 'Sense-Data', *Inquiry*, 10 (1968), 225–44.

Moore, G. E., 'A Defence of Common Sense', in *Philosophical Papers*, London: Allen and Unwin, 1959, pp. 32–59.

Moore, G. E., 'The Nature and Reality of Objects of Perception', in *Philosophical Studies*, London: Routledge and Kegan Paul, 1960, pp. 31–96.

Nagel, Thomas, 'Physicalism', *Philosophical Review*, 74 (1965), 339–56.

Noren, Stephen J., 'Smart's Materialism: The Identity Theory and Translation', *Australasian Journal of Philosophy*, 48 (1970), 54–66.

Pap, Arthur, *Semantics and Necessary Truth*, New Haven: Yale University Press, 1958.

Parsons, Terence, 'Some Problems concerning the Logic of Grammatical Modifiers', *Synthese*, 21 (1970), 320–34.

Paul, G. A., 'Is There A Problem About Sense-Data?', in *Perceiving, Sensing, and Knowing*, ed. R. J. Swartz, New York: Doubleday, 1965, pp. 271–87.

Pitcher, George, 'Minds and Ideas in Berkeley', *American Philosophical Quarterly*, 6 (1969), 198–207.

Pitcher, George, *A Theory of Perception*, New Jersey: Princeton University Press, 1971.

Plantinga, Alvin, *God and Other Minds*, Ithaca: Cornell University Press, 1967.

Price, H. H., *Perception*, London: Methuen, 1954.

Quine, W. V., 'Notes on Existence and Necessity', *Journal of Philosophy*, 40 (1943), 113–27.

Quine, W. V., *Word and Object*, Cambridge, Mass.: MIT Press, 1960.

Quine, W. V., 'Two Dogmas of Empiricism', in *From a Logical Point of View*, New York: Harper and Row, 2nd ed. 1961, ch. 2.

Quine, W. V., 'Three Grades of Modal Involvement', n *The Ways of Paradox*, New York: Random House, 1966, pp. 156–74.

Quinton, Anthony M., 'The Problem of Perception', *Mind*, 64 (1955), 28–51.

Roxbee-Cox, J. W., 'Distinguishing the Senses', *Mind*, 79 (1970), 530–50.

Roxbee-Cox, J. W., 'An Analysis of Perceiving in Terms of the Causation of Beliefs I', in *Perception: A Philosophical Symposium*, ed. F. N. Sibley, London: Methuen, 1971, pp. 23–64.

Ryle, Gilbert, *The Concept of Mind*, London: Hutchinson, 1949.

Ryle, Gilbert, *Dilemmas*, Cambridge: Cambridge University Press, 1960.

Schlesinger, George, 'It is False that Overnight Everything has Doubled in Size', *Philosophical Studies*, 15 (1964), 65–71.

Sellars, Wilfred, 'Reply to Aune', in *Intentionality, Minds, and Perception*, ed. H. Casteñeda, Detroit: Wayne State University Press, 1966, pp. 286–300.

Sellars, Wilfred, 'The Adverbial Theory of the Objects of Sensation', *Metaphilosophy*, 6 (1975), 144–60.

Sellars, Wilfred, *Science and Metaphysics*, London: Routledge and Kegan Paul, 1968.

Shaffer, Jerome, *Philosophy of Mind*, Englewood Cliffs: Prentice-Hall, 1968.

Skyrms, Brian, 'The Explication of "X Knows that p"', *Journal of Philosophy*, 64 (1967), 373–89.

Smart, J. J. C., 'Colours', *Philosophy*, 36 (1961), 128–42.

Smart, J. J. C., *Philosophy and Scientific Realism*, London: Routledge and Kegan Paul, 1963.

Smart, J. J. C., 'Comments on the Papers', in *Identity Theory of Mind*, ed. C. F. Presley, Brisbane: Queensland University Press, 1967, pp. 84–93.

Smart, J. J. C., 'On Some Criticisms of a Physicalist Theory of Colours', in *Philosophical Aspects of the Mind–Body Problem*, ed. Chung-Ying Cheng, Honolulu: University Press of Hawaii, 1975, pp. 54–63.

Sprigge, T. L. S., *Facts, Words, and Beliefs*, London: Routledge and Kegan Paul, 1972.

Suchting, W. A., 'Perception and The Time-Gap Argument', *Philosophical Quarterly*, 19 (1969), 46–56.

Teichman, Jenny, *The Mind and The Soul*, London: Routledge and Kegan Paul, 1974.

Tye, Michael, 'The Adverbial Theory: A Defence of Sellars against Jackson', *Metaphilosophy*, 6 (1975), 136–43.

Vesey, G. N. A., *Perception*, London: Macmillan, 1971.

Vesey, G. N. A., 'Analysing Seeing II', in *Perception: A Philosophical Symposium*, ed. F. N. Sibley, London: Methuen, 1971, pp. 133–8.

Warnock, G. J., *Berkeley*, London: Penguin, 1953.

Warnock, G. J., 'Seeing', *Proc. Aristotelian Society*, new series, vol. LV (1954–55), 201–18.

Warnock, G. J., 'On What is Seen I', in *Perception: A Philosophical Symposium*, ed. F. N. Sibley, London: Methuen, 1971, pp. 1–12.

White, Alan, *G. E. Moore*, Oxford: Blackwell, 1958.

White, Morton, *Toward Reunion in Philosophy*, New York: Atheneum, 1963.

Wittgenstein, Ludwig, *Philosophical Investigations*, trans. G. E. M. Anscombe, Oxford: Blackwell, 2nd ed., 1963.

Wittgenstein, Ludwig, *Blue and Brown Books*, trans. G. E. M. Anscombe, Oxford: Blackwell, 1964.

Wyburn, G. M., R. W. Pickford, and R. J. Hirst, *Human Senses and Perception*, Edinburgh: Oliver and Boyd, 1964.

Index